编委会

普通高等学校"十四五"规划旅游管理类精品教材
教育部旅游管理专业本科综合改革试点项目配套规划教材

总主编

马 勇　教育部高等学校旅游管理类专业教学指导委员会副主任
　　　　中国旅游协会教育分会副会长
　　　　中组部国家"万人计划"教学名师
　　　　湖北大学旅游发展研究院院长，教授、博士生导师

编 委（排名不分先后）

田 里　教育部高等学校旅游管理类专业教学指导委员会主任
　　　　云南大学工商管理与旅游管理学院原院长，教授、博士生导师
高 峻　教育部高等学校旅游管理类专业教学指导委员会副主任
　　　　上海师范大学环境与地理学院院长，教授、博士生导师
韩玉灵　全国旅游职业教育教学指导委员会秘书长
　　　　北京第二外国语学院旅游管理学院教授
罗兹柏　中国旅游未来研究会副会长，重庆旅游发展研究中心主任，教授
郑耀星　中国旅游协会理事，福建师范大学旅游学院教授、博士生导师
董观志　暨南大学旅游规划设计研究院副院长，教授、博士生导师
薛兵旺　武汉商学院旅游与酒店管理学院院长，教授
姜 红　上海商学院酒店管理学院院长，教授
舒伯阳　中南财经政法大学工商管理学院教授、博士生导师
朱运海　湖北文理学院资源环境与旅游学院副院长
罗伊玲　昆明学院旅游管理专业副教授
杨振之　四川大学中国休闲与旅游研究中心主任，四川大学旅游学院教授、博士生导师
黄安民　华侨大学城市建设与经济发展研究院常务副院长，教授
张胜男　首都师范大学资源环境与旅游学院教授
魏 卫　华南理工大学经济与贸易学院教授、博士生导师
张 瑛　国际旅游学会（ITSA）中国区副主席，中央民族大学管理学院教授，博士生导师
毕斗斗　华南理工大学经济与贸易学院副教授
史万震　常熟理工学院商学院营销与旅游系副教授
黄光文　南昌大学旅游学院副教授
窦志萍　昆明学院旅游学院教授，《旅游研究》杂志主编
李 玺　澳门城市大学国际旅游与管理学院院长，教授、博士生导师
王春雷　上海对外经贸大学会展与旅游学院院长，教授
朱 伟　天津农学院人文学院副教授
邓爱民　中南财经政法大学旅游发展研究院院长，教授、博士生导师
程丛喜　武汉轻工大学旅游管理系主任，教授
周 霄　武汉轻工大学旅游研究中心主任，副教授
黄其新　江汉大学商学院副院长，副教授
何 彪　海南大学旅游学院副院长，副教授

普通高等学校"十四五"规划旅游管理类精品教材
教育部旅游管理专业本科综合改革试点项目配套规划教材

总主编 ◎ 马 勇

旅游英语
Tourism English

主　编 ◎ 张 瑛
副主编 ◎ 肖 瑶　郑倩倩　贾雯雯

华中科技大学出版社
http://press.hust.edu.cn
中国·武汉

内 容 提 要

本教材主要介绍旅游相关内容。教材主选内容参考国际上较为权威、较为经典、较受欢迎的旅游教材,并与中国国情相结合,涵盖旅游管理所涉及的主要行业和部门,由浅入深,知识体系完整,并融入旅游热点问题。教材设计了知识阅读、对话、案例研究、行业知识拓展等栏目,在侧重旅游实务英语的同时,还将章节中所涉及的内容与旅游研究相结合,设计了学术提升部分,并推荐《旅游管理》(*Tourism Management*)等国际旅游研究顶尖期刊的经典文章作为扩展阅读,进一步提升旅游英语教材的深度和广度。教材每一章都设有导读、本章目标、阅读材料、案例研究、行业知识拓展、对话(配有音频)、学术思考/论文导读、思考题、关键术语和在线答题等栏目,并配有教学PPT。本教材是高等院校旅游管理专业、旅游英语专业,特别是旅游管理硕士(MTA)的理想教学用书,也可作为旅游行业从业人员和广大旅游爱好者的参考读物。

图书在版编目(CIP)数据

旅游英语/张瑛主编. —武汉:华中科技大学出版社,2022.9(2023.8 重印)
ISBN 978-7-5680-7365-3

Ⅰ.①旅… Ⅱ.①张… Ⅲ.①旅游-英语 Ⅳ.①F59

中国版本图书馆 CIP 数据核字(2022)第 174434 号

旅游英语 张瑛 主编
Lüyou Yingyu

策划编辑:王 乾
责任编辑:陈 然
封面设计:原色设计
责任校对:曾 婷
责任监印:周治超

出版发行:华中科技大学出版社(中国·武汉) 电话:(027)81321913
武汉市东湖新技术开发区华工科技园 邮编:430223
录 排:华中科技大学惠友文印中心
印 刷:武汉科源印刷设计有限公司
开 本:787mm×1092mm 1/16
印 张:14.75 插页:2
字 数:452千字
版 次:2023年8月第1版第2次印刷
定 价:59.80元

本书若有印装质量问题,请向出版社营销中心调换
全国免费服务热线:400-6679-118 竭诚为您服务
版权所有 侵权必究

伴随着我国社会和经济步入新发展阶段,我国的旅游业也进入转型升级与结构调整的重要时期。旅游业将在推动形成以国内经济大循环为主体、国内国际双循环相互促进的新发展格局中发挥独特的作用。旅游业的大发展在客观上对我国高等旅游教育和人才培养提出了更高的要求,同时也希望高等旅游教育和人才培养能在促进我国旅游业高质量发展中发挥更大更好的作用。

《中国教育现代化2035》明确提出:推动高等教育内涵式发展,形成高水平人才培养体系。以"双一流"建设和"双万计划"的启动为标志,中国高等旅游教育发展进入新阶段。

这些新局面有力推动着我国高等旅游教育在"十四五"期间迈入发展新阶段,未来旅游业发展对各类中高级旅游人才的需求将十分旺盛。因此,出版一套把握时代新趋势、面向未来的高品质和高水准规划教材则成为我国高等旅游教育和人才培养的迫切需要。

基于此,在教育部高等学校旅游管理类专业教学指导委员会的大力支持和指导下,教育部直属的全国重点大学出版社——华中科技大学出版社——汇聚了一大批国内高水平旅游院校的国家教学名师、资深教授及中青年旅游学科带头人,在成功组编出版了"普通高等院校旅游管理专业类'十三五'规划教材"的基础上,再次联合编撰出版"普通高等学校'十四五'规划旅游管理类精品教材"。本套教材从选题策划到成稿出版,从编写团队到出版团队,从主题选择到内容编排,均作出积极的创新和突破,具有以下特点:

一、基于新国标率先出版并不断沉淀和改版

教育部2018年颁布《普通高等学校本科专业类教学质量国家标准》后,华中科技大学出版社特邀教育部高等学校旅游管理类专业教学指导委员会副主

任、国家"万人计划"教学名师马勇教授担任总主编，同时邀请了全国近百所开设旅游管理类本科专业的高校知名教授、博导、学科带头人和一线骨干专业教师，以及旅游行业专家、海外专业师资联合编撰了"普通高等院校旅游管理专业类'十三五'规划教材"。该套教材紧扣新国标要点，融合数字科技新技术，配套立体化教学资源，于新国标颁布后在全国率先出版，被全国数百所高等学校选用后获得良好反响。编委会在出版后积极收集院校的一线教学反馈，紧扣行业新变化，吸纳新知识点，不断地对教材内容及配套教育资源进行更新升级。"普通高等学校'十四五'规划旅游管理类精品教材"正是在此基础上沉淀和提升编撰而成。《旅游接待业（第二版）》《旅游消费者行为（第二版）》《旅游目的地管理（第二版）》等核心课程优质规划教材陆续推出，以期为全国高等院校旅游专业创建国家级一流本科专业和国家级一流"金课"助力。

二、对标国家级一流本科课程进行高水平建设

本套教材积极研判"双万计划"对旅游管理类专业课程的建设要求，对标国家级一流本科课程的高水平建设，进行内容优化与编撰，以期促进广大旅游院校的教学高质量建设与特色化发展。其中《旅游规划与开发》《酒店管理概论》《酒店督导管理》等教材已成为教育部授予的首批国家级一流本科"金课"配套教材。《节事活动策划与管理》等教材获得国家级和省级教学类奖项。

三、全面配套教学资源，打造立体化互动教材

华中科技大学出版社为本套教材建设了内容全面的线上教材课程资源服务平台：在横向资源配套上，提供全系列教学计划书、教学课件、习题库、案例库、参考答案、教学视频等配套教学资源；在纵向资源开发上，构建了覆盖课程开发、习题管理、学生评论、班级管理等集开发、使用、管理、评价于一体的教学生态链，打造了线上线下、课堂内外的新形态立体化互动教材。

在旅游教育发展的新时代，主编出版一套高质量规划教材是一项重要的教学出版工程，更是一份重要的责任。本套教材在组织策划及编写出版过程中，得到了全国广大院校旅游管理类专家教授、企业精英，以及华中科技大学出版社的大力支持，在此一并致谢！衷心希望本套教材能够为全国高等院校的旅游学界、业界和对旅游知识充满渴望的社会大众带来真正的精神和知识营养，为我国旅游教育教材建设贡献力量。也希望并诚挚邀请更多高等院校旅游管理专业的学者加入我们的编者和读者队伍，为我们共同的事业——我国高等旅游教育高质量发展——而奋斗！

总主编

序
Foreword

  2019年底以来席卷全球的新冠疫情，已经让世界的许多方面发生了许多改变：至少在全球旅行方面，出国旅行变得不再那么容易，实际上是变得非常困难，从事旅游接待的目的地国家的经济发展受到了致命的打击，从事这一关联面非常广泛的行业的人们的生计，也受到了严重的影响。从这个角度看，国际旅游、跨国旅行和旅游服务，是不是变得不再必要、不再需要重视了呢？并非如此，如今疫情过后，信息化、全球化、移动化的世界潮流很快就恢复了其旺盛的生命力，人类已重新回归正常的生活，国际旅游事业仍然会蓬勃发展。

  国际旅游的正常运行离不开基于通用语言的国际交流。虽然汉语、英语、西班牙语、法语和阿拉伯语是世界上使用人数最多的五种语言，但是就跨语言交流来说，英语确实是全球最为流行的国际交流工具。虽然大家都会说英语，但是在旅游行业内，由于其知识领域、术语体系和主要目的地国家的地理环境与传统文化存在巨大差异，决定了旅游行业的英语有其自身的独特性。对于将来有志于投身旅游行业的院校师生，或者对旅游行业有兴趣的一般读者来说，旅游英语就是一个值得高度重视的专业知识领域。从这个角度看，旅游英语是从事旅游服务、提升业务能力、进行学术研究和促进文化传播的重要工具。

  为了传授旅游英语这一特定知识体系，就需要撰写高质量的教材。优秀的旅游英语教材，可以满足教学需求，可以提高学生的专业岗位技能和职业素养，可以提升学术能力和专业水准。在"十四五"时期坚持高质量发展，坚持实施更大范围、更宽领域、更深层次对外开放的大环境下，需要一本较好的旅游英语教材来满足这些需求。

  好的教材需要好的编撰者。一本好的旅游英语教材的编撰者，最好既是旅游专家，又有较深厚的英语功底；既熟悉中国的旅游状况，又有宽广的国际视野；既有丰富的教学经验，又有良好的学术功底和成果。能够满足这些复合要求的人还真不易找到，就我所了解的专业人士中，中央民族大学的教授，也是北大校友的张瑛博士，就是这样一位难得的执笔者。张瑛教授本科是英语文学专业，硕士阶段主攻旅游人类学，其后考取北京大学城市与环境学院攻读博士学位，再到中央民族大学民族学博士后流动站进行博士后研究，出站后留校从事旅游管理教学和研究工作，两次获得中央民族大学教学基本功大赛一等奖，并担任十多年的中央民族大学国际合作处副处长。博士毕业后近20年时间里，她分别在瑞士恺撒里兹酒店管理学院担任高级访问教授，从事酒店管理教学和科研工作；先后在美国加州大学伯克利分校、美国俄克拉荷马州立大学、英国剑桥大学沃尔森学院和牛津大学奥利尔学院访学。鉴于她丰富的阅历和学术建树，连续两届被聘为国际旅游学会（International Tourism Studies Association，ITSA）中国区副主席。在学术兼职方面，她被聘为首届中国旅游协会学科建设专家委员会委员、中国太平洋学会太平洋岛国研究分会常务理事等。

本教材分为8章，第1章对旅游进行了概述，后7章分别从旅游交通、旅游吸引物、旅游服务、旅游营销、文化旅游、可持续旅游和旅游的未来进行介绍，由浅入深，知识体系完整，并融入旅游热点问题，兼具系统性、实践性和专业性。就其知识结构来讲，本教材既可以视为旅游英语的语言类教材，也可以视为以专业英语为工具撰写的旅游学概论教材。虽然不是尽善尽美，但编撰者将其丰富的国际国内教学经历和经验融入教材的知识体系当中，英文表达标准地道，教学内容和形式丰富多样，兼有知识性、实用性、学术性、前沿性和趣味性，是一本非常好的旅游英语教材。

就教材的特色来讲，本教材为每一章的内容构建了导论、本章目标、阅读材料、案例研究专栏、对话、行业知识拓展、学术思考/论文导读、关键术语的知识框架。阅读材料侧重主题的宏观解读，案例研究专栏侧重通过情景故事动态把握教学内容，行业知识拓展侧重扩大学生知识面，学术思考/论文导读侧重对学生学术思维的训练，对话侧重具体场景中的应用。在支持任课教师教学开展方面，本教材还贴心地为任课教师提供了教学PPT，配备了外籍专家听力录音、思考题和在线答题，方便教师和相关教学人员使用，既是高等院校旅游管理专业的理想教学用书，也是旅游行业从业人员和广大旅游爱好者的参考读物。

作为国际旅游学会的创会主席，本人虽然并非英语方面的专业人士，但对旅游研究的国内外进展和教材特点的评估，还是略有积累。基于这样的知识背景，在初步翻阅了张瑛教授的《旅游英语》教材书稿之后，我非常高兴向广大

读者和旅游相关专业的师生推荐她多年悉心钻研、在长期积累基础上撰写的这本教材。

国际旅游学会创会主席
国际旅游研究院院士
北京大学城市与环境学院旅游研究与规划中心主任、教授

前言
Preface

　　旅游英语是旅游专业的主要课程。在"十四五"时期坚持高质量发展，坚持实施更大范围、更宽领域、更深层次对外开放的大环境下，亟需一本科学性、合理性、系统性、应用性和学术性相结合的旅游英语教材为旅游管理专业师生及相关专业人员服务。本教材具有以下特点：

　　第一，教材内容具有系统性、前瞻性、应用性和补缺性的特点。考虑到旅游专业的特性，本教材增加了以下几个方面的设计。首先，教材每章设有案例研究专栏(Case Study)，通过真实而经典的事件帮助学生从实际情景的描述中，通过对问题和情景的思考，加强对教学内容的动态把握。其次，教材每章设计了和教学内容相关的对话，以满足应用场景中实际操作的需要。再次，为拓宽学生识面，每章节还设计了行业知识拓展(Tips)部分，以拓展每个章节内容的相关知识。最后，考虑到国家高质量发展和旅游管理专业高质量教学的需求，本教材增设和每一章内容相关的学术思考/论文导读(Academic Thinking)内容，以期能帮助学生从实践中增加学术思维。学术论文大多从近几年国际顶尖期刊中精选，具有较高的国际学术水准且代表学术前沿。

　　第二，教材具有阅读材料经典权威、与时俱进且可读性强、启发性强、实用性强的特点。例如，教材将"一部手机游云南"、新冠肺炎疫情后迅速发展的直播和"云旅游"(Cloud Tourism)作为案例，入选本书学术思考/论文导读栏目。教材框架合理，教学资源丰富，除设计了导论(Introduction)、本章目标、关键术语(Key Words and Terms)、阅读材料(Reading)、对话(Dialogues)等部分外，还有案例研究(Case Study)、行业知识拓展(Tips)、学术思考/论文导读(Academic Thinking)，并有思考题和在线答题(配有参考答案)等，有利于激发读者的学习兴趣并扩充知识量。

　　本教材分为8章，由张瑛教授总策划、总设计、提供教材资料、撰写内容提要和前言,主持课题组成员进行多次讨论和修改并最终审稿校稿。课题组成员分工如下:第一章由宋杰航编写;第二、三章由张瑛、夏文轩编写;第四章由张瑛、方灵娟编写;第五章由芮雪怡、张瑛编写;第六章由刘彤瑶、张瑛编写;第七章由方灵娟编写;第八章由靳晶、张瑛编写。

目录
Contents

Chapter 1	What is Tourism	/001
Chapter 2	Transportation	/023
Chapter 3	Tourism Attractions	/051
Chapter 4	Tourism Service	/083
Chapter 5	Marketing for Tourism	/106
Chapter 6	Cultural Tourism	/139
Chapter 7	Sustainable Tourism	/171
Chapter 8	Trends and Future of Tourism	/191
参考文献		/218

Chapter 1
What is Tourism

I Chapter Introduction

Welcome to the study of one of the world's fastest growing industry—tourism! Tourism is the business of travel and hospitality. As an indispensable part of today's world, tourism touches all aspects of our life and plays a vital role in economic, cultural and social development of most nations. From the so-called frivolous and shallow activity to modern ritual, from luxury to necessity, tourism now evolves into all kinds: leisure travel, business travel, sightseeing trips, vacations for rest and relaxation, cultural pursuits, adventure, or visits with friends and relatives, etc. Subsequently, airplanes, hotels, car rentals and trains that are in place to serve the tourists. In countries like Mexico, Jamaica and Spain, tourism is the linchpin for the economy. For countries lacking valuable resources or heavy industry, tourism represents hope in breaking a spiral of poverty and misery. Closer to home, there are countless examples of communities where tourism stands for the base for the economy. Also, tourism industry makes commerce, diplomacy, and exchanges of ideas and cultures possible. "The world is becoming a global village," said Pope John Paul. Tourism can help overcome real prejudices and foster bonds. Tourism can be a real force of world peace.

This chapter will introduce basic concepts of tourism, including its definitions, classifications and development, etc. Through this, you may find tourism both a career worth engaging in and a valuable subject.

II Chapter Objectives

1. Understand and describe the definitions and classifications of tourism.
2. Understand the history of tourism and major features of each period.
3. Identify the major elements of tourism system.

4. Know some main tourism organizations and research journals.

Ⅲ Reading

1. Tourism Definitions

1.1 Economic Definition

Undoubtedly, tourism is an identifiable nationally important industry. The industry involves a wide cross section of component activities. Tourism refers to the provision of transportation, accommodation, recreation, food, and related services for domestic and overseas travelers. It involves travel for all purposes, including recreation and business. One economic definition recognizes that tourism involves more than the business components themselves, it has a qualitative facet: Tourism can be defined as the science, art and business of attracting and transporting visitors, accommodating them and graciously catering to their needs and wants. The economic approaches to a definition can be criticized. They state nothing explicitly about the tourist, the human element, who is arguably the focal point of the subject. Nor do they recognize spatial or temporal elements, which are equally significant.

1.2 Technical Definition

Since the 1930s, governments and tourist industry organizations have tried to monitor the size and characteristics of tourist markets. To do this they needed a definition of a tourist, to demarcate him from other travelers and to have a common base by which to collect comparable statistics.

Naturally, various definitions have taken radically different lines in the three elements in the definition of the tourist: purpose of trip, distance travelled and duration. The first of these tourist definitions was adopted by the League of Nations Statistical Committee in 1937 and referred to an international tourist, who "visits a country other than that in which he habitually lives for a period of at least twenty-four hours". This has been the basis of later definitions.

In 1963, the United Nations sponsored a conference on travel and tourism in Rome. The conference recommended definitions of "visitor" and "tourist" for use in compiling international statistics: For statistical purposes, the term "visitor" describes any person visiting a country other than that in which he has his usual place of residence, for any reason other than following an occupation remunerated from within the country visited. This definition covers: Tourists, i.e. temporary visitors staying at least twenty-four hours in the country visited and the purpose of whose journey can be classified under one of the following headings: (a) leisure (recreation, holiday, health, study, religion and sport), (b) business, family, mission, meeting.

Excursionists, i. e. temporary visitors staying less than twenty-four hours in the country visited (including travelers on cruise ships). In 1968, the International Union of Official Travel Organizations (now the World Tourism Organization) approved the definition given in 1963 and has since encouraged countries to use it. It is notable that as a result, statistical data on international tourists includes trips for purposes beyond the popular use of the word. The public and most employees of firms in the industry do not regard trips for business and some other purposes as constituting tourism. Statistical definitions of the tourist in a domestic setting (travelling within the country of residence) have varied among countries and regions, but have generally included the three elements of the standard international definition: distance travelled, duration and purpose. Partly because of a pre-occupation with measuring the size and nature of tourist markets, and partly because of the difficulties of coming to grips with the multiple facets of tourism, many definitions of tourism are framed by stating a particular definition of a tourist and extending it by implication to tourism generally. This is noticeable in submissions to governments. A British work of tourism has noted the confusion which arises from this: In endeavoring to define tourism, it is useful to distinguish between the concept and the technical definitions. The concept provides a notional, theoretical framework, which identifies the essential characteristics, and which distinguishes tourism from similar, often related, but different phenomena.

1.3 Holistic Definition

Holistic definitions attempt to embrace "the whole" essence of a subject. Two Swiss academics defined tourism in a 1942 study as: "The sum of the phenomena and relationships arising from the travel and stay of non-residents, in so far as they do not lead to permanent residence and are not connected to any earning activity." This definition has been recognized by various international organizations. Its feature is its scope, recognizing that tourism embraces many facets centering around the principal one, tourists. Because it is not framed in the terminology of an academic discipline, this definition allows interdisciplinary and multidisciplinary approaches to the study of tourism. While its approach is sound, the phrase "sum of phenomena and relationships" is criticized for being too vague and not indicating methodical applications or extensions.

The editor of *Annals of Tourism Research* has seen the need to incorporate into the study of tourism theories and concepts from the affiliated fields, e.g. anthropology, sociology, economics, geography, political science, ecology and urban studies. That list could be extended to include marketing, law, management, psychology and others. He also proposed another holistic approach, "Tourism is the study of man away from his usual habitat, of the industry which responds to his needs, and of the impacts that both he and the industry have on the host's socio-cultural, economic and

physical environments".

A third holistic approach appeared in a study of the design of tourist regions. It presented a model which can be viewed as a definition of tourism, claiming that the designer has an opportunity for a closed system of tourism environment made up of the five components: people in a market area with desire and ability to participate; attractions that offer activities for user participation; services and facilities for users or that support the activities; transportation that moves people to and from the attraction destinations; and information and direction that assists users in knowing, finding, enjoying.

Tourism defined in a system framework would enable each of its basic facets to be identified. They become the elements of the system. Such an approach would facilitate multidisciplinary studies of particular aspects of tourism and more significantly would give interdisciplinary studies of various facets and perspectives: common point of reference; the division between the two camps of academic scholarship could be bridged. Before starting a new system definition, it is necessary to identify and define its elements. From the earlier discussion, it suggested that four facets are involved: tourists, geographical components, an industrial component, and various interactions with broader environments.

2. Tourism Classifications

Figure 1.1 shows the tourism classifications.

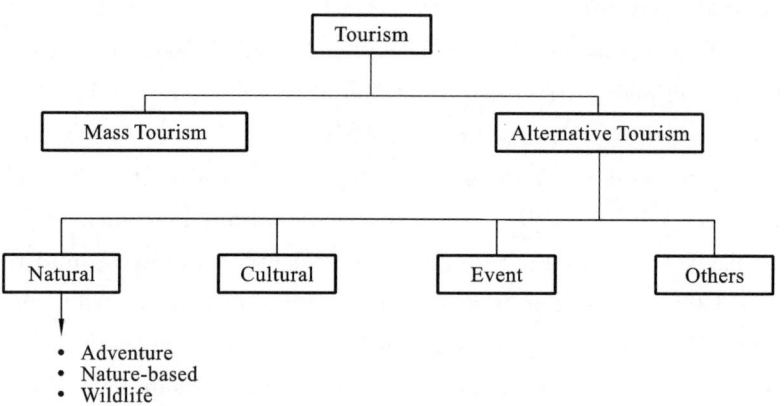

Figure 1.1 Tourism classifications

2.1 Mass Tourism

Mass tourism is related to two main characteristics: (a) participation of large numbers of people in tourism; and (b) the holiday is standardized, rigidly packaged and inflexible. The number of international tourist arrivals is expected to continue to grow, and with it the phenomenon of mass tourism. Benefits and costs of tourism can be measured at different levels: national, regional or local. In all cases, a social cost-benefit analysis is the adequate approach. In such an approach, paid and unpaid benefits and costs and side effects are taken into account. The key benefits of mass tourism are income and employment generation. For both benefits input-output analysis is the best method of assessment. The key cost items are the so-called incidental costs. These lead to quality-of-life costs and public or fiscal costs. To cope with the negative impacts, attention should be paid to: (a) staggering of holidays in time, space and product; (b) tolerable numbers as a central issue in tourism planning; and (c) a better behaved kind of tourist. For sustainable tourism a region should put environment first. This means building responsible tourism, fostering a culture of conservation and developing an environmental focus.

What does mass tourism mean exactly? Is it a package tour? Is it a concentration of tourists in a resort or region? Is it tourism with a low profile? These are only some aspects of the phenomenon. The basic elements of mass tourism are:

(1) participation of large numbers of people;

(2) mainly collective organization of travelling;

(3) collective accommodation;

(4) conscious integration of the holidaymaker in a travelling group.

A more general and workable definition was found with Burkart and Medlik (1992): Mass tourism refers to the participation of large numbers of people in tourism. In this sense the term is used in contrast to the limited participation of people in some specialist forms of tourist activity, such as yachting, or in contrast to the situation in developing countries or in countries with extreme inequalities of income and wealth or, indeed, to the limited extent of tourist activity everywhere until a few decades ago. Mass tourism is essentially a quantitative notion, based on the proportion of the population participating in tourism or on the volume of tourist activity.

The notion of mass tourism should be distinguished from the notion of popular and social tourism. Once again to refer to Burkart and Medlik (1992): Popular tourism denotes tourist activities meeting with a wide acceptance by people, because of their attractiveness and availability. The acceptance may be due to meeting the needs or tastes of people or more particularly to being available at a low price. Popular tourism is, therefore, essentially a qualitative notion, although by its nature it may give rise to mass tourism.

As distinct from the former two examples, social tourism is concerned specifically with the participation in tourism of people of limited means and with the measures to encourage this participation and to make it possible. From these definitions two main features can be derived:

(1) The participation of large numbers of people in tourism, whatever the tourist activity may be.

(2) The holiday is mainly standardized, rigidly packaged and inflexible.

2.2 Alternative Tourism

As a concept, alternative tourism is surprisingly broad. It is fundamentally problematic when subject to analysis and brings out many emotional responses, a common feature of tourism as a subject. There is not one single or absolute definition, although there are a number of very good attempts, and many writers give a list of criteria against which it should be assessed. It remains an important issue to be dealt with, not the least because of its relationship to basic problems that human society must confront: environmental destruction, wealth inequalities, and irresponsible development among others. It is also growing in popularity as fashions change and tourists seek different experiences. Just as it has been promoted as a development tool and a means of protecting nature, so it has also been seen as an attractive way to pass leisure time without causing ecological damage.

This part is a critical inquiry into the character of alternative tourism and its impact and is composed of two major sections. The first section deals with its meaning as can be ascertained from surveying and comparing the works of different scholars; the second deals with its impact, in which the influences described by various scholars are compared, including detailed case studies. Finally, the conclusion challenges the viability of the term "alternative tourism" and proposes a new approach. It also attempts to revise our understanding of the impact of this type of tourism, critiquing earlier models and stressing the powerful influences that it has had on the environment and the host populations. Throughout this discussion, problems are highlighted and suggestions are made for future research.

For Cohen (1987), alternative tourism is not even a single general concept, but composed of two principal conceptions. First, it is seen as a reaction to modern consumerism, a counter-cultural response to mass tourism composed of such characters as the adventurer, drifter, traveler, or those looking for spontaneity or romantically searching for a lost paradise. He suggests that these types occasionally create their own cultural enclaves involving drugs and sex, treating local people as oddities, and initiating a diminution of the culture of hospitality amongst the host community. There is also the incipient creation of an alternative tourism "establishment" which leads to a further reduction in difference between alternative and mass tourism. Second, it is conceived as "concerned alternative tourism" which is in essence a reaction to the exploitation of the Third World in which the notion of a "just" tourism arises, furthering mutual understanding and preventing environmental or cultural degradation and exploitation. In this type of tourism small groups interact with local people, and small-scale projects involving local consultation and participation are the principal means of promotion. Cohen offered a good working definition, drawing attention to two central aspects, and has added a healthy air of critical judgment.

It is suggested that alternative tourism is underpinned by a number of principles:

(1) It should be built on dialogue with local people who ought to be aware of its effects and have political weight concerning the matter.

(2) It should be established on sound environmental principles, sensitive to local culture and religious tradition.

(3) It should be a means of giving the poor a reasonable and more equal share in the gains.

(4) The scale of tourism should be tailored to match the capacity of the local area to cope, measured in aesthetic and ecological terms.

3. Tourism Development

Tourism has a history colored with both success and failure. For the most part, tourism is a story of rapid change effected by industrial and technological advances. In summary, the history of tourism is filled with social, economic and political currents that move the industry forward. The understanding of the history of tourism is the mix of people's motivations and the availability of attractions. Travel patterns change with the times, technology and policies, but do not stop. The spark of adventure first experienced by prehistoric travelers has been passed from the visitors to the Nile, to pilgrims and crusaders, to the first tourists on a Cook's tour, and on to the modern day traveler who enjoys the luxury of cruising or flying by civic aviation flights. From a historical point of view, progress in tourism has been spectacular.

3.1 Tourism in Prehistoric Times

Early humans lived hard lives. Evidence from the latter part of the Paleolithic Age suggests that all human activity focused upon day-to-day survival. The search for basic necessities—food, water and shelter—kept early hunters and gatherers on the move. This often meant difficult and dangerous travel for families or entire communities. People traveled by foot over paths. Foot trails were useful when available. More often, early humans had to travel to new, unfamiliar locations, which meant breaking new trails. Movement across the landscape was a perilous adventure that required caution and skill. Like the animals they hunted, prehistoric humans had to cope with dangerous predators including other hunting and gathering tribes. Once a hospitable region was explored, foot paths were developed that led to hunting grounds and to seasonal sources of food and water. The discovery and control of fire, the use of tools, and the ability to build shelters broadened the range of travel. The ability to use tools and build shelters permitted prehistoric humans to travel to new hunting grounds and food gathering locations even in extreme or unpredictable weather.

Although traveling was rigorous and unsafe, it did not stop early people from migrating all over the globe. Although we may be uncomfortable with the company we keep as world travelers, the point is proven: Humans have traveled since the beginning of time.

3.2 Tourism in Neolithic Times

The Neolithic Age refers to a time of change which began about 10000 years ago. During this period, primitive people settled in more permanent areas, formed agricultural communities and developed elementary cultures. These agricultural communities had many advantages over the nomadic tribes of the Paleolithic Age. For one, the community was more likely to have a reliable food source. In addition, food could be stored and consumed at a later date, which reduced the need to migrate to new hunting grounds.

Several innovations during the Neolithic Age changed the nature of travel forever. Sailing vessels were built in Egypt around 4000 BC. During this period, animals were being domesticated and trained to carry supplies, community members, weapons and tools; the Sumerians invented the wheel around 3500 BC and used it to move materials, people, military might, and to make pottery and tools. Each development alone, and in combination, dramatically affected travel. The burdens of travel were considerably reduced and the distance which a person, a group, or whole community could travel expanded from a few miles to hundreds.

Most early travel was associated with the trade and exchange of goods. Growing agricultural communities were able to maintain reliable sources of food and water, offered some measure of safety and stability for travelers. This security fostered exchanges of surplus food, artifacts, tools and weapons among neighboring communities and cultures. Innovations in the means of travel also made trading a realistic venture for some community members.

Related to the rise of travel for trade was the development of media of exchange between communities. Before coins were invented, valuables such as attractive jewelry, knives and implements for lighting fires served as exchange media. The first coins were developed around 680 BC. They were irregular and round in shape with official imprints stamped by the issuing government. With the coin, travel costs could be managed without transporting cumbersome, perishable, and often heavy bundles of valuables for barter.

The unique cultures and religions which emerged during the Neolithic Revolution fostered travel for religious and spiritual purposes. While early hunters and gatherers traveled to survive, the people of primitive agricultural communities were able to set aside regular time for spiritual events and festivals. Some members of the community traveled to shrines, burial grounds, sacred locations, and places of exceptional beauty or mystery.

The leisure time required for pleasure travel was very scarce in primitive societies, even in the first agricultural communities. As these communities stabilized, and as surplus food supplies and trade increased, leisure time did appear for some people. The quality of life for community members was significantly higher than members of earlier hunting and gathering tribes. Gradually, the number of options increased in terms of how people could choose to spend their time and their resources.

3.3 Tourism in Ancient Civilizations: Ancient Greece, Egypt and Rome

Many historians and anthropologists consider travel for trade and commerce a common activity in ancient civilizations. Civilizations of great power, long duration and extensive dominion were also known for sophisticated levels of commerce. As commerce grew, so did travel for pleasure. The societies of ancient Greece, Egypt and Rome openly encouraged pleasure travel by providing necessary ways and means. With such support, travel contributed to the success of each of these great empires.

3.3.1 Conditions for Travel

The ever-increasing specialization of labor within ancient civilizations fostered the growth of travel. As ancient communities grew in size, the tasks and roles of the population became more specialized and skilled. This made it possible for communities to develop an array of products that increased in quality with each generation. Craftsmen honed their skills and passed them on to family members or others willing to learn. Such division of skills meant that people needed to exchange goods to survive. For example, a craftsperson busy producing pottery would not have time to plant and harvest crops for food. This scarcity of time required the craftsperson to obtain such necessities through barter and trade with the person who specialized in planting and harvesting crops.

The exchange of products and currency required travel. Caravans and trade expeditions moved people, products and ideas between cultures. The oceans provided the major routes of travel for the cultures centered in the Mediterranean, particularly the Greek, Egyptian and Roman empires. Roads, too, supported the swift deployment of military power and facilitated the exchange of goods over vast distances. Over time, the earliest foot trails became overland trade routes. As these routes were maintained and improved, they became the basis for extensive road systems.

Road systems were quite advanced in several ancient civilizations. The Romans were excellent road builders. Well-maintained road systems were extremely important to the Roman Empire because they supported rapid communication across the republic. Road systems, too, enabled swift and effective military movement which kept the empire intact. In fact, the quality of life for citizens within the Roman Empire was partly due to the diversity of goods, foods and services made possible by an effective road system.

Based upon the history and quality of these road systems, we can assume that travel was an important part of commerce, government and cultural exchange during the rule of the Romans. In the latter years of the Roman Empire, the road system included inns, stables for animals, crude maps or itineraries. Travel was on foot, on horseback, in carriages of various types, or in a litter—a covered or curtained couch carried by slaves or servants.

Travel technologies and the ability to support commerce and trade over long distances resulted in improvements for travel of all types, including pleasure, communications and military travel. After conflicts and wars, the victor usually absorbed the best innovations, social behaviors, tools and implements of the conquered. Conquered lands had to be managed, controlled, supplied and that required those in power to settle within the new lands and adapt to a new setting, new land and people. Travel blossomed as those in power and the new citizens moved back and forth between territories. With peace established, military routes became routes of commerce, and of political, social and religious exchange.

3.3.2 Early Pleasure and Religious Travel

While military and commercial goals may have been major stimuli for early travel, the wonders of travel itself were not lost on the peoples of ancient societies. Ancient travelers were lured to new lands to discover beautiful places, to experience natural attractions, and to obtain curios. However, the majority of pleasure travel was allowed or affordable only to those in power or with sufficient resources.

Those with the necessary resources frequently traveled for religious purposes. The monuments to the gods became travel destinations that people visited out of religious motives or curiosity. Ancient Egyptians traveled to religious centers up and down the Nile, Greeks traveled to Mount Olympus, and the early Christians traveled to the holy cities of Jerusalem and Rome.

Cultural events often developed from religious festivals and became attractions in their own right. Examples from Greece included classical drama and the Olympic Games. These popular events attracted local residents from the countryside and the foreign visitor. Some Greek plays had religious overtones while the games originated in a spiritual festival in honor of Zeus. Greek literature and philosophy also underscored leisure and travel in the pursuit of self-enrichment and exploration. Philosophers Plato and Aristotle both stressed the importance of leisure to society, arguing that such activities helped develop better citizens and political leaders. Now here is the Greek fascination for travel more clearly illustrated than in the *Iliad* and the *Odyssey*—epics written by Homer around 700 BC.

The Romans, too, traveled for a variety of reasons and enjoyed such attractions. The Romans had safe access to Egypt, Asia Minor, Greece and extensive parts of present-day Europe and Africa. Travel for business, pleasure, religion and sport was recognized as an important use of a well-to-do Roman's leisure time and discretionary resources.

The primary conditions that nurtured travel were present during the time of the Roman Empire. The Roman citizens had the resources and time for travel. The empire, too, provided the support services such as roads, inns, slaves and a host of consumer goods. Holidays were plentiful. All the gods needed to be celebrated and, of course, a military victory was an excellent reason for celebration. At one point nearly one third of the days in a year were set aside for holidays.

As the Roman Empire was awash in the pleasures of games, festivals and leisure, another movement was emerging as the next dominant force to control leisure and travel behavior—Christianity. The stability of the Roman Empire permitted relatively free flow of travel for the teachers of this new religion. In the time immediately after the life of Christ, the Apostles moved about the Roman Empire, taking advantage of the safe, qualified road system.

3.4 Tourism in Middle Ages: the Crusades and Pilgrimages

The fall of the Roman Empire between 400 AD and 500 AD ushered in changes that profoundly affected travel. In the centuries that followed, to about 1000 AD, the safety, services and comforts of travel disappeared. Local travel continued in response to limited bartering and trade. However civil wars, changes in leadership and shifting political and military boundaries made travel difficult and dangerous. Limited trade among the European feudal communities represented most of the significant travel that occurred.

These Middle Ages or Dark Ages were indeed dark times for travel. The luxury of vacation travel disappeared. Resources required for the common person travel were no longer available. The new rulers of the old Roman lands did not continue to develop leisure activities for the masses. The common person was subjected to a life of toil in the service of land owners in return for food, shelter and protection. During these times, the Roman Catholic Church became a central force throughout Europe. The Roman festivals, games and holidays gave way to Catholic holy days. A person's time was to be spent in religious thought of heavenly rewards, not in worldly pleasure.

The only major travel activities of the period included crusades and pilgrimages. During the Middle Ages, pilgrimages were undertaken for a variety of purposes. Some individuals traveled to religious sites for the forgiveness of their sins, others to receive a divine cure for their health problems. While religion was the primary purpose for a pilgrimage, adventure, learning and merriment were also enjoyed on the trip.

Travel was by foot or horseback; when possible, pilgrims traveled by boat on horse-drawn coach. The mass pilgrimages required communities near the shrines or along popular routes to provide accommodations for these spiritual travelers. Some inns catered only to particular nationalities; others varied by location and in terms of the resources of the traveler.

By the thirteenth and fourteenth centuries, pilgrimage was a mass phenomenon. A growing industry of charitable hospices and mass-produced indulgence handbooks

served the travelers. Eventually, the religious nature of travel gave way to more secular pleasures, education and sightseeing. Significant social changes began to shape a new sense of the individual. People began to search for a better quality of life, and acknowledged the importance of education, culture, art and science. This important period was called the Renaissance.

3.5 Tourism in the Renaissance: the Grand Tour

The Renaissance was a time of enlightenment, change and exploration from the fourteenth to the seventeenth century. During this period, the Grand Tour of Europe emerged as one of the first manifestations of upper-class travel. It is here, too, that we see the beginnings of modern tourism.

The Grand Tour began as an educational experience for the sons of the English aristocracy. Generally, the tour started in England and had the major cultural cities of Italy as its ultimate destination. A typical tour took the young traveler, his servants and tutors to France, to Rome, and then back to England via Germany and the Netherlands.

The Grand Tour encompassed the period from 1500 to about 1820. During its early years, the Grand Tour could last as long as 40 months because of the extensive amount of study involved. For example, the young aristocrat could spend an entire year studying a new language or a particular type of literature. In the time of the Grand Tour, travel purposes went beyond commerce, trade, religion and military expeditions. Education, culture, health, pleasure, curiosity, science, career development, art and scenery became motives for traveling—motives very different from those of the Middle Ages. People traveled to experience culture, and to learn about the new scientific discoveries. These same scientific findings turned into technologies that facilitated travel. Ship building, geographical analyses, navigational skills and training, and map making were making travel safer over longer distances. Traveling to observe scenery also emerged as an important travel motivation in the latter part of the Grand Tour era. In the late 1700s, writers, artists and philosophers began to argue for the value, inherent beauty and the sublime characteristics of nature which all people could see and appreciate.

Near the end of the Grand Tour era, the trip lasted a mere four months, and the age of the average traveler had increased. By the 1800s, the Grand Tour, for the most part, was taken by members of the upper and middle classes. These individuals traveled more for pleasure than for an extended educational tour.

Transportation was always a concern for the traveling party. Crossing the Alps drained the most devoted travelers. Marshes, waterways and poor roads yielded physical punishment. Road villains and thieves also posed a threat. The traveler could cross Europe via postal or mail coach system, canal or river vessel, on horse, or by foot. By the time the steamboat and railroads revolutionized travel in the early 1800s, the Grand Tour was fading as a phenomenon.

During the latter part of the Grand Tour, travel was facilitated by transportation rentals. An important transportation advance in the 1700s was the "all-inclusive" rental or purchase agreement. Upon arriving on the continent, English tourists could purchase or rent a carriage that they later returned or sold back to the original establishment. In 1820, carriages could be rented at hotels for travel throughout Europe, much like rental cars can today. In 1829, a travel merchant in London offered one of the first all-inclusive trips to Switzerland for 16 days covering all transportation, food and lodging. Thus, the all-inclusive package tour was born.

3.6 Tourism in Industrial Age

During the Industrial Age, the economies of nations shifted from rural agriculture to urban-based industry. The structure of employment, class and affluence shifted as well. More and more people were able to travel for health, pleasure and curiosity. Expanding railroads, distant travel by sea and the coach system all contributed to the democratization of travel.

Health and pleasure were strong travel motivations during the seventeenth and eighteenth centuries. Strong motivations for travel were also generated through a movement in literature and the arts. Through the early 1800s, writers, poets, artists and explorers extolled the virtues of the natural world. This love of nature, beauty and the sublime represented the romantic period or romanticism in Europe and America. Stories of beautiful landscapes, majestic mountains and vast oceans were passed on to the masses for their enjoyment; through these stories, the public developed an interest in faraway places and unknown lands. In other words, the precursor for travel was set in the minds of people.

The most important travel developments during the Industrial Age occurred in transportation. The expansion of the coach system was as much a by-product of the development of the postal service as it was a response to the increasing demands tourism and business travel. In England, early attempts to schedule coach service between two cities began around 1669. Nearly 100 years later, England had a fairly comprehensive postal service and a nearly complete coach service between cities. However, not all cities were connected nor was travel easy and convenient.

Travel by water offered more alternatives than coach travel as migration and colonization developed, and was considered more pleasurable. Travel on the high seas was advancing in terms of technology, safety, speed and convenience, but even in the 1800s, sea travel was still an ordeal.

In the 1820s, regular ferry service was initiated across the English Channel. Before this time, steamboats traveled on the rivers of France and America. In 1787, steamboat was tested on the Potomac. This foreshadowed the extensive use of America's waterways as courses of commerce, as boundaries for settlements, and a

relatively smooth means of travel. By 1800, many rivers were essentially the "highways" of the new world.

Travel by ship soon became an important means of travel for the Europeans. As the ships plowed the seas, the steam engine made railroads the symbol of mass travel by land. The Liverpool and Manchester Railway opened in England in 1830. Trains soon become a major force in travel and development.

The fine art and business skill of developing the inclusive group tour can be credited to Thomas Cook of England. While others may have used the concept earlier, Cook made the group tour a true business venture that appealed to the public. As an active member of the Temperance Society, he put together the first group trip by train in July 1841. He arranged a trip by rail of nearly 600 people to a large temperance meeting.

Some four years later, Cook began arranging tours as a commercial business. He began with small tours within England, taking school children, mothers, women, couples and common people to places they had not been able to visit before the development of the train and inexpensive tours.

Cook's success rested in his ability to understand the travel possibilities of his time. He saw the need, the desire and the motivations for travel and capitalized on all three through his tours. Cook recognized how new industries were changing the social and economic structure of his day. He saw how people were moving off the land and into the cities for employment and livelihood. He saw how rails and waterways moved manufacturing materials in and out of the cities. And finally, Cook saw how these same rails and waterways could be used to move people. Also, his service contributed to his success. Cook handled all the matters related to tours such as connections, tickets and timetables. He handled currency exchanges for trips abroad and even published travel guides and tour timetables at his printing company. By doing so, Cook developed strong loyalties with his customers. These customers, in turn, would tell friends or relatives about the joys of a Cook's tour. By today's jargon, what Cook had done was to build for himself an effective word-of-mouth marketing program.

The Cook's Tours between 1850 and 1900 foreshadowed the true age of travel for the masses. However, it is difficult to say exactly when such tourism and travel truly became available. Certainly, the advent of railroads, large safe ships and Cook's package tours gave millions of middle-class people an opportunity to travel beyond their own communities. A world was now open to the middle class that was once open only to the very rich. But even so, tourism required more than money, it required time, which is truly scarce.

3.7 Modern Mass Tourism

A series of key technological, political and social events during the first 50 years of the twentieth century finally made tourism a major worldwide business and leisure

experience for the middle class. While travel was greatly limited during the two world wars, the desire to travel seemed to increase.

However, it was not so much the economy that reduced sea travel as it was the emergence of the automobile and the airplane. Both became reliable modes of travel for a large middle class, a middle class which had the financial means and leisure time for travel. In this sense, modern mass tourism had come into its own.

Historically, holy days created free time for the masses to travel, relax and be away from work. After the World War I, industries within several countries considered granting holidays for their employees. In England, while labor unions were obtaining benefits such as paid holidays, youth movements—such as the Cooperative Holidays Association and the Workers Travel Association—were organizing for travel to foster personal development and culture. In the United States, the work week was shrinking, holidays were expanding, and the paid vacation was being considered.

Throughout the history of tourism, the common theme has been that the phenomenon affects the rich first, the middle class second, and the working class third. The public began to travel in earnest when paid vacations and holidays became available for all classes of workers. By the 1920s, the two-week vacation was being accepted for the middle-class workers, but not yet for the working class.

The shorter workweek, paid holidays and longer vacations were condition that facilitated mass tourism. In addition, the increase in real incomes for the working class and middle class contributed to the arrival of mass leisure and tourism after the World War II. Travel and tourism has continued its transformation in more recent times. As general travel took off with the airlines in the 1960s, other changes occurred around the world that altered the course of tourism.

4. Tourism Model

The model presented in Figure 1.2 was developed to highlight important participants and forces that shape the tourism industry.

This model can be used as a reference throughout the entire text. Let's begin our study of tourism by looking at travelers (tourists), who serve as the focal point for all tourism activities and form the center of our model. Radiating from this focal point are three large bands containing several interdependent groups of tourism participants and organizations. Tourism suppliers may provide these services independently; they may compete with each other; and, at times, they may work together. For example, airline, bus, railroad, cruise ship and car rental companies may compete individually for a traveler's business. However, they may also team up to provide cooperative packages such as fly-ride, fly-cruise, and fly-drive alternatives. Airlines establish strategic alliances with many other carriers to provide seamless travel across states, nations and continents. Hotels and resorts may also compete against each other for the same traveler's patronage yet cooperate with transportation providers to attract

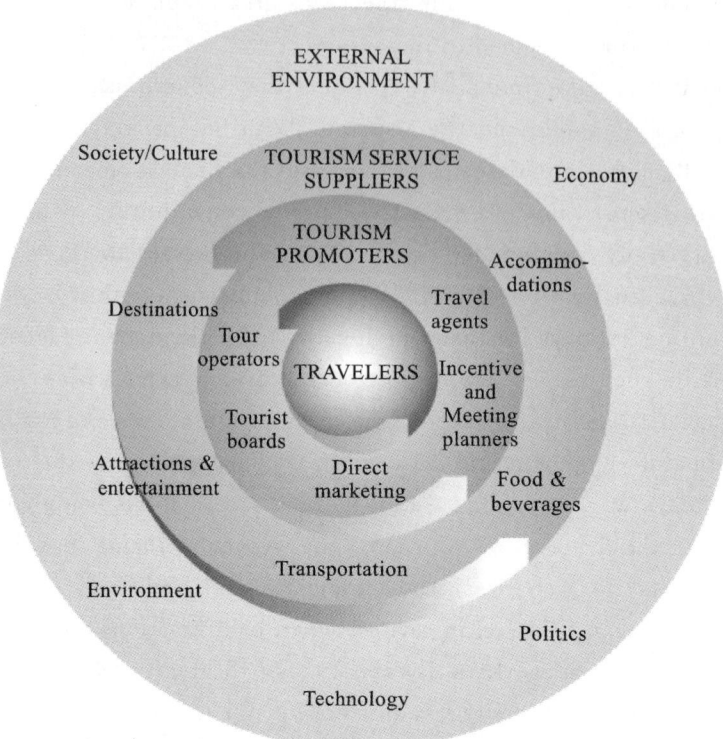

Figure 1.2 An Integrated Model of Tourism

tourists to a specific location. Service providers representing all segments of the tourism industry may often work together to develop promotional packages designed to attract tourists to destinations.

How closely these individuals and organizations work together is ultimately influenced by the forces shaping the face of tourism activities. All participants of the tourism industry are constantly responding to a variety of social/cultural, political, environmental, economic and technological forces. These forces may range from subtle changes, which are noticeable only after many years, to more dramatic changes, which have immediate and visible impacts. Examples of these forces can be found all around us.

Let's look at how our model might work. Suppose you (a tourist) want to visit a sunny beach or a snow-covered mountain. You might begin planning your trip by browsing the websites of different airlines, condominiums, hotels, or resorts (tourism service suppliers) searching for possible flight schedules and accommodation options. You could simply call a travel agent (tourism promoter) who would search out the best alternatives to meet your needs, rather than spending time and money contacting each supplier. Another option would be taking a "virtual trip" to your desired destination by browsing offerings on the Internet. Finally, you could contact your preferred destinations' local chambers of commerce or visitors' bureaus to learn more about their offerings.

As you progress through this book, we will focus our attention on specific features of our model, learning more about each component and how it interacts with other components of the tourism industry.

 Ⅳ Case Study

Phone in hand, Yunnan to go

Background

Yunnan Province is located in southwestern China and has lots of natural attractions and rich ethnic culture. The unique tourism resources fascinate thousands of tourists from all over the world. However, the phenomenon of compulsory shopping and brutal tour guides in Yunnan tourism has been criticized, the restrictions from government win little success. Tourists' rights cannot be protected, leading to the decline of tourism experience as well as tourism satisfaction. Yunnan's tourism image is severely damaged. How will the government deal with the situation?

Countermeasures

In September 2017, led by governor Ruan Chengfa, Yunnan Province cooperated with Tencent to establish a provincial-level tourism App named "Tour Yunnan", which is the first province-wide intelligent tourism platform in China. Jointly led by Yunnan Province and Tencent, this App integrates more than 3000 government agencies and more than 300 destination resources in the province. "Tour Yunnan" relies on a number of core technologies such as the Internet of Things (IoT), cloud computing, big data, Artificial Intelligence (AI), face recognition, applets, Tencent Cloud, WeChat payment, etc., to open the entire chain of tourism industries such as hotels, restaurants, scenic spots, commerce and provide tourists with service in the whole process of the tour.

In October 2018, "Tour Yunnan" was officially launched with the slogan "Yunnan has only one scenic spot called Yunnan". Users as tourists can download it from the mobile App store to get an overview of the tourism resources of the 16 cities in Yunnan, and experience various functions such as the heat map of the scenic spot, face swiping into the park, audio guide, toilet navigation, etc. Among its diverse functions, what is most important is when encountering problems or treated unfairly during travel, tourists can complain to the departments concerned at any time through "Tour Yunnan" and receive feedback within 24 hours.

Effect

Now, through the App, domestic and foreign tourists can enjoy immersive tourism experience of tourist destinations, ticket purchase, car rental, tour guides, face recognition, boarding and hotel check-in, as well as finding toilets, taking photos and shopping. Users can also choose English language service to truly realize "tour Yunnan with your mobile phone, and walk away without worry". The core is to focus on solving the pain points and difficulties of tourists with the help of government and new technologies. This App has fully digitized tourism elements and provided tourists with safer, more effective, affordable and environmentally friendly personalized services.

On the 2019 CITM (China International Travel Mart) co-hosted by Ministry of Culture and Tourism and Yunnan Province, "Tour Yunnan" App was introduced to all attendants as the benchmark of smart tourism. It also won the Project Management Institute's award in 2019.

In the next step, "Tour Yunnan" will help Yunnan to fully try out innovative applications in the 5G environment, combining identity recognition and face recognition to achieve unimpeded "brushing" applications in Yunnan, while actively promoting car networking and automatic driving; using digital means to build the Western Yunnan Tourism Circle into a 5G smart tourism test field and a unique tourist destination in the world, and strive to build Yunnan into a world-class smart tourism destination through the development of digital cultural tourism and government-industry-university-research collaboration.

V Tips

What is UNWTO?

The World Tourism Organization (UNWTO) has been the United Nations specialized agency from 2003. Formed in November 1974, it is the leading international organization in the field of tourism, which promotes tourism as a driver of economic growth, inclusive development and environmental sustainability. It serves as a global forum for tourism policy issues and a practical source of tourism knowledge. Zurab Pololikashvili became UNWTO Secretary-General in 2018. By far membership of the UNWTO includes 158 states, six territories, and two permanent observers worldwide. And now its headquarters are in Madrid.

The objectives of the UNWTO are to promote and develop sustainable tourism to contribute to economic development, international understanding, peace, prosperity without distinction as to race, gender, language or religion. The main tasks of

UNWTO are to formulate international tourism conventions and rules, study global tourism policies, collect and analyze tourism data, and provide statistical data to member countries on a regular basis.

What is WTTC?

The World Travel & Tourism Council (WTTC) is a forum for the travel and tourism industry. It is made up of members from the global business community and works with governments to raise awareness about the travel and tourism industry. It is known for being the only forum to represent the private sector in all parts of the industry worldwide. Its activities include research on the economic and social impact of the industry and its organization of global and regional summits focused on issues and developments relevant to the industry.

 Ⅵ Dialogue

Tourism Routes and Attractions Consulting

(Here is a woman speaking with a travel agent officer and consults with some tourism routes.)

Travel Agent: Good morning, World Tours. My name is Jamie. How can I help you?

Andrea: Good morning. This is Andrea Brown. I want some information on self-drive tours in the USA. Could you send me a brochure and introduce some main spots?

Travel Agent: Of course, I'll get the brochures in the post to you, but can I give you some information over the phone? What kinds of things do you want to do on your holiday?

Andrea: I'm interested in going to California with my family. I've got two children and we want to hire a car.

Travel Agent: OK. We have a couple of self-drive tours there visiting different places of interest in California. The first one begins in Los Angeles and there's plenty of time to visit some of the theme parks there, for example, the Disneyland.

Andrea: That's something on my children's list so I want to include that.

Travel Agent: Good. Then you drive to San Francisco. From San Francisco you can drive to Yosemite Park where you spend a couple of nights. You can choose to stay in a lodge or on the campsite.

Andrea: I don't like the idea of staying in a tent. It'd be too hot.

Travel Agent: Right. And the tour ends in Las Vegas.

Andrea: OK.

Travel Agent: The other trip we can arrange is slightly different. It starts in San Francisco. Then you drive south to Florida.

Andrea: Someone told me there's a really nice heritage farm near Florida. We will go near that?

Travel Agent: Fiddy Working Heritage Farm is on that road so you could stop there. This open-air museum gives you the experience of agriculture and rural life in the English countryside at the end of the nineteenth century so you'll see a typical farm of that period.

Andrea: Good. I'd like to do that. Does this trip also go into the desert?

Travel Agent: No, it continues to Santa Monica where most people like to stop and do some shopping. There are some shopping centers in commercial districts.

Andrea: We have enough of that at home so that doesn't interest us.

Travel Agent: OK. Well, you could go straight on to San Diego. Then you may as well go to the museum, one with a remarkable range of exhibits, which I'm sure you'll enjoy.

Andrea: Well, I see. So how many days are the trips and how much do they cost?

Travel Agent: The first one I told you about is a self-drive tour through California which lasts twelve days and covers 2020 kilometers. The cost is £525 per person. That includes accommodation, car rental and a flight but no meals.

Andrea: OK. And the other trip?

Travel Agent: That lasts nine days but you spend only three days on the road. You cover about 980 kilometers altogether and the fee is £385 per person.

Andrea: OK. Well, thank you very much. I'll be in touch when I've had a chance to look at the brochure.

Travel Agent: I'm pleased to help. Goodbye.

Andrea: Bye.

Ⅶ Academic Thinking

A Review of Research into Automation in Tourism:
Launching the *Annals of Tourism Research Curated Collection on Artificial Intelligence and Robotics* in Tourism

Author: Iis Tussyadiah

Journal: *Annals of Tourism Research*

Abstract:

Driven by the advancements in artificial intelligence (AI) and its related technologies, the application of intelligent automation in travel and tourism is expected to increase in the future. This paper unpacks the need to shape an automated future of tourism as a social phenomenon and an economic activity, hence contributes to theory and practice by providing directions for future research in this area. Four research priorities are suggested: designing beneficial AI, facilitating adoption, assessing the impacts of intelligent automation, and creating a sustainable future with artificial intelligence. Research in these areas will allow for a systematic knowledge production that reflects a concerted effort from the scientific community to ensure the beneficial applications of intelligent automation in tourism. The article also launches the *Annals of Tourism Research Curated Collection on Artificial Intelligence and Robotics*. The collection contains all past articles published in *Annals of Tourism Research* on the topic, and continues to grow as new articles are added.

旅游自动化研究综述:《旅游研究年鉴人工智能与机器人技术精选文集》发布

在人工智能及其相关技术发展的推动下,未来智能自动化在旅游领域的应用将越来越广泛。本文将旅游业作为一种社会现象和经济活动来塑造一个自动化的未来,从而为这一领域的未来研究提供理论和实践指导。本文提出了四个研究方向:设计有益的人工智能、提高人工智能使用率、评估智能自动化的影响,以及用人工智能创造可持续的未来。在这些领域的研究将允许系统的知识生产,反映出科学界的一致努力,以确保智能自动化在旅游业中的有益应用。这篇文章还推出了《旅游研究年鉴人工智能与机器人技术研究精选文集》。该文集包含所有过去发表在《旅游研究年鉴》上的相关文章,并随着新的文章的增加而继续增加。

Ⅷ Questions(扫码看答案)

1. What do you think is the most important driving force to stimulate the development of tourism from Prehistoric Times through Modern Times? Why?

2. Could you please give some basic research issues in current tourism study?

Ⅸ Key Words and Terms

WTO (World Tourism Organization)	世界旅游组织
WTTC (World Travel and Tourism Council)	世界旅行和旅游理事会
PATA (Pacific Asia Travel Association)	亚太旅游协会
UFTAA (Universal Federation of Travel Agent's Association)	世界旅行社协会联合会
WTCF (World Tourism Cities Federation)	世界旅游城市联合会

IHA (International Hotel Association) 国际饭店协会
ICAO (International Civil Aviation Organization) 国际民用航空组织
IATA (International Air Transport Association) 国际航空运输协会
AIEST (International Association of Scientific Experts in Tourism) 国际旅游科学专家协会
IMTA (International Mountain Tourism Alliance) 国际山地旅游联盟
WATA (World Association of Travel Agencies) 世界旅行社协会
ETC (European Travel Commission) 欧洲旅游委员会
Annals of Tourism Research 《旅游研究年鉴》
Tourism Management 《旅游管理》
Journal of Travel Research 《旅行研究期刊》
Journal of Sustainable Tourism 《可持续旅游期刊》
Journal of Leisure Research 《休闲研究期刊》
Asia Pacific Journal of Tourism Research 《亚太旅游研究期刊》
Leisure Studies 《休闲研究》
Cornell Hotel and Restaurant Administration Quarterly 《康奈尔酒店与餐馆管理季刊》
Tourism Economics 《旅游经济》

X Single Choice Questions

Chapter 2
Transportation

I Chapter Introduction

Although we may not think about it, the tourism industry would cease to function without an efficient and effective transportation system; trains, automobiles and airplanes are just a few of the more obvious parts of this system. There are many other modes of transportation in addition to planes, trains and automobiles from which to choose. The components of this system can be conveniently classified and placed into two broad categories: surface (land and water) and air. Transportation is often intermodal, with travelers relying on several different modes of transportation to reach their final destinations. Intermodal transportation options can be found throughout the transportation system, but airports provide a focused glimpse into the importance of all transportation modes. Providing a variety of transportation connection options to feed passengers into airports, inter-modality has become increasingly important as air traffic volumes have soared.

How did this system of interconnectivity develop and how does it function today? Modes of transportation evolved slowly until the 19th and 20th centuries.

II Chapter Objectives

1. Explain the importance of transportation to the tourism industry.
2. Identify and describe the major components of the tourism transportation system.
3. Explain the differences between passenger railroad operations within and outside the United States.
4. Explain the importance of automobiles and motor coaches to the tourism transportation system.
5. Describe the role and importance of water transportation in the movement of

travelers.

6. Describe how airlines operate in a deregulated and competitive environment.

Ⅲ Reading

1. Air Transportation

The first scheduled passenger flight debuted in Europe on August 25, 1919, with a route between London and Paris, and jet passenger service was inaugurated on May 2, 1952, with a flight between London and Johannesburg, South Africa. The Civil Aviation Administration of China (CAAC), also called the General Administration of Civil Aviation of China, was established as a government agency in 1949 to operate China's commercial air fleet. In 1988 CAAC's operational fleet was transferred to new, semiautonomous airlines and has served since as a regulatory agency. The International Civil Aviation Organization reported that between 2009 and 2017, the number of air passengers carried in China increased by 140% from 229062099 to 551234509.

As with all tourism service providers, competition among airlines is intense. In an attempt to attract more customers and to develop brand loyalty, American Airlines pioneered a frequent-flyer marketing program in 1981. This program was soon copied by other major carriers as well as regional and low-cost carriers. Research into why consumers participate in frequent-flyer benefit programs found three perceived dimensions: recognition, convenience and exploration. These benefits relate to multiple consumer motivations: utilitarian (convenience benefits), hedonic (exploration benefits) and symbolic (acknowledgment/recognition benefits).

These programs have increased customer loyalty, with passengers often going out of their way or taking inconvenient flights to obtain frequent-flyer miles, yet few actually cash in their mileage for awards. Airlines are also partnering with a multitude of other organizations both inside and outside the tourism industry by offering miles for purchase to generate additional revenues, increase brand awareness, and heighten customer loyalty.

Airlines, like most other service providers in the tourism industry, operate on very thin profit margins. In fact, since the inception of commercial air service, airlines have collectively lost more money than they have ever made. Therefore, controlling costs and maximizing revenues are major concerns and absolute necessities for survival and profitability. The most significant expenses as a percentage of sales in the airline industry are operating costs and equipment. Because costs other than labor are difficult to control, airline companies attempt to maximize revenues. This can be accomplished by obtaining the highest possible load factor per revenue passenger mile on each flight.

In the United States, the leader in low-cost airlines, Southwest Airlines has achieved what seems to be an amazing operational cost per seat mile flown of six cents. However, Air Asia has eclipsed this efficiency benchmark by flying its planes at a cost per seat mile of three cents. Combining low cost with maximizing available seat miles (ASMs) has led to profitability for these selected few carriers in an industry filled with competition that struggles even to achieve break-even.

1.1 Decoding the Language of the Airline

All participants in the tourism industry have their own particular set of terms they use to describe operating issues, but the airline industry has more than most. To understand the airline industry, it is important to be familiar with some of the more common terms.

(1) Every airline has its own two-letter identification code. Examples of these codes for the largest airlines in the world are American Airlines (AA), Air Canada (AC), Air China (CA), British Airways (BA), Korean Air (KE), Lufthansa (LH), Qantas (QF), Singapore Airlines (SQ) and United Airlines (UA).

(2) Every city with scheduled passenger service has its own three-letter airport code to identify the airport that is served. Examples of these airport codes are Seoul/Gimpo (GMP); New York/Kennedy International Airport (JFK); Orlando International, Florida (MCO); Orly, Paris, France (ORY); Narita, Tokyo, Japan (NRT); and Toronto Airport, Toronto, Ontario, Canada (YTO).

(3) Every airline uses codes to identify class of service. Examples: First Class (F), Business Class Discounted (D), Business Class Premium (J), Business Class (C), Coach Economy Class (Y), Coach Economy Premium Class (W) (Q), and Advance Purchase Excursion (APEX).

(4) Airline service is also classified as nonstop, direct or through, and connecting. Nonstop flights are from the point of origin to a destination with no intermediate stops. Direct or through flights are from the point of origin to a destination with one or more intermediate stops. Connecting flights require passengers to change planes to a connecting flight between the point of origin and final destination.

(5) There are also several types of trips that passengers can book. Examples: one-way—a trip from origin to destination without a return to origin; round-trip—a trip from origin to destination with a return to origin; circle-trip—similar to a round-trip except that the outbound and the return trips follow different routes and possibly use different airlines; open-jaw—a round-trip that allows the passenger to utilize different points of origin or return.

1.2 Airports

We can't leave our discussion of transportation without taking a look at

terminals. Passengers pass through many different types of terminals during their journeys: rail, bus, car rental, ferry, cruise, or air. In fact, the number of travelers passing through terminals is staggering. For an idea of how big these volumes are, just think about the fact that over 255 million people passed through the world's three busiest airports—Atlanta, GA; Beijing, China and London, United Kingdom in 2014.

One key service provider in the transportation industry, airports, has now realized that passengers using their terminals hold the potential of substantially increased revenues. However, it has only been since the 2000s that airport operators have shifted their attention from simply providing facilities and services to meet basic needs to enhancing the airport experience with a broad array of design and operational amenities focused on increasing revenues.

According to industry research findings, satisfied passengers spend more time and money in airports than less satisfied passengers leading to increased economic benefits and profitability. With money to be made on not only departing and arriving passengers who are passing through their facilities, but also passengers who are passing through on connecting flights and passengers who are enjoying the time-saving convenience of using airports as primary destinations for business meetings.

A prime example of putting all the pieces together to create a sense of place, space and destination for passengers can be found at the Seoul Incheon International Airport serving Seoul, Korea. This airport has the typical amenities you would expect such as a variety of retail shops, food and beverage outlets, but you will also find a casino, a golf course, hotel rooms, an ice-skating rink, indoor gardens, a spa, and the Museum of Korean Culture.

2. Water-based Transportation

Just like modern travelers, early travelers probably used both land and water. Modern modes of surface transportation were ushered in with the development of sailing vessels and then passenger railroads, and grew with increased personal ownership of automobiles, availability of rental vehicles, and the convenience of coach services. We will briefly examine important historical developments as well as key issues associated with each of these modes of transportation.

2.1 Ferries

Like most of the early technological innovations in transportation, steam-powered ships originated in Europe. In 1838, two passenger ships (the Sirus and the Great Western) crossed the Atlantic from Ireland and Great Britain to the United States. By today's standards, and even compared with the speed of clipper ships, their 19-day and 15-day crossings were slow. But they ushered in a new age of dependable scheduled service whereby travelers had some assurance that they would arrive at their destinations on time.

Transatlantic passenger traffic grew rapidly until 1957 when another technological innovation—the jet engine—heralded the demise of point-to-point ocean crossings. Although Cunard Line still runs scheduled routes between Southampton, England, and New York City, and some cruise ships at times carry passengers on point-to-point crossings, ocean-going transportation is now limited. Long-distance cruise ship crossings are typically restricted to repositioning cruises, in which cruise ships are being moved from one location to another. For example, a cruise line will move ships from the Caribbean to the Mediterranean to take advantage of seasonal changes and passenger demands. Cruise ships are such a significant sector of the tourism industry that we will take an in-depth look at cruising.

When mentioned water transportation, most people think about cruise ships or a brief hop on a ferry when they cross a river, lake, or other short distance on a waterway. Water transportation, especially ferry services, is still an important link in the total transportation system. Passenger ferries have evolved over time and have become more sophisticated, offering a wide range of services. They are now designed to do more than just carry passengers and vehicles. Some ferries also offer sleeping cabins, restaurants, lounges, casinos, movie theaters, shops and child-care services.

Passenger ferry routes have been designed to tie in with rail and road systems to facilitate intermodal transportation. These routes create important links in the transportation system for many residents and visitors in North American locations such as Alaska, British Columbia, Newfoundland, Nova Scotia and Washington State. British Columbia, for example, has an extensive system of ferries calling on 42 coastal ports. For the millions of people who travel throughout Asia and the European community, water transportation is not a luxury but a necessity and a key driver of tourism.

Technological advances in ferry design and construction have increased both speeds and operating efficiencies. These high-speed ferries are particularly noticeable in high-traffic tourist areas such as the Bahamas, Catalina Island, Tasmania, and along the Massachusetts coastline. These locations are all served by high-speed catamarans that can transport passengers at aspeed of up to 42 miles per hour.

2.2 Cruise Ships

Cruising is booming as record numbers of vacationers select cruise vacations. And why not? Cruising is fun! Cruises of all durations have been experiencing growth, with the largest increase recorded in the 2-day to 5-day category. Very long cruises, 21 or more days in length, are also proving to be very popular. However, 7-day itineraries still remain the most in demand. The Caribbean continues to be the favorite cruising destination, and the Mediterranean and other European routes are the second most purchased cruising itineraries. Alaska and the coast of Mexico also remain popular with cruise passengers. River cruising has gained momentum, especially in

Europe, Asia and the United States, and cruise lines are adding ships at a rapid pace to keep up with the growing demand.

Cruise passengers sail on either one-way or round-trip itineraries. On a one-way itinerary they will begin and end their journey to and from different ports. One-way itineraries are very common on river cruises and Alaskan routes. For example, passengers begin their journey by flying to Paris where they transfer to a coach traveling to Trier, board a river barge and cruise the Moselle, Rhine, and Main Rivers to Nuremberg then transfer to another coach finishing their journey in Prague. Alaskan cruise passengers begin their inside passage journey by boarding their cruise at ports in either Vancouver, B. C., or Seward, Alaska. Seward is just a short train or bus ride away from Anchorage. On a round-trip itinerary, passengers begin and end their journey from the same port.

Expanded fleets of ships combined with new amenities and effective marketing efforts have helped to reposition the cruise experience in consumers' minds as destination resorts rather than as transportation. Growth in the number of cruises has led to other changes as cruise line operators continue their efforts to improve service and expand their marketing reach.

The number of ports and the quality of facilities where passengers may embark and disembark have grown and improved. Cruise-line companies have also expanded the number of available cruising options and targeted specific market segments. Because of the flexibility provided in cruise-line operations, each cruise can be designed to meet the tastes and needs of a specific cruising audience, with focused activities such as fitness, big band or rock music, and mystery parties. Cruise ships come in a variety of types and offer different experiences. Cruising was originally available on classic ocean liners, such as the "Queen Mary" and the "Queen Elizabeth" (Ⅰ and Ⅱ). But most cruising now takes place on vessels that fit one of the following categories:

(1) Megaships. Most of the ships are extremely large, weighing up to 250000 Gross Registered Tons (GRT), carrying up to 7000 passengers or more, and having 12 or more decks. These ships are virtually floating resorts, usually offering an array of entertainment and dining options onboard.

(2) Midsize ships. Luxury ships, older cruise ships, and ships that primarily sail select regions, for example, Europe and the Mediterranean, accommodate 950 to 2000 passengers. These ships offer amenities but on a smaller scale than those featured on the megaships.

(3) Small ships. Carrying fewer than 950 passengers, these ships offer a more intimate, less frenzied cruise experience. Most are used for niche markets, such as education-based, ultra-luxury, or adventure cruises.

(4) Sailing ships. Serving a distinct market segment, masted ships provide

passengers with the opportunity to cruise in the original style—using wind power! Frequently, passengers act as part of the crew and aid in the sailing of the vessel.

(5) Riverboats and barges. An additional style of nostalgia cruising is provided by the riverboat. In the United States, riverboats designed to look like Mark Twain paddle wheelers ply the Mississippi, the Missouri and the Columbia rivers. In Europe, modern riverboats, built low to the water to glide under bridges, travel on rivers such as the Danube and the Rhine.

(6) Multipurpose ships. Some ships, like those that transit the Scandinavian fjords, carry leisure travelers along with cargo or local commuters.

(7) Superyachts. These large luxury yachts, also called megayachts, are usually over 24 meters in length and can reach up to 110 meters. Typical occupancy onboard is approximately 200 passengers, and all cabins are classically well-appointed suites or estate rooms.

A ship's size will impact the space ratio or how much space is allocated to each passenger. You can find the space ratio by dividing the GRT of a ship by the number of passengers it can accommodate. The greater the space ratio, the roomier and less crowded the ship will feel. Space ratios of 25 to 40 are fairly common on today's ships.

Cruise ships have an operational advantage over destinations that are anchored to a specific geographic location and must suffer through changing weather patterns. Sailing itineraries can be changed through repositioning cruises to take advantage of the best seasonal patterns and passenger demand anywhere in the world. In addition, "Cruise ships are an operator's dream. They run at 95% of capacity or higher, when hotels are pressed to manage 70%. And cruise passengers, unlike hotel guests, cannot wander off to eat their dinner elsewhere."

With the flexibility to meet vacationer and meeting-goer needs, cruise lines are now targeting many of the same people and groups who previously stayed in traditional destination resorts. The primary geographic markets for U.S. cruise-line passengers are California, Florida, New York, Illinois, Pennsylvania and Texas; and the primary ports for cruise ships serving U.S. and Canadian markets are located in Miami, New York, Port Everglades, Los Angeles, San Francisco, Seattle and Vancouver. Most cruise ships sailing from these ports go southward to Mexico, the Caribbean, and the Panama Canal, or northward to Alaska.

3. Land-based Transportation

The term highway came into use as roads were built up from the paths they followed to raise them out of the mud and make them usable on a year-round basis. Innovations in road construction that were pioneered by the French and English soon spread throughout the world. Road construction has continued to progress and now plays a central role in the transportation systems of all developed countries. For

example, the first multilane highway, the Autobahn, built in Germany during the 1930s, still serves as a vital link in that country's transportation system. These improvements in road systems allowed travelers to move from horses and carts and stagecoaches to automobiles and coaches.

3.1　Automobiles

The availability of affordable automobiles and an expansive highway system have made automobile travel the most popular form of transportation in Canada and the United States. The vast majority of domestic trips in the United States were taken over the highways. In addition, 84% of all overnight weekend travelers drove to their destinations. Self-driving tourism provides a flexible space for the tourists in the selection of objects, participation in the process and experience of freedom. Self-driving has become a dominant form of short-distance tourist travel as it enables to extend and expand the depth and breadth of tourist activities.

Both Canada and the United States have focused government attention and resources on the development of highway systems rather than rail systems. The Trans-Canada Highway spans 4860 miles between Victoria, Vancouver Island, British Columbia, and St. John's, Newfoundland. The interstate highway system in the United States has resulted in an intricate web of 42800 miles of divided highways connecting every major city in the country. This system is truly remarkable because it accounts for only 1% of all roads in the United States but carries over 20% of all highway traffic.

An overview of the growth of the American and Chinese highway systems underlines different growth sequences and rates(Figure 2.1). From its inception, the American Interstate highway system expanded substantially, but at a declining rate as the system neared its planned size (74000 km). By 1991, after more than three decades of construction, the system was considered completed, with a total cost of about 129 billion dollars. Between 1954 and 2001, 370 billion dollars were invested by the federal government in the construction and maintenance of the system. Close to three-quarters of the financing came from fuel taxes, which created a positive feedback loop as the more interstate roads were available, the more fuel consumption and thus tax collection. However, the interstate highway is facing diminishing returns due to high construction and maintenance costs, which is forcing many state governments to consider privatization of several highway segments. Construction costs went from 4 million dollars per mile in 1959 to 20 million dollars in 1979. Still, the system has returned more than 6 dollars in economic productivity for each dollar it costs, placing it at the core of American economic productivity gains in the second half of the 20th century.

The Chinese expressway system was developed later but at a much faster rate. Prior to 1989, there were no highways in China, but as the economy opened up, the

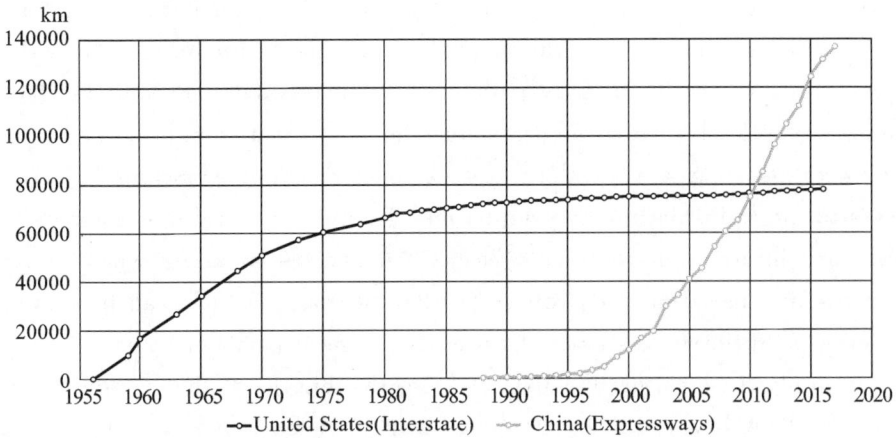

Figure 2.1 Length of the interstate highway system in the
United States and of the Chinese expressway system, 1959-2017

Source: Federal Highway Administration & National Bureau of Statistics of China.

development of a national system of expressways was seen as a priority. To facilitate the fast construction of the system, almost all expressways are toll roads financed by private companies under contract from provincial governments, commonly as public-private partnerships. The debt contracted for expressway construction is expected to be recovered through toll collection. Unlike the United States, China did not implement a national fuel tax road financing mechanism. This mode of financing thus differs from the publicly funded highway systems built in Europe and North America. A significant landmark was achieved in 2011 when the length of the Chinese expressway system surpassed that of the American interstate system. The planned length of the expressway system was set at 85000 km but was exceeded since the system surpassed 100000 km in 2013. The construction of new expressways will likely slow down afterward, underlining that at this point China will have achieved an important step in its motorization transition. It remains to be assessed in light of the significant urban population, rising levels of national production and consumption and the fast growth of car ownership, to what extent the national expressway network will be sufficient to effectively support China's mobility needs. Further, such rapid growth will incur very high maintenance costs as the highway infrastructure ages.

Why do travelers rely on their personal motor vehicles for so many of their trips? Reasons vary but include the relatively inexpensive cost of vehicle travel compared with that of other modes, especially for families. In addition, cars, trucks and recreational vehicles offer the convenience of having a vehicle at the destination, the ability to alter the route and pace, and the opportunity to explore new places "up close".

Supporting all of these over-the-road travelers is the American Automobile Association, commonly known as AAA.

Although automobiles may be the desired form of personal transportation in the United States, less than 20% of the population has ever rented a car. Growth in the rental car business has historically paralleled or exceeded the growth in air travel, with almost two-thirds of car rental revenues being derived from airline passengers.

Logistics also play a key role in successful car rental operations in getting the right cars to the right place at the right time. Recent software developments provide the necessary information for employees and managers to know when to refuse a short-term rental based on the probability that the same vehicle can be rented for a longer term to a different customer. Car rental revenue management needs to take into account not only the existing bookings but also the lengths of the existing rentals and the capacity flexibility via fleet shuttling, which yields a high-dimensional system state space. Still, cars must be moved to meet seasonal demand, creating inexpensive repositioning rentals as fleets must be moved from high demand area. Can economies of scale make a difference? The answer is yes.

In this highly competitive industry, price is important, but it is often the little things, things such as how quickly you get your car, that make a difference. Surveys show that customers want to cut as many hassles out of rental car returns as possible. Car rental companies are responding to these requests by enhancing their services to include valet delivery and parking services to avoid shuttle buses, equipping cars with onboard computerized navigation systems, providing drop boxes for the return of keys and rental forms, and equipping service personnel with handheld computers to complete rental transactions at the point of return.

The rental transportation options in some tourism areas have diversified to include many alternatives other than rental cars. For example, in Kitakyushu City, Japan, users can choose from ultra-lightweight vehicles (ULVs), electric-assisted bicycles, electric scooters and electric four-wheel carts. When consumers have options for rentals in short transportation situations such as this, which option do they choose? It was not the car, but the ULV.

While car sharing in North America was in a commercial mainstreaming stage, active members of the car-sharing service in Hangzhou, China was still in an upward trend in general. However, the scale and the relative usage level of the Chinese car-sharing and service was far smaller than those in North America market.

3.2 Coach and Bus

Coaches have come a long way since their predecessor (stagecoaches) bounced across the countryside. There are now two primary categories of coach (often called bus) transportation—scheduled intercity travel and charter/tour groups. Intercity bus travel, like rail travel, has continued to command less and less of the scheduled travel market in the United States. As with railroads, the importance of scheduled bus service in the United States peaked in the 1940s, and the decline continues today. In

1980, bus travel accounted for 12% of all interstate travel, but it now accounts for only about 6% of that market segment. Although the number of passengers utilizing interstate buses has continued a gradual downward trend, this mode of transportation still provides a vital link in domestic and international transportation systems.

In the United States, schedules, fares, and routes of intercity buses were closely regulated by the Interstate Commerce Commission (ICC) until passage of the Bus Regulatory Reform Act of 1982, which eliminated most regulations except those pertaining to safety. In this deregulated environment, intercity bus lines have continued to consolidate and pare their schedules and now focus primarily on trips of less than 250 miles. Greyhound Lines is now the dominant intercity bus service provider in North America carrying over 20000 passengers daily in Canada and the United States. Although the primary market segment served remains visiting friends and relatives, several diverse target markets, including lower-income groups and riders under the age of 24 or over the age of 65, are proved to be fertile ground for future growth.

As Greyhound continues to rationalize its routes, many rural communities have found themselves without bus services and miles away from any rail or air connections. Luckily, many of these abandoned routes have been picked up by regional carriers. Coaches provide.

The regional carriers often rely on government subsidies to meet expenses. Through interline agreements passengers are able to buy one ticket and transfer between multiple coach carriers for long distance trips.

While intercity bus travel is common in many parts of the world, for many North Americans it is considered to be demeaning. This move away from bus travel occurred in North America in the mid-20th century as a result of rising living standards, suburban growth and sprawl, growth in airline capacity, and increased car production. All of these factors came together to change the demand for scheduled intercity bus service. It became a transportation choice used mainly by poor whites, African Americans, Hispanics, recent immigrant women, and low-income males who could not afford car ownership.

New life is being breathed into the North American market by upgrades at Greyhound and a variety of start-up carriers serving paired cities like New York-Washington, D.C., Los Angeles-San Francisco, and Chicago-Milwaukee. Using concepts such as yield management and hub-and-spoke systems, bus companies are finding new niches and growth opportunities.

Although intercity bus travel in the United States has declined, coach usage in general has increased owing to its popularity among tour and charter operators because of flexibility and economy of operation. In addition, intercity bus travel remains an attractive alternative to rail travel in many countries with high population densities.

Additional growth opportunities for coach travel can be found in the mature traveler market segment. During the past two decades, the first wave of baby boomers began to enter their senior years, making them a prime target for the domestic coach market. Their primary considerations in selecting coach tours will be service, quality and comfort. Coach executives predict that health, spa, special event, entertainment, and golf and ski packages will be the primary tours sought by these demanding groups in the future.

As profiles of individuals using coaches have changed, so have the coaches. "Seats are wider. Views are better. There's stereo music and often an integrated video system showing the latest movies, just like the airlines. Increasingly, there's a hot beverage service or even a full galley with a microwave oven." The standard coach has grown from 40 feet to as much as 45 feet in length, and passenger capacity has increased from 47 to 55.

Coach operators such as Gray Line highlight their ability to provide a wide range of ground transportation services especially suited to coaches, from sightseeing tours and charter services to airport services on six continents at 150 destinations. Coach operations, whether intercity (bus) or charter (tour operators), have many of the same operational concerns that face every participant in the tourism industry. Because operators in this industry are privately owned, financial data are not available.

Competition and government involvement in intercity bus transportation varies widely outside the United States. In some countries, such as Spain, bus transportation is more important than rail transportation; in other countries, such as Iceland, there is no train service, only bus service; and in Japan, the Japan Rail Pass includes unlimited travel on the bus as well as the train. Therefore, because of the country-specific nature of intercity bus transportation, we will leave the investigation of availability and operations in specific geographic locations up to your exploration.

Coaches usually serve many more locations than trains, which are confined to specific routes because of their fixed tracks. They are frequently less expensive to ride and can often take you to places not served by trains, although they are generally slower. However, there are several exceptions to this general rule. In southern European countries, including Portugal, Greece, Spain and Turkey, bus service may be faster but more expensive than trains. The long-distance bus networks of Great Britain, Ireland, Portugal, Morocco, Greece, Turkey and the Czech Republic are more extensive, more efficient, and often more comfortable than trains. The Eurobus programs provide direct competition to train-pass programs, with two months of unlimited travel on buses accompanied by an English-speaking driver and guide. Destinations in continental Europe include Paris, Amsterdam, Cologne, Prague, Munich, Venice, Rome and Milan. As with rail passes, passengers get on and off at their leisure. As researchers studied intercity bus travel in the United States and

Germany, they determined that the spatial distribution (distances) between cities was a key determinant in the supply of intercity bus services.

In most major tourism active metropolitan areas, such as Paris, London, Sydney and Shanghai, city tour buses are available to take visitors around major tourist attractions within the city. Passengers can purchase a single day or multi-day pass and "hop on, hop off" as often as they wish. These bus tours are often known as loop tours; because the buses drive around town in a loop, provide a quick and convenient way to get an overview of a city.

3.3 Rail Travel

Passenger rail service had its origins in Europe. The first railway service for passengers was inaugurated in Europe on September 17, 1825, when the Stockton and Darlington Railway began offering regularly scheduled service in England. Passenger rail service arrived in North America in 1829, when the South Carolina and Canal Railroad began carrying passengers between Charleston, South Carolina, and Hamburg, Georgia, with steam-powered locomotives. Transcontinental service in the United States began in 1869 and in Canada in 1885. Long-distance rail travel was given a boost in the United States when George Pullman developed the Pullman coach, with sleeping facilities for overnight travel. The addition of dining cars and legitimate food and lodging facilities pioneered by Fred Harvey heralded the golden age of passenger railroad service in the United States. Dissatisfied with poor food and service, Harvey arranged in 1875 to provide food service for the Atchison, Topeka and Santa Fe Railroad at its Topeka, Kansas, depot. He became so well known for quality and service that the railroad eventually awarded him all of its dining car services.

3.3.1 Canada and the United States Rail Service

Rail passenger service followed similar tracks of decline in both Canada and the United States until public interest in salvaging long-distance passenger train service resulted in government intervention. Amtrak was formed in 1971 and VIA Rail Canada in 1978 to reduce the number of routes and points served while upgrading the remaining passenger rail systems. Although in different countries, there are many similarities between these two passenger-rail-operating companies.

Amtrak is the marketing name for the National Railroad Passenger Corporation, which is a combination of the passenger rail services of U.S. railroads. Amtrak trains now serve 45 states, with stops in hundreds of communities. (Note: the popular Alaska Railroad is not part of the Amtrak system.) VIA Rail Canada is the marketing name for Canada's passenger train network, which links over 400 communities throughout the country. Although they both receive governmental financial support, neither Amtrak nor VIA Rail Canada is a government agency; they are corporations structured and managed like other large businesses.

Passenger rail service in Canada and the United States, where passenger and freight trains share the same rails, still faces an uncertain future and will probably continue to rely on some form of government subsidies. However, with increased urban growth and new airports being constructed farther and farther from city centers, rail service may grow in importance. Because train terminals were originally built in the center of cities, they now provide a convenient central location and, in many cases, faster and easier transportation in crowded corridors. This is especially true between major cities in close proximity to each other, such as Montreal and Toronto, New York and Boston, Kansas City and St. Louis, and Los Angeles and San Francisco.

Recent improvements in Amtrak service can be attributed to several factors: introduction of improved service and scheduling in the high-traffic Northeast corridors, aggressive marketing and packaging of vacation trips including rail passes (All Aboard America Fares) and fly/rail packages, membership in the Airlines Reporting Corporation (ARC), and listings on airline computer reservation systems. Amtrak service has been further enhanced by the addition of high-speed trains (top speeds of 150 mph) on major passenger routes and routes that serve as feeders to major hub airports. In fact, in some city pairs, transit time is shorter via Amtrak service than by air service.

Similar steps such as rail passes (Canrailpass), fly/drive packages, special tour packages, and lodging partnerships have been taken by VIA Rail Canada to enhance customer service and ridership.

3.3.2 Asian and European Rail Service

Although train travel has declined in Canada and the United States, it has continued to be an important mode of intercity transportation in Asia and Europe. At present, the countries with the largest number of train passengers are China, Germany, India and Japan. Heavy population concentrations and attention to roadbeds and tracks dedicated solely to passenger traffic have led to the development of high-speed rail service. China, Japan, Korea, France, Great Britain, Italy, Germany, Sweden and Spain are just a few of the countries where passengers can travel by train at a speed averaging up to 220 miles per hour (350 kilometers per hour). The technology for high-speed rail travel is continually evolving, and trains that can travel at a speed of up to 270 miles per hour are being put into service.

Between major population centers within European countries, train travel has also become so fast and efficient that it is often more convenient and less expensive than travel by plane when travel to the airport, check-in, and baggage handling times are considered. By comparison rail service in Canada and the United States is more expensive and very difficult to piece together for long distance journeys.

One of the most exciting developments in rail transportation was the inauguration of high-speed passenger rail service between London, England, and Paris, France. The Euro-star, which travels through the channel tunnel or "Chunnel," allows passengers to make the entire trip in just less than two hours at aspeed of close to 200 mph, cutting the time in half when compared with ferry crossings.

Passenger rail service in Europe has been further enhanced through expansion of the Eurailpass. A number of European countries—Austria, Belgium, Denmark, France, Germany, Italy, Luxembourg, the Netherlands, Norway, Portugal, Spain, Sweden and Switzerland—introduced the first Eurailpass in 1959. Finland, Greece, and Ireland were added later. With the fall of the Berlin Wall and the end of the Cold War, the pass became valid throughout the entire German Republic as well as the Czech Republic and Hungary. Trains have become so significant in Europe that they move more than 40 times more passengers every day than in the United States.

The Eurailpass is used as a marketing tool to attract international visitors from outside the European community because it is available only to non-European tourists. Pass holders are allowed unlimited travel for varying periods of time throughout Western Europe, with the exception of Great Britain. Recognizing the importance of rail travel to their total tourism package, individual countries such as Great Britain (BritRail pass), Germany (German Railpass), Switzerland (Swiss Pass), Spain (Spain Railpass), and Greece (Greek Railpass) are providing similar services.

Most countries consider passenger rail transportation to be of vital national importance and continue to retain government control. Therefore, information on operating results (other than ridership) and the financial condition of most passenger railroads is not available. This may all change in the future as a trend toward private ownership and reduced subsidies has emerged in European countries, especially Great Britain and Germany. Managers there find themselves venturing into unfamiliar territory, requiring marketing skills to maintain and increase ridership and financial skills to attract the necessary capital to maintain and improve service quality while controlling costs.

High-speed rail (HSR) in China consists of a network of passenger-dedicated railways designed for speeds of 250-350 km/h (155-217 mph). It is the world's longest high-speed railway network, and is also the most extensively used. China's HSR accounts for two-thirds of the world's total high-speed railway networks. In 2019, China started testing a magnetic levitation ("maglev") prototype train that runs at 600 km/h.

By December 29, 2019, HSR extended to 32 (31) of the country's 34 (33) provincial-level administrative divisions, the exceptions being Macau and Tibet, although Ningxia and Hainan currently only have isolated high-speed lines. The national network reached 35000 km in total length, accounting for about two-thirds of the world's high-speed rail tracks in commercial service. The HSR building boom

continues with the HSR network set to reach 38000 km in 2025. Almost all HSR trains, track and service are owned and operated by the China Railway Corporation under the brand China Railway High-Speed (CRH). The CRH train service was introduced in April 2007 featuring high-speed train sets called Hexie Hao (simplified Chinese：和谐号；lit.：Harmony) and Fuxing Hao (simplified Chinese：复兴号；lit.：Rejuvenation) running at speed from 250 km/h to 350 km/h on upgraded/dedicated high-speed track. The Beijing-Tianjin intercity rail, which opened in August 2008 and could carry high-speed trains at 350 km/h (217 mph), was the first passenger dedicated HSR line.

China's early high-speed trains were imported or built under technology transfer agreements with foreign train-makers including Alstom, Siemens, Bombardier and Kawasaki Heavy Industries. Since the initial technological support, Chinese engineers have re-designed internal train components and built indigenous trains manufactured by the state-owned CRRC Corporation.

The advent of high-speed rail in China has greatly reduced travel time and has transformed Chinese society and economy. A World Bank study found "a broad range of travelers of different income levels choose HSR for its comfort, convenience, safety and punctuality".

Notable HSR lines in China include the Beijing-Guangzhou high-speed railway which at 2298 km is the world's longest HSR line in operation, the Beijing-Shanghai high-speed railway with the world's fastest operating conventional train services and the Shanghai Maglev, the world's first high-speed commercial magnetic levitation line, whose trains run on non-conventional track and reach a top speed of 430 km/h (267 mph).

The fastest train service measured by peak operational speed is the Shanghai Maglev Train which can reach 431 km/h (268 mph). Due to the limited length of the Shanghai Maglev track (30 km), the maglev train's average trip speed is only 245.5 km/h (152.5 mph).

The fastest train service measured by average trip speed from 2009 until 2011 was on the Wuhan-Guangzhou high-speed railway, where from December 2009 until July 1, 2011, the CRH3/CRH2 coupled-train sets averaged 312.5 km/h (194.2 mph) on the 922 km route from Wuhan to Guangzhou North. However, on July 1, 2011 in order to save energy and reduce operating costs, the maximum speed of Chinese high-speed trains was reduced to 300 km/h, and the average speed of the fastest trains on the Wuhan-Guangzhou high-speed railway was reduced to 272.68 km/h (169 mph).

After the speed reduction in 2011 the fastest services are found running between Shijiazhuang and Zhengzhou East where they achieve an average speed of 283.4 km/h (176.1 mph) in each direction in 2015.

350 km/h operation was restored in late 2017 with the introduction of Fuxing

Hao trains for services running on the Beijing-Shanghai high-speed railway in late 2017 making the CRH network once again having the fastest operating speed in the world. Several services to complete the 1302 km journey between Shanghai Hongqiao and Beijing South in 4 hours and 24 minutes or with an average speed of 291.9 km/h (181.4 mph) making it the fastest train service measured by average trip speed in the world.

In 2019, the fastest timetabled start-to-stop runs between a station pair in the world are trains G17/G39 on the Beijing-Shanghai high-speed railway averaging 317.7 km/h (197.4 mph) running non-stop between Beijing South to Nanjing South before continuing to other destinations.

The top speed attained by a non-maglev train in China is 487.3 km/h (302.8 mph) by a CRH380BL train on the Beijing-Shanghai high-speed railway during a testing run on January 10, 2011.

3.3.3 Scenic Railroads

In addition to the ready availability of passenger rail service for basic transportation in most developed countries, there are several specialty trains with particular appeal to tourists. The Orient Express is without a doubt the most famous of all luxurious or scenic trains. With its magnificently restored cars, it runs from London, England, to Istanbul, Turkey. Another classic train, the Blue Train, can be found traveling between Cape Town and Johannesburg, South Africa. With its gold-tinted windows and fine dining, the Blue Train is also renowned for its mystique and romanticism. China's Sky Train carries passengers across the Tibetan Plateau from Xining to Lhasa, Tibet, using three locomotives to cross the 16640-foot Tangula Pass. Other trains such as the Copper Canyon in Mexico, the Palace on Wheels in India, and the Indian-Pacific in Australia are just a few of the many specialty trains that can be found throughout the world.

In addition to these long-haul scenic trains, you will find many historic trains that have been preserved for tourist enjoyment. Although many of these trains may be considered to be attractions, these vintage trains carry an amazing number of tourists on trips of nostalgia each year.

Founded in 1990, Rocky Mountaineer offers three train journeys through British Columbia and Alberta to Banff, Lake Louise, Jasper, and Calgary, and one train excursion from Vancouver to Whistler. In 2013, Rocky Mountaineer introduced Coastal Passage, a new route connecting Seattle to the Canadian Rockies that can be added to any two-day or more rail journey (Rocky Mountaineer, 2014).

While the industry overall has been in a decline, touring companies like Rocky Mountaineer have found a financially successful model by shifting the focus from transportation to the sightseeing experience. The company has weathered financial storms by refusing to discount their luxury product, instead focusing on the unique

experiences. The long planning cycle for scenic rail packages has helped the company stand their ground in terms of pricing.

3.4 Cycling

The bicycle is arguably the most sustainable form of tourist transportation (Lumsdon and Tolley, 2004): it is non-motorized and it does not require fuel while having a minimal impact on the built and physical environment, with the exception of mountain biking, where it constitutes a recreational activity with resource impacts. As Lumsdon and Tolley (2004) argue, after walking, cycling is the most important form of transportation globally, given its significance for leisure use in developing countries such as China where it comprises 65% of all trips made. In a European context, cycling remains a popular form of transportation in Denmark, Germany and the Netherlands, even though motorized transportation has dominated transportation policy in the inter-war and postwar period in most westernized countries. Up until the 1990s, cycling symbolized many of the key principles of sustainable tourism, with minimal environmental impacts and limited infrastructure requirements. Since the late 1990s, cycling has become part of a wider renaissance of interest in walking and cycling in North America, Australasia, and in Eastern Europe where the issue of quality of life is moving higher up the political agenda in contrast to developing countries seeking to emulate symbols of modernization and affluence such as car ownership. Yet the major change, in recreational terms, in the late 1990s has been the demand for purpose-built infrastructure such as dedicated bike lanes, marked cycling routes, multiuse pathways to accommodate local commuters and urban visitors, as well as cycle tourism in scenic rural, coastal and mountain landscapes.

3.5 Important Transportation Links

The final link in the surface transportation system is composed of many modes such as subways, trolleys, intracity buses, water taxis and light-rail systems. Although each of these forms of transportation is important to the overall transportation system, we will not examine them in this book because they are used primarily for daily commuting to and from work and do not fall within our definition of tourism. However, they do fill an important transportation need for many individuals who do not want to be burdened with automobiles as they travel.

If short distances are involved or individuals do not need a car while at their destination, then they may rely on taxi, limousine, ride-sharing or shuttle services. Taxis fill an important transportation function by efficiently moving large numbers of people within cities, especially in crowded urban areas, as well as to and from airports and railway stations. One of the most significant changes in the tourism industry has been the intermodal tour that combines coach, air travel, railroad and water travel.

A highly valued transportation link for air travelers is transport to and from the air terminal. In 1983, SuperShuttle pioneered door-to-door ground transportation by offering shared ride vans for travel to the Los Angeles airport. Today, SuperShuttle provides service for over 20000 air travelers a day. Reserving a ride on one of SuperShuttle's blue vans is as easy as picking up the phone or clicking on its website. Finally, more and more travelers are tapping into the convenience of ride-sharing services such as Uber, Lyft and Didi through easy-to-use mobile Apps.

4. Transportation Transformations

Significant changes will be noticed in all forms of transportation. Speed and efficiency will increase thanks to advances in technologies and materials. Every form of transportation from automobiles to ferries will see change. For example, ferry transportation, which has been an old standby, should become more prevalent and popular in the face of increasing demands for energy efficiency. New high-speed ferries cut down on travel time by taking shorter across-the-water routes than land-based alternatives or over shorter routes that would be prohibitively expensive for air service. For example, introduced in 2004, the Lake Express ferries cross Lake Michigan from Milwaukee to Muskegon in just two and one-half hours.

Expanded rail service will also provide additional relief to crowded transportation corridors. Proliferation of high-speed rail service will be the hallmark of this transportation mode for years to come. Although speeds of 100 miles per hour are commonplace, plans are already being tested to produce trains that travel at much higher speeds. Magnetic levitation (Maglev) trains, especially on shorter high-traffic routes, will replace traditional track-based trains. Maglev trains generate their own energy from the friction created over their magnetic lines and will travel at speeds in excess of 300 miles per hour. As the convenience and comfort of magnetic levitation technology spreads from its experimental status to the norm for high-speed rail travel, more and more passengers will be drawn from the airports to the ground.

To get an idea of how efficient train travel could be, think about the following proposal. Brad Swartzwelter, a conductor for Amtrak, has suggested that the solution to transportation problems within the United States could be solved by underground trains. He proposes that tunnels be dug, connecting points A and B, and a magnetic levitation system be installed to carry travelers between these points at speeds up to 900 miles per hour. Future technological advances could lead to a transcontinental trip that could be completed in approximately three hours.

In the meantime, in the United States and throughout the world, you can expect that more high-speed trains will be put into service as demand continues to be fueled by the efficiencies of point-to-point service in high-demand corridors prompted by fuel costs, security delays, and continuing customer-service problems at crowded airports. Noticeable increases in this type of service in China and India have been seen as the appetite for travel explodes.

Connector trains will become the norm for mass transit in densely populated corridors and as connectors for newly built airports. As you will see next, there will be a boom in new airport construction. In these new facilities, ticket counters, parking, and baggage checking will be located at substantial distances from the airports, which will be built far outside of urban areas to alleviate noise, road traffic, and airspace congestion. These new airports will become destinations in themselves, featuring a wide variety of entertainment options for locals and travelers alike.

The future of air travel presents a picture that at first seems to be incongruous. As airline fleets are upgraded, these new planes will be larger or smaller, faster or slower, and be designed to fly more direct routes. First, you will see more of the double-decker super jumbo jets, the 555-seat A380, serving long-haul trans-Pacific and trans atlantic routes. These extremely large aircrafts can serve routes only between airports that have made infrastructure investments to handle the weight of the planes on the runways, and the large number of passengers during arrivals and departures. At the same time, you will also be seeing smaller planes, like the regional jets, as airlines are finding that it is more profitable to serve many markets through direct routes that can produce passenger traffic to fill planes with fewer than 100 seats. In an effort to conserve fuel, more and larger turboprop aircraft, with lower operating costs, will be placed into service, replacing jets.

Because of new technology, air traffic control centers may become a thing of the past. Pilots in the future will determine their own routes, aided by computers calculating their planes' and other air traffic positions each second. As a matter of fact, planes may fly without pilots. Most commercial aircraft already fly "pilotless" from just after takeoff to just prior to landing. Another new concept, tilt-rotor planes, may make it possible for aircraft to take off and land with little to no runway.

Increases in size and speed of aircraft will be absolutely necessary to satisfy future demand for air travel. While worldwide, 2.4 billion passengers were carried in 2010; this number is projected to grow to 16 billion by 2050! The demands on aircraft and the supporting infrastructure will be enormous.

As for airline services, polarization in service offerings also appears to be the norm for the future. On one hand, the service in business and first class will continue to become more upscale and elaborate. Some long-haul first class suites now are configured like a hotel room, with a comfortable double bed and a seating area. Passengers can enjoy comfort and privacy while traveling. Most large airlines also offer menus designed by well-known chefs and wines selected by sommeliers. On the other hand, low-cost carriers will continue to expand rapidly, especially in developing countries where domestic and regional travel have grown and will continue to grow exponentially. When safety permits, on some short-haul flights, the least expensive "seats" will not be seats at all, as passengers will simply stand the same way they do on crowded subways during rush hours.

Finally, even with all of the improvements being made in other forms of transportation, automobiles will still be the most popular means of getting from one place to another, but they will definitely be more efficient. The future of automobile travel is already with us; all electric vehicles, hydrogen fueled cars, hybrid vehicles, and driverless cars will continue to shape the futures of our roadways. As technologies take over human decisions for driving and routing, roadways will also become safer.

5. Summary

Passenger transportation, whether on land, over the water, or in the air, is the lifeblood of the tourism industry. Water transportation was the first mode of transportation to move travelers rapidly over long distances, but many other modes have since evolved to meet time and distance requirements. Geography and governmental policies and subsidies combined to create a host of transportation alternatives that vary greatly by country and location.

When it comes to transportation, travelers have the choice of plying the waves, riding the rails, cruising the highways, or soaring through the skies. Which one they choose will depend on where they are going, their budget, and the amount of flexibility they desire.

Ocean-going passenger service, which was once popular crossing the Atlantic, declined as jet air service increased. However, water transportation alternatives, including ferry services, which are designed to carry everything from passengers to trains, coaches and automobiles, are still very important in many parts of the world.

Land transportation revolves around rail service, automobiles and coaches. Passenger rail service, which originated in the European countries, has continued to improve in efficiency and still meets the needs of those travelers, but it is also popular in other countries, especially those in Asia, with high population concentrations and large cities located in close proximity to each other. In other countries, such as Canada and the United States, automobiles account for the majority of all travel away from home. Taxis, shuttles, limousine services, and light rail systems fill important transportation needs for travelers everywhere. In addition, the flexibility and economy of operations of coaches that can serve scheduled routes and organized tours continue to meet the needs of travelers worldwide.

Transportation as tourism occurs where the form of transportation is integral to the over-all experience of tourism such as cruising or taking a scenic railway journey. This is reflected in T. S. Eliot's famous quotation "The journey, not the arrival, matters".

Air transportation has proven to be the driving force behind the explosive growth in domestic and international travel. As governmental regulations are removed from air transportation, international barriers fall, and major airlines vie for an increasing

number of passengers, competition as well as passenger traffic will continue to increase.

With the growth in air transportation, the number of travelers passing through terminals has also exploded. When these travelers are combined with those passing through rails, ferries and cruise terminals, the number of potential customers is compounded.

IV Case Study

Rovos Rail Celebrates 30 Years on the 29th of April 2019

Since its first overnight journey with a seven-coach train to what was then the Eastern Transvaal, Rovos Rail has expanded exponentially and now offers eight trips around South Africa with more trains that can accommodate 72 passengers. Journeys range from 48 hours to 15 days with the newest route, Trail of Two Oceans, departing for its maiden voyage in July this year from Dares Salaam to Lobito in Angola. It will be the first time in history that a passenger train will travel the east-to-west copper trail.

"Our new route coincides nicely with our 30th birthday. I'd like to say it was planned but I can't take credit for the serendipitous timing," says Rohan Vos, owner and CEO of Rovos Rail Tours.

Also in the Rovos fleet is the Shongololo Express that was purchased and renovated in 2016. Three journeys are on offer ranging from 12 to 15 days with the train travelling for over 300 days of the year. "That train just goes and goes with very few issues—mostly I think due to the relaxed itineraries. It's quite amazing," comments Vos.

Asked if he ever thought Rovos Rail would progress this far, Vos responds, "Not at all. We lost so much money in the early days and we knew nothing about hospitality. In my naivety I believed what we were offering was so unique that tickets would sell easily. Boy, I was mistaken."

With his wife Anthea at his side, Vos travelled the world attending travel shows and calling on leading travel agents and tour operators. "It was both invigorating and exhausting," says Anthea. "We were starting out at the same time as the Vartys from Londolozi and the late Liz McGrath as well as a few others. We all used to lose our voices from punting our offerings so vigorously!"

It took a decade for the company to break-even. "We managed to side-step bankruptcy more than once," says Vos. "I was inexperienced and had no idea just how expensive trains would be to operate."

An auspicious moment arrived in 1993 when Vos formed a relationship with

Phillip Morrell from Jules Verne in the United Kingdom. Together they plotted a route from Cape Town to Victoria Falls. "We had no money at the time for any advertising but we placed an ad in the *Sunday Telegraph* nonetheless. It was December and I didn't hold much hope." However, much to his surprise, the advertisement worked and the maiden voyage sold out. When Phillip called to share the good news, Vos's words to him were "Send cash!" The new Victoria Falls journey proved successful.

When Rovos Rail did eventually start making some headway, the company—like many others—was impacted by events such as a volcanic ash cloud, airline strikes, the Ebola outbreak and a crippling global recession.

"It's certainly been a challenging and interesting ride but one has to play to one's strengths and luckily I thrive under pressure and I'm a good crisis manager. I also don't like being told I can't do something," he smiles.

There is a great deal that Vos would like to say about local politics and how it affects his business on a weekly basis but in short: "The railway infrastructure on which we are 100% reliant needs attention to enable our services to run efficiently. We have procured our own electric and diesel locomotives so that one day we may become independent of Transnet in this department. Our goal is to be as self-reliant as possible," says Vos.

The business now employs 440 staff members at Rovos Rail Station, the impressive private railway station and headquarters in Pretoria. In 1999, the derelict 60-acre property was rehabilitated and renovated to become the home of everything from the on-site laundry and kitchen to the locomotive and coach maintenance workshops, reservations and the finance department. "We also have our own little museum that pays homage to our 30 years of operation and also South Africa's railway history," says Vos.

A sixth train set is in production with completion aimed for December 2019. This means that the company will be able to have five Rovos Rail trains out at once on any of the eight journeys it offers along with Shongololo Express running on one of its three trips.

What's next for Rovos Rail? "Consolidation," says Vos. "Once we've launched our sixth train, we need to focus on maintaining all the coaches, training staff and persevering in our pursuit to be independent," he adds. "Our daughters are also actively involved in the business and I imagine there will be significant change over the next few years as they work with me to propel us forward."

The company also has long-standing, amicable and prosperous relationships with many travel agents and tour operators around the world. "Without them we would not be here so I feel this is as much their celebration as it is ours," says Vos.

Like many in the hospitality industry, Rovos Rail has had to weather its fair share of turbulence and even though the company has grown substantially, the

determined and family-orientated spirit that started the business 30 years ago is still very much at its core. "We have staff members here who have been with us since the beginning and over 100 employees who have been here for over 20 years," says Vos. "It's quite incredible and unheard of these days so for this I am truly thankful," he smiles.

Ⅴ Tips

Self-driving Car is Actually a Tiny Hotel Suite on Wheels

The future of travel may be in outer space, or it could be in a self-driving car. That's the hope of the Autonomous Travel Suite, a driverless mobile hotel room that provides door to door transportation.

Recently named one of three finalists in this year's Radical Innovation Awards, the Autonomous Travel Suite was developed by Steve Lee of Los Angeles-based Aprilli Design Studio. Instead of heading to the airport, Lee envisions vehicles picking up travelers from their homes in solar-powered electric vehicles that shuttle them to their destination in micro hotel rooms.

Each mobile hotel room features a memory foam mattress for sleeping, a kitchen and mini bar, storage for luggage, a washroom, a toilet, and a seating area for working or entertainment. The car's windows use smart glass that can dim for privacy, and the Autonomous Travel Suite could be available in different room types (single, family, pets, etc.) and various unit sizes at different price points. Customized equipment—like a TV or an extra bed—could also be available upon request, allowing travelers to work on the road and avoid stopping for bathroom breaks.

Each suite contains a sleeping area, washroom and toilet, and a work/entertainment area(Figure 2.2).

Once at your destination, the Autonomous Travel Suite would arrive at an Autonomous Hotel (Figure 2.3) facility and dock into what Lee calls a "parent suite". Together, the car and the parent suite would become a larger, standard hotel room, and the Autonomous Hotel would provide expected amenities like a gym, spa, meeting rooms and dining facilities.

Lee contends that the Autonomous Travel Suite would be cheaper than many hotels because it combines the price for transportation and room stays. The self-driving suites would also provide unlimited luggage space for traveling, privacy and flexibility for families or groups, and eliminate security or flight delays.

Fully autonomous cars may have not truly hit the road in significant numbers yet, but it's not far off. As we've reported, autonomous vehicles promise to decrease car

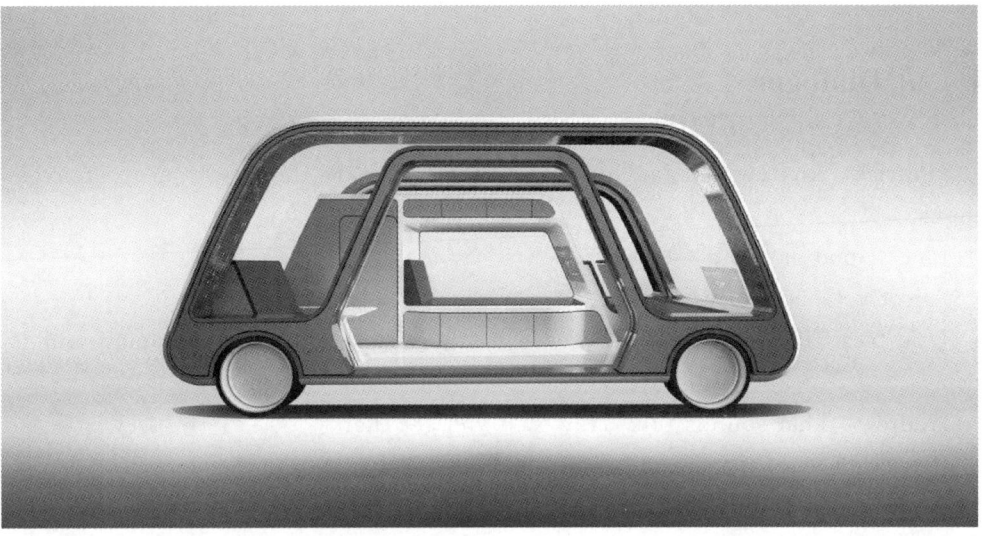

Figure 2.2 Mobile hotel room

Figure 2.3 Autonomous Hotel

ownership, narrow streets and eliminate parking lots, and dramatically reshape our cities. A few cities already have driverless cars on the streets, albeit in test mode; Las Vegas has a Navya self-driving minibus, San Francisco boasts General Motors' Cruise ride-hailing service, and Waymo's family-focused Chandler, Arizona-based pilot program uses no human operators in its Chrysler Pacifica minivans.

The Autonomous Travel Suite would likely be most successful once more self-driving cars and electric cars are on the road. It could also be limited to regions of the country that are the most dense since it requires driving long distances between large cities, and there's no real explanation for how you might recharge the car if there's not enough sun and don't have an Autonomous Hotel nearby. But the idea is interesting, if nothing else because it rethinks what the future of travel might look like.

Ⅵ Dialogue

(Patrick, Andrew and Jane discuss how to travel to the city from the university campus.)

Jane: Good morning, Andrew.

Andrew: Good morning, Jane. Are you going somewhere?

Jane: Yes. Patrick and I are going to the city to do some shopping and have lunch.

Andrew: That sounds fun. How will you get there?

Patrick: I want to take the train, but Jane prefers to ride her bicycle.

Andrew: Don't you like using the train, Jane?

Jane: The train station is far away and riding my bicycle does not cost anything.

Patrick: OK. Jane, why don't we travel by bus, there is a bus stop just behind the university.

Jane: It might take longer. I think we will need to take two buses to the city center.

Andrew: Jane is right. There is not a direct bus into the city. Why don't you use a taxi?

Patrick: That will be quick, but expensive. Can you rollerblade?

Jane: I hope you don't mean we should rollerblade to the city.

Andrew: Is rollerblading popular in America, Patrick?

Patrick: Yes. People often use roller skates. There is even a designated lane for it.

Jane: In UK we can't do that, the path is just for walking on.

Andrew: I need to go to the train station to buy some tickets. I can give you both a lift in my car.

Jane: That would be wonderful, Andrew. Thanks so much.

Patrick: That is very kind of you, Andrew. Let's go to the city center!

Ⅶ Academic Thinking

Visitors' Attitudes towards Bicycle Use in the Teide National Park

Author: Rosa Marina González, Concepción Román and Ángel Simón Marrero

Journal: *Sustainability*

Abstract:

Few studies have examined visitor preferences with regard to public bike-sharing inside national parks. Here, we present a case study of the Teide National Park (TNP), the most visited national park in Spain. The TNP is a clear example of a natural site suffering the effects of mass tourism, largely due to the fact that 70% of visitors access the TNP by car. This puts the park's sustainability under considerable pressure, may well affect visitor enjoyment, and highlights the need to implement alternative transportation systems. The main aim of this paper is to assess the attitudes of visitors to the TNP towards the implementation of a public bike-sharing system. To do so, we combine information on revealed and stated preferences and estimate ordered logit models to establish the determinants of the propensity to choose the bicycle to move around the park. Our findings suggest that the bicycle has potential as a means of transport in this setting. The results have implications for the design of mobility management measures aiming to increase visit quality and reduce the negative externalities associated with mobility patterns in national parks.

游客对泰德国家公园自行车使用的态度

近年来，欧洲游客对自行车的使用迅速增加。但是很少有研究检查游客对国家公园内公共自行车共享的偏好。在这里，作者以泰德国家公园（TNP）这一西班牙访问量最大的国家公园为例。泰德国家公园是自然景点受大规模旅游业影响的一个明显例子，主要是由于70%的游客是乘车前往泰德国家公园，给公园的可持续发展带来了巨大压力，也给游客体验造成负面影响，因此实施替代交通系统具有必要性。本文的主要目的是评估泰德国家公园访客对实施公共自行车共享系统的态度。作者结合了游客所陈述的偏好信息，估计了有序logit模型，以确定选择自行车作为公园内交通工具的倾向性的决定因素。研究结果表明，自行车具有作为交通工具的潜力。结果对提高访问质量并为减少国家公园出行方式的负面外部影响制定出行管理措施具有意义。

扫码看答案

Ⅷ Questions

1. What are the major modes of transportation, and why is each of these modes important to the current and future success of the tourism industry?

2. Why is Europe's passenger rail service at a more advanced stage of development compared with that of the United States?

3. Why are motor coaches experiencing renewed growth in Europe?

4. Discuss how low-cost airlines have changed the European airline industry.

5. Why are airlines considered to be the backbone of travel?

Ⅸ Key Words and Terms

airport code	机场代码
banks of flights	飞行坡度
circle-trip flight	往返航班
code-share	代码共享
concession	减价票
connecting flight	转机航班
direct flight	直航
intermodal	联运
international Air Transport Association (IATA)	国际航空运输协会
legacy carrier	传统航空公司
nonstop flight	直飞航班
one-way flight	单程航班
overbooking	超额预订
point-to-point	点对点
round-trip flight	往返航班
spoke route	辐条路线
terminal	航站楼

Ⅹ Single Choice Questions

Chapter 3
Tourism Attractions

I Chapter Introduction

People have always been attracted to new, unusual, or awe-inspiring attractions and events in every corner of the world. In the days before recorded history, travelers may have journeyed for miles just to experience the beauty of the setting sun across a mountain valley or to participate in a religious festival in honor of bountiful harvests. Today, we may expect more, but we are still inspired to travel by the appeal of special attractions and events. No matter whether it is the chance to attend a rock concert, to witness Shakespeare being performed in the rebuilt Globe Theatre, to climb to the top of the Eiffel Tower, or to view the solitude and majesty of Uluru (Ayers Rock), tourists are constantly seeking new sights, sounds and experiences as well as the opportunity to participate in a variety of leisure activities.

Tourists, whether visiting friends and relatives, traveling for pleasure, conducting business, or attending a professional meeting, tend to seek out a variety of attractions and entertainment alternatives to fill their leisure time. When traveling, we may continue to participate in many of our favorite leisure and recreational activities, but we also seek to see, do, and experience new things.

II Chapter Objectives

1. Describe the major classifications of attractions and entertainment in the tourism industry.
2. Understand the differences among heritage attractions, commercial attractions and live entertainment.
3. Identify key marketing, management and financial issues facing attractions and entertainment operations.
4. Describe major types of heritage attractions.

5. Describe major types of commercial attractions.
6. Describe major types of live entertainment alternatives.

Ⅲ Reading

1. Foundations for Understanding Attractions and Entertainment

What is attraction? Lew (1987) believes that in essence, tourist attractions consist of all those elements of a "non-home" place that draw discretionary travelers away from their homes. They usually include landscapes to observe, activities to participate in, and experiences to remember. Yet it can sometimes be difficult to differentiate between attractions and non-attractions. Pearce (1991) finds that attractions are famous places with special human and natural features, which can get tourists and managers' focus. Lawton (2005) followed Pearce and defined tourist attractions as named events, sites, areasor linear phenomena with specific human or natural features that provide the focus of manager and visitor attention. Though definition varies, attractions are the core element of the tourism system and a primary influence on destination success.

There has also been discussion in relation to the differentiation between visitor attractions and destinations, with Swarbrooke (2002) stating that "Attractions are generally single units easily delimited geographical areas based on a single key feature. Destinations are larger areas that include a number of individual attractions together with the support services required by tourists". Leask (2008) developed a classification of VAs that identifies the principal features of attractions and the diversity of their product internationally, demonstrating the breadth of resource, visitor markets and objectives involved. Leask(2010) later offered a summary of the generally accepted categories of visitors attractions.

Attractions are similar in some ways to live entertainment alternatives. Visiting attractions or enjoying entertainment opportunities require travelers to make choices about how they will use their leisure time. Some attractions are planned around historic sites and natural settings, whereas others are designed and constructed around planned activities, themes and events. Depending on the purpose or setting, they may be controlled and operated by not-for-profit organizations that are dedicated to preservation and interpretation or by commercial organizations dedicated to meeting guests' needs while making a profit. Live entertainment opportunities may also be found in these same settings and may be operated on a not-for-profit or a for-profit basis. However, there are some key differences between attractions and live entertainment venues.

Attractions are natural locations, objects or constructed facilities that have a special appeal to both tourists and local visitors. In addition to these attractions, tourists and other visitors are also drawn to see and be part of a variety of live entertainment opportunities. Although most attractions are permanent, entertainment alternatives are often temporary. In contrast, events such as fairs and festivals are temporary attractions that include a variety of activities, sights and live entertainment venues. In addition, visitor attendance, as well as the financial fortunes of almost all attractions, is influenced by seasonal changes, whereas entertainment venues can be planned to take advantage of seasons and tourism flows. Even at a popular location such as the White House, there are definite highs and lows in attendance patterns.

Although many heritage attractions as well as amusement and theme parks are heavily used during the summer months, they may experience much less traffic in the winter months and so they close down. Even commercial attractions that were originally intended to be open all the year round, such as Sea World in San Antonio, Texas, saw their visitor numbers drop so much during the colder months that it was no longer profitable to operate on a year-round basis. Yet, these attractions may still have very appealing shoulder seasons, which can meet the needs of many visitors and still generate sufficient revenues to cover operating expenses or generate a profit.

This seasonality of demand raises some key operating concerns for attractions. First, from a marketing perspective, how can more visitors be attracted during less popular shoulder seasons and how can they be encouraged to spend more time and money during their visits? Second, from a management perspective, how can large numbers of employees be recruited and trained in a short period of time to deliver high-quality customer service? Finally, from a financial perspective, how can cash flow be managed so that enough money is available to meet payroll and other operating expenses during the busy periods while retaining enough funds to meet maintenance and administrative expenses that occur on a year-round basis? Attraction operators have a variety of alternatives to address these concerns.

In an attempt to address the slump in attendance and revenues during off-peak periods, attractions are developing and using special events to attract more visitors. To generate shoulder season attendance, marketing efforts have been altered to target groups of potential visitors with flexible schedules such as mature travelers and families with students on year-round education calendars. In addition, activities have been added to match the seasons. For example, winter snow sport resorts have added mountain biking and alpine slides to attract summer visitors, while amusement and theme parks are hosting large groups at special promotional prices during traditionally slow shoulder seasons. Attractions are also cooperating in their marketing efforts. "To help boost attendance, the Toronto Metro Zoo has entered into cross-promotions with Paramount's Canada's Wonderland, a large amusement park located about 30 minutes from the zoo."

Attracting and retaining the traditional pool of high school and college-aged employees through the entire busy season has been accomplished through implementing wage scales that increase as the season progresses and the payment of completion bonuses if an employee stays through a specified target date. In response to fluctuating demand, many seasonal operations are also finding it helpful to recruit older workers, especially retirees who still want to be active in the workforce or simply want to supplement their incomes. No matter what the source of employees, managers must maintain a continuous recruiting and training process to fill vacant slots created by employee turnover.

When the gates to an amusement park open or a ski lift starts running, guests arrive and expect to find a staff ready to meet their needs. They also expect the same array of foods, gifts, and other goods and amenities that they would find if they had arrived a month later when the season was in full swing. Because most attractions operate on a cash basis from admission receipts, initial payroll and supply expenses must be paid before revenues are received. Planning and creative thinking are required to ensure that adequate funds are available at the start of the busy season as new employees are hired and supplies are received in anticipation of arriving guests. Selling season passes at a discount at the end of the season or before the season begins and negotiating a line of credit and extended payment terms with suppliers can help to ease the cash flow squeeze. As you will soon see, these are just a few of the problems and solutions facing tourism service suppliers in this segment of the industry.

In the following sections, we will describe and explore many of the heritage attractions, commercial attractions and live entertainment alternatives that are available for people to enjoy as they travel. You may be amazed by the variety of opportunities available in each of these categories.

2. Heritage Attractions

Heritage attractions can be found in a variety of shapes, sizes and locations throughout the world. These attractions may range from a small community museum dedicated to preserving memories and experiences to incredible feats of human ingenuity and determination such as the Great Wall of China and other world heritage sites. But heritage attractions are more than just museums, monuments and archaeological treasures. They also include showplaces for natural wonders such as botanical gardens and aquariums as well as parks and preserves that are dedicated to public enjoyment and the protection of natural resources. In addition, fairs and festivals create special venues for celebrating and sharing a variety of accomplishments and cultural activities.

2.1 Museums and Historical Sites

Archaeological evidence shows that once people began to live in communities, they began collecting, preserving and displaying various items of interest from a cultural and historical perspective. These collections have provided a means of displaying history and passing on important information to future generations as well as "outsiders". Our continuing fascination with the past has created a growing demand for museums and cultural heritage sites. Although the majority of these sites are operated on a non-profit basis, they serve as major tourist attractions, generating important cultural and economic benefits.

Today people are attracted by the diverse cultures of other people and the past that are displayed in museums. The number, types and locations of museums can be counted in the hundreds of thousands, and the list of people who visit these museums each year can be measured in the millions.

Research shows that when visiting museums, most visitors expect an experience that can be described as "easiness and fun". However, there are differences in what these visitors expect based on demographic segments. For example, females with a higher educational level usually expect a museum-visiting experience like most others of easiness and fun; whereas older and married participants with higher incomes often expect historical reminiscences.

The number of available museums throughout the world continues to grow. For example, in Europe, for every museum that existed in 1950, there are now more than four. The list of museum types is extensive, but the following list provides some examples of the more common options from which visitors can choose: general, art, history, science and technology, military and natural history. Whether there are too few or too many museums is the subject of much debate. However, as societies grow and change, museums provide a valuable foundation for studying the past and thinking about what the future may hold.

You may have heard of or even visited Colonial Williamsburg, Virginia, or Old Quebec and recognize that they are major historic attractions. These are just two examples of historic sites, yet there are many other places beckoning tourists and dependent on tourism revenues to continue preservation activities. Sites such as Historic Deerfield and others throughout the world are attracting record numbers of visitors, especially international tourists. More and more communities and countries are taking steps to preserve historic treasures and attract visitors through active restoration and interpretive programs. New life and uses are even being found for old industrial sites. "The owners of the Dürnberg salt mine in Hallein, Austria, which has been hosting visitors since at least 1700, decided in 1989 that salt was no longer profitable and closed down the mine."

For visitors to have a quality experience museums must promote a positive but accurate external image, provide a sense of occasion on arrival, welcome them as equals, meet the highest possible standards of service and do their best to encourage audience motivation to become involved. From the moment of arrival, operational

quality also means ensuring that belief in, commitment to and enthusiasm for the site and collections shine through.

Many museums over the world provide visitors with devices enabling them to listen to audio content that describes the artifacts exhibited in the museum. VR has also been actively adopted in cultural tourism because some of its characteristics help to achieve the tourism industry's goal of providing tourists with unique and enhanced experiences. In using new technology, museums can virtually overlay educational or entertaining content without modifying the physical space thus creating a new layer through which to connect with visitors.

2.2 Zoos and Aquariums

Large collections of animals, which were originally called menageries, have served as magnets for visitors since the times of the ancient Chinese, Egyptians, Babylonians and Aztecs. Modern zoos (sometimes referred to as zoological parks) now come in many sizes and can be found throughout the world. The Philadelphia Zoo was the first (1859) location in the United States dedicated to the large-scale collection and display of animals. Although this facility is still of great importance, it has been eclipsed by more spectacular zoos such as the Bronx Zoo and the San Diego Zoo. Other notable zoos around the world can be found in Montreal, Vancouver, Frankfurt, London, Paris, Moscow, New Delhi, Tokyo and Sydney.

Some of these zoos are very large, creating a great deal of public interest and publicity as well as generating significant international tourism traffic. This interest and traffic is based on unusual exhibits, collections of animal species, and efforts to re-create the natural setting found in the wild. Even the Walt Disney Company is banking on the continued draw of zoos. Disney's Animal Kingdom Theme Park, which features a blend of live displays of existing animal species and animatronic displays of species from the past, such as dinosaurs, has proven to be an attractive tourism destination. From both a management and marketing perspective, research shows that improving the zoo environment and demonstrating a concern for animal welfare were important for achieving overall visitor satisfaction levels.

The first public aquarium was established in London at the Regent's Park in 1853. It eventually failed because of poor design and management, but the idea of a preservation attraction devoted to water life has proven to be successful. Although aquariums are only about half as popular as zoos and wild animal parks combined, they are increasing in number, size and attendance. The Lisbon Oceanarium, Portugal, which opened as the flagship attraction of Expo 1998, represents Europe's largest and possibly the most spectacular of the world's hundreds of aquariums. The Manila Ocean Park in the Philippines, which opened in 2008, combines not only an expansive oceanarium but also shopping and food to round out its attractiveness to visitors.

Many aquariums are supported and managed as not-for-profit foundations, such as Canada's largest, the Vancouver Aquarium. Others have been developed as for-profit enterprises, such as the chain of SeaWorld Parks. Recently, many cities, such as Camden, New Jersey, Long Beach, California, have funded aquariums to help revitalize waterfront areas by attracting tourists and residents to oceanside regions of these cities. One of the most successful aquariums, Baltimore's National Aquarium, helped ensure the success of that city's redeveloped Inner Harbor.

The non-profit National Aquarium opened in 1981, the jewel of Baltimore City's Inner Harbor redevelopment. With a mission to inspire conservation of the world's aquatic treasures, the Aquarium is consistently ranked as one of the nation's top three aquariums and has hosted over 51 million guests since opening. It is Maryland's largest paid tourist attraction, with 20000 fishes, birds, amphibians, reptiles and marine mammals living in award-winning habitats.

The National Aquarium—also known as National Aquarium in Baltimore and formerly known as Baltimore Aquarium—is a non-profit public aquarium located at 501 East Pratt Street on Pier 3 in the Inner Harbor area of downtown Baltimore, Maryland, in the United States. Constructed during a period of urban renewal in Baltimore, the aquarium opened on August 8, 1981. The aquarium has an annual attendance of 1.5 million visitors and is the largest tourism attraction in the state of Maryland. The aquarium holds more than 2200000 US gallons of water, and has more than 17000 specimens representing over 750 species. The National Aquarium's mission is to inspire conservation of the world's aquatic treasures. The aquarium's stated vision is to confront pressing issues facing global aquatic habitats through pioneering science, conservation and educational programming.

Today, the National Aquarium builds on a 35-plus-year history of local, regional and global conservation initiatives that provide real solutions for protecting aquatic and marine life alongside human communities.

Based on a 2017 analysis by Sage Policy Group, the Aquarium annually generates nearly $455 million in economic activity across Maryland, with an impact of more than $360 million in Baltimore City, and this economic activity supports approximately 4500 jobs.

2.3 Parks and Preserves

Every park and preserve is a little bit different. They may range from famous urban parks such as Central Park in New York City or Hyde Park in London to forests and preserves such as Prince Albert National Park in Canada and Nairobi National Park in Kenya. Although they may be different in appearance and purpose, they are dedicated to protecting the natural beauty of landscapes, plants and animals for future generations as well as providing visitors with open spaces for rest, relaxation and recreation. Achieving this balance requires meeting the needs of visitors while

maintaining the resources contained within the lands that have been set aside for public use. To serve all these needs, the potential impacts of all activities must be monitored and managed. For example, day-use areas and campsites that are accessible by motorized vehicles and have full sanitary facilities require more upkeep and labor than wilderness areas that are accessible by foot or on horseback only.

The importance of parks as major tourist attractions was ushered in with the dedication of Yellowstone National Park in 1872. The U. S. national park service has now expanded to include a variety of sites dedicated to the preservation of nature and heritage. The 411 units within the park system are grouped into 20 designations including national parks, national monuments, national scenic trails and national preserves. The idea of national parks soon spread north to Canada, where in 1887, the first national park was established with the opening of Banff National Park. National parks can now be found throughout the world as countries strive to preserve and protect their more pristine natural treasures. The grandeur and importance of some of these national parks, such as Jasper National Park in Canada and Grand Canyon National Park in the United States, have become legendary and draw millions of visitors each year to enjoy their breathtaking beauty.

Some attractions such as Nairobi and Tsavo National Parks in Kenya and Serengeti National Park in Tanzania have gained such international acclaim that they serve as some of these countries' primary tourist attractions. Although people from around the world are drawn to these well-known national parks, there are also millions of acres of land that have been set aside for public enjoyment on the state, provincial and local levels. From these giant parks to the small pocket parks tucked away in the corner of a city, not a day goes by that visitors and locals alike are not relaxing or taking in a little bit of nature.

The U. S. National Park Service is a large operation in itself, with over 28000 employees and 2. 4 million volunteers, and spending over $2. 7 billion to serve approximately 11. 7 billion visitors a year. As a not-for-profit government agency, the National Park Service depends on appropriations as well as other sources of revenues. These other sources include admission (user) fees as well as revenues generated from over 650 concessionaires that supply a wide range of goods and services from food and lodging to transportation and souvenirs. However, the majority of operating funds (65% in 2008) still come from appropriations. Even with what may seem to a significant government appropriation, the park service is having difficulty finding funds for maintenance and is exploring the possibility of corporate sponsorship in the form of advertising in the parks to generate additional funding. With the number of units in the national park service having increased from 391 to 412 from 2009 to 2016, this funding problem is sure to persist.

Botanical gardens are another important part of the tourism attraction mix for many communities. Some botanical gardens are renowned for their magnificent displays and they draw visitors from all over the world. The oldest botanical garden was established at the University of Pisa in Italy in 1544. The Royal Botanical Gardens in Edinburgh, the Munich Botanical Gardens, the Montreal Botanical Gardens and the Missouri Botanical Gardens in St. Louis are just a few examples of some of the more popular and frequently visited botanical gardens.

2.4 Fairs and Festivals

While this debate has continued with regards to the inclusion or otherwise of events and festivals, fairs and festivals hold unique positions in the attractions and entertainment segment of the tourism industry because they are a little bit of everything—heritage attractions, commercial attractions and live entertainment. A fair was originally a temporary marketplace set up with the idea of stimulating commerce by creating an event that would bring together buyers and sellers. On one hand, you might recognize the modern-day version of the original fair as a flea market. Festivals, on the other hand, were gatherings devoted to times of celebration.

Up through the Middle Ages, there were fairly distinct differences between fairs and festivals. However, over time, many of the same types of activities such as food, shows and musical entertainment could be found at both fairs and festivals. The idea of having fun at these events is probably not surprising because the word fair comes from the Latin word feria, meaning "holiday".

As commerce grew, so did the idea of fairs that were designed to be large and last for longer periods of time, maybe as long as several months. Many major exhibitions highlighting achievements and industries were held before the first "World's Fair". Two of these were the Paris Exhibition of 1889 and the 1904 Louisiana Purchase Exhibition in St. Louis, Missouri.

The idea of these very large fairs that bring together exhibitors and visitors from all over the world proved to be so popular that international leaders decided to bring some uniformity to the concept. With the signing of a diplomatic convention in Paris in 1928, 43 countries agreed to the frequency and basic operational goals of events that would officially be recognized as World's Fairs. This agreement created the International Bureau of Exhibitions (BIE), which divided the world into three zones: Europe, North and South America, and the rest of the globe. It also stipulated that fairs would not be held in consecutive years in any one country and that no fees would be charged for the exhibits of foreign governments. Since its formation, there have been a number of notable World's Fairs including the New York World's Fair (1939); Brussels Universal and International Exhibition (1958); Expo 1967 in Montreal, Canada; Expo 1970 in Osaka, Japan; Expo 1992 in Seville, Spain; Expo 2000 in Hanover, Germany; Expo 2005 in Aichi, Japan; Expo 2010 in Shanghai, China; and

Expo 2015 in Milan, Italy.

Another very popular visitor attraction is the regional, state, or county fair. Most of these have evolved around the display of agricultural and livestock exhibits, but they often include industrial exhibits and many other entertainment activities. The Eastern States Exhibition, or "The Big E" as it is called, is an annual regional 10-day fair held each summer in West Springfield, Massachusetts; it celebrates the crafts, industries and agricultural products of the northeastern states of the United States. Some of these fairs, such as the Canadian National Exhibition in Toronto, the State Fair of Texas, and the National Western Livestock Show in Denver, draw tens of millions of visitors. However, whether it is a World's Fair, state fair, or county fair, people still travel from all over to exhibit and participate in the festivities.

Festivals celebrate a variety of special occasions and holidays. Some are derived from religious observances, such as New Orleans' and Rio de Janeiro's huge Mardi Gras festivals. Other festivals focus on activities as peaceful as ballooning (the Albuquerque Balloon Festival) or as terrifying as the running of the bulls in Pamplona, Spain. Often, festivals center on the cultural heritage of an area, such as the clan festivals that are prominent in the North Atlantic province of Nova Scotia. Seasons are also reasons for festivals such as the Harbin International Ice and Snow Festival in China, Winter Carnival held in Quebec City, or Milwaukee's Summerfest. More recently, food has become the center of attention at locations such as the Taste of Chicago, the National Cherry Festival in Traverse City, Michigan, or the Garlic Festival in Gilroy, California.

Any time people visit a fair or a festival, it is a time of celebration, and what celebration would be complete without fun and food? From the Oktoberfest in Munich to Hawaii's oldest food festival, the Kona Coffee Cultural Festival, tourists and locals can expect to find a tempting array of music, food and drinks. Community leaders have discovered that tourists can be drawn to even the smallest communities for fun-filled events. The National Cluck-off held during Chicken Days in Wayne, Nebraska, and the Oatmeal Cook-off held at the Oatmeal Days in Oatmeal, Texas, attest to people's desires to attend and be a part of festivals from the sophisticated to the seemingly silly.

In addition to these many heritage attractions, culture provides innumerable other methods to attract visitors.

3. Commercial Attractions

In addition to the heritage attractions just discussed, a host of commercial attractions have been developed to meet travelers' leisure-time needs. Whether it's the thrill of the roller-coaster plunge, the excitement of gaming, or the joy of an armload of boxes after a day at the mall, both tourists and locals welcome the opportunity to visit and enjoy these attractions.

3.1 Amusement Parks

The first amusement parks, which were called pleasure gardens, were built in England and France. Some of the largest and most popular amusement parks such as Gardaland on Italy's Lake Garda and Tivoli in Denmark attract millions of visitors each year. As the name "pleasure garden" implies, these attractions began as manicured gardens designed to provide a temporary escape for city dwellers from the everyday drudgeries of life. Rides such as carousels, games, and food and drink stands were added to these pleasure gardens to meet guest needs.

The idea of parks with rides and other entertainment activities soon found its way to the United States. Interest in amusements in the United States heightened when the Ferris wheel was introduced at the 1893 Chicago World's Fair. The name for this new amusement that became the centerpiece of most early amusement parks was taken from its inventor, George Washington Gales Ferris.

Lights, sounds, rides, games of chance, food, and a flurry of activities proved to be natural draws for those early thrill-seeking visitors to such places as Coney Island in Brooklyn or the Steel Pier in Atlantic City. Many smaller amusement parks in the United States were originally located at the edge of towns, where the trolley lines stopped. These amusement parks, called "trolley parks", were established as marketing tools to encourage ridership during the slow weekend periods. As automobiles and buses replaced trolleys, these and other amusement parks faded in popularity as their captive audiences disappeared. However, the concept of family fun and amusement was kept alive during the first half of the 20th century by traveling carnivals that moved across the country as a source of entertainment at many fairs and festivals until a landmark event that occurred in 1955. That year marked the opening of Disneyland in Anaheim, California.

Disneyland was much more than an amusement park. Although it drew on some of the basic attributes of an amusement park, Disneyland was the first theme park, and its opening served to rekindle respectability and interest in amusement parks. Since that time, the operations of amusement parks have become more sophisticated, with technology playing a far more important role. However, the basics of fun, excitement, and fantasy remain the keys to amusement park successes.

Amusement parks, family entertainment centers and water parks serve as important recreational outlets for their host communities and also attract considerable tourism interest from the region. Some of the larger amusement parks that may be recognizable to you include Six Flags/Elitch's Garden in Denver; Kentucky Kingdom in Louisville; Kennywood Park (one of the original trolley parks) in West Miffin, Pennsylvania; Grand Slam Canyon in Las Vegas; and Cedar Point in Sandusky, Ohio (the largest in North America). Like so many tourism service providers, there is no industry-specific classification system for these entertainment attractions.

3.2 Theme Parks

The distinction between amusement parks and theme parks is beginning to blur, but there are several unique characteristics that set them apart. Theme parks create a destination in themselves. By combining entertainment, food and beverages and an environment different from that found outside the gates, visitors are allowed to escape reality as they enter. Through the magic of technology and elaborate staging, theme parks can replicate almost any location in the world. As visitors are transported into this simulated environment, they are afforded the luxury of being in another location without the expense or any of the potential problems of faraway travel. It is predicted that, "The popularity of theme parks and attractions will continue to grow as theme parks and attractions are more and more associated with the new vacation experience that includes the convenience of on-property accommodations, food services, recreation, shopping, recreational and entertainment activities, and other tourist services."

There may be a tendency on the part of North Americans to think that they are the center of amusement park attractions. However, remember that the idea was imported from Europe and a trip to that continent will show that it has not lost its place in the theme park spotlight. Disneyland Paris; Europa Park in Rust, Germany; De Efteling Leisure Park in Kaatsheuvel, the Netherlands; and Port Aventura in Salou, Spain, etc., are Europe's most popular theme parks. Other park locations around the world. such as Tokyo Disneyland in Japan; Dreamworld at Coomera on Australia's Gold Coast; Lotte World in Seoul, Korea; Ferrari World Abu Dhabi; Hopi Hari in Sao Paulo, Brazil; Window of the World in Shenzhen, China; and Burlington Amusement Park on Prince Edward Island, Canada, serve to highlight the international appeal of these attractions.

Increasingly, in the creation of theme parks, we see labor, expertise, capital, and management flowing freely around the world.

"The contemporary American typically associates theme parks with concepts of permanence, gardened park-like settings and single price admission." Theme parks meeting these criteria range from elaborate parks such as Disney World in Florida and Canada's Wonderland in Toronto to local and specialty theme parks such as Worlds of Fun in Kansas City, Missouri, and Six Flags over Georgia, in Atlanta, providing a wide range of choices for the consumer. To differentiate product offerings and compete successfully, theme park operators must become more aware of consumer perceptions and concerns. In today's global market, the basics of parks development and management remain the same, but attention to detail is vital. "Whether the project is in your native country, or a continent away, it is imperative to be up to date on the demographics of your target market, what appeals to them and how to communicate with them."

From an operating point of view, parks must create a fun atmosphere and be clean and visually pleasing. There are several core conditions that must be met by theme park operators to retain repeat patronage and attract new patrons. In addition to visually pleasing and exciting park facilities designed based on the preferences of your target markets, all the service quality principles apply. For example, employees need to have good product knowledge, be able to think and feel from customers' perspective, and deliver consistency in products, services, and funs! Good communication skills by park employees are also pertinent to maintain visitors' interest and excitement. The ability to control crowds and work out the logistics of people flow are other essential components.

Park designers must provide a wide variety of rides, especially roller coasters and water rides, while reducing the perception of crowding. In addition to activities with an educational focus, new rides and features must be added on a periodic basis to maintain guest interest and ensure repeat patronage.

4. Gaming

Casino gaming has always been popular and available in many parts of the world, but it has experienced explosive growth in popularity and availability in the United States, China, Singapore and Canada during the past few years. When gaming was legalized in Nevada in 1931 to attract tourists during the Depression, few would have envisioned that some type of gaming operation would one day be found within easy access of so many people in so many locations. The same type of phenomenon happened in Macao in 2003 when China eased visa requirements, and gaming exploded as tourists flooded in.

The increasing availability and ease of access to gaming locations just in the United States has resulted in more Americans visiting casinos than attending major league and collegiate football games, arena concerts symphony concerts and Broadway shows combined.

From New Mexico to Connecticut, casinos all over the country are in the midst of a high-stakes gamble: remaking themselves into full-service, if not luxury, vacation destinations. Taking their cue from Vegas, they're throwing up plush hotels, highend shopping malls and even kiddie amusement parks, all in an unprecedented bid for the family-vacation dollar.

Five basic factors combine to explain the current success and future prospects of the gaming industry. First, voters have been increasingly willing to approve new gaming alternatives because these activities have come to be viewed as a "voluntary tax" or form of economic development while politicians have been unwilling or unable to pursue new taxes. Second, more people than ever before are choosing casino gaming as an acceptable leisure activity. Four out of five adults now report that they consider casino gaming to be a "fun night out". Third, retirees constitute the single

largest segment of the casino market and their numbers continue to grow. Fourth, casinos have devised marketing programs to attract the previously ignored "low roller". And fifth, expanded availability of gaming opportunities is attracting many individuals who have never before visited casinos for entertainment.

With the advent of more locations, accessibility and new technologies, the characteristics of gaming as a leisure-time activity have changed. Currently, there are five broad categories of gaming alternatives:

(1) Traditional, full-scale casino gaming, including well-established locations in Atlantic City, Las Vegas, London, Macao and Monte Carlo.

(2) Historic, limited-stakes operations such as those in Colorado's mining towns.

(3) "Dockside" (riverboat) casinos, such as those operating in Missouri and Illinois, and on the Mississippi Gulf Coast.

(4) Gaming on Native American reservations varies all the way from limited-stakes, small-scale operations such as the Sky Ute Casino in Ignacio, Colorado, to largescale Vegas-style operations such as Foxwoods on the Mashantucket Pequot reservation in Connecticut.

(5) Casino on ocean cruises where the slot machines and gaming tables begin operation when the cruises reach international waters.

Casino gaming is one of the most regulated businesses around the world. Gaming businesses must comply with local, state and federal regulations. These include complying with tax laws, treasury department regulations, rules governing alcohol consumption, types of games allowed, and sizes of bets. The size of casino operations is measured by gross gambling revenues (GGR). GGR is the amount wagered minus the winnings returned to players.

The development of new games and expanded gaming availability have given rise to several gaming segments, each with a profile somewhat different from the others and each with different benefits sought from gaming. Four broad segments appear to be emerging:

(1) High rollers. This segment is composed of sophisticated gamblers (both domestic and foreign), to whom traditional gaming was originally targeted. These players tend to be wealthy, older and male. High rollers tend to play games of skill rather than luck. Gaming venues outside of the United States have been especially adept at serving this segment.

(2) Day-trippers. Retirees dominate this segment. These players make several short duration trips to operations within easy driving distance and wager relatively significant amounts per trip but tend to play slots and other video gaming options.

(3) Low-stakes/new adopters. Players in this segment have discovered and accepted gaming as an interesting day or evening diversion when it is close to home or

when traveling. Members of this segment include the growing cadre of aging baby boomers and their retiree parents, with the time and money to enjoy the entertainment associated with gaming. Other players in this segment are younger adults who grew up with computers and playing video games.

(4) Family vacationers. Owing in part to the development of complementary tourism attractions such as theme parks, this segment tends to play as an offshoot of a family vacation.

Through the use of customer loyalty programs, casinos are collecting marketing data to target each segment and cross-sell related products and services.

5. Shopping

Shopping may be part of the travel experience or it may be the primary focus of travel. Shopping is an activity that crosses all market segments. "As long as cities have existed, the pattern of 'going into towns' has included a leisure experience, and visiting towns is an essential part of the tourist market." Whereas some visitors, simply pick up necessities or souvenirs as reminders of their travels, gifts for friends and relatives, or conversation pieces and evidences, others may travel to specific locations for the primary purpose of shopping. "Nearly nine out of ten, or 87%, of overseas travelers report that they shopped during their visits to the United States, according to a study conducted by the U. S. Department of Commerce and Taubman Centers Inc."

"Shop till you drop." This statement applies to more than just local shoppers as more and more malls are turning to tourists in search of new customers and growth. Shopping malls have increasingly become popular tourist attractions. Despite "placelessness" (homogenized, modern, synthetic landscapes) assumptions, shopping malls, and the experiences they facilitate do increasingly matter to those visiting them. For some travelers, a visit to a mega-shopping mall has become reason enough to take a trip, especially as these malls are transforming themselves into tourist destinations by adding amusement parks and other cultural attractions and entertainment activities.

In fact, the number-one tourist attraction in Minnesota is a shopping mall. The Mall of America in Bloomington, Minnesota, attracts over 43 million visitors a year. Based on its resounding success as a tourist attraction, plans are underway to more than double the size of the mall by adding more retail and office space, and entertainment opportunities as well as additional hotel rooms and other services.

What brings visitors from far and wide to these shopping meccas? It's more than just the wide array of retail shopping alternatives. For example, the Mall of America comes complete with an 18-hole miniature golf course, a 14-screen theater, and 9 nightclubs. But as successful as the retailing and attraction mix is at the Mall of America, management is not counting on its past decisions for future success.

Additions like Underwater World, a 1.2-million-gallon walk-through aquarium, provide just one more reason for shoppers to plan a trip to experience a unique mall environment.

Other malls, such as Woodfield Mall in Schaumburg, Illinois, and Gurnee Mills Mall in Gurnee, Illinois, do not rely on added attractions to draw in visitors, just good, solid shopping opportunities. And does this work? The answer is a definite yes, as these two malls are Illinois' number-one and two tourist attractions, drawing in over 28 million visitors a year. Marketing efforts that provide incentives to tour operators and support from tourist bureaus keep the shoppers coming back in record numbers.

All of these malls pale in comparison to the roster of megamalls that dot the Asian continent. Nine of the ten largest malls can be found on this continent. Based on leasable space, only the West Edmonton Mall can be found in the top 10. The others are located in China, Malaysia, the Philippines and Turkey. In addition to shopping, food service and theaters, these attractions include everything from ski slopes, casinos and human-made beaches to aquariums, theme parks, spas, hotels, performing arts venues and IMAX theaters.

When you think of a trip to the Big Apple you probably imagine visiting its famous sites, such as the Empire State Building and the Statue of Liberty. But international visitors think of New York City as a shoppers' paradise. Shopping is the number-one activity for overseas visitors to New York City, who account for over 70% of visitor retail sales. In fact, Bloomingdale's claims that it is the city's third largest tourist attraction.

When it comes to shopping, the motto "build it and they will come" works! Ontario Mills Mall, located 60 miles east of Los Angeles, California, attracts over 20 million shoppers each year. About 40% of these shoppers are tourists, coming from as far away as Australia, China, Japan, Malaysia and the Philippines, while tour buses, approximately 2000 a year, bring in the not-so-distant tourists. All of this tourist traffic doesn't just happen by accident. The mall has an office of tourism and marketing staff targeting not only countries but also tour operators, airlines and other travel industry representatives.

The importance of shopping to tourism has become so significant in recent years that it has given rise to a distinct category of travel with a purpose: shopping tourism. Although the activity is distinct and growing, there is still some disagreement on how it should be defined. Even though there may be some disagreement as to a common definition, there seems to be one common theme: shopping is the main purpose of the trip. "Studies on the role of shopping in tourist destination choice and experience identify four types of tourists (i.e., serious shoppers, non-shoppers, arts-and-crafts shoppers and not-so-serious shoppers) based on a combination of the importance of shopping in destination choice and actual participation in shopping activities."

The Biggest Malls on Earth

Vast shopping centres give one-quit shopping to anything possible. Our rundown of the biggest shopping centres on the planet depends on the measure of "Gross Leasable Area". This is the number of square feet the property has for income producing exercises like retail, eating and beguilement. The building blast in Asia, where land is shabby and work costs are low has created the biggest shopping centres. On the list of top 10 largest malls around the world, only two shopping malls on this list are located outside Asia. China has the largest shopping mall in the world.

Top 1: New South China Mall (659612 m^2)

New South China Mall, in Dongguan, China, is the biggest shopping centre on the planet when estimated as far as a gross leasable zone, and second regarding all-out region to the Dubai Mall (which has broad non-shopping space including a zoo, a lodging complex and an amusement park). New South China Mall opened in 2005 and for over 10 years it was, for the most part, empty a couple of shippers at any point joined, driving it to be named a dead shopping centre.

As indicated by another article distributed in January 2018, after overtime of high opening, most retail spaces had been filled and the shopping centre highlighted an IMAX-style film and amusement park. The shopping centre was based on previous farmlands in the Wanjiang District of Dongguan in southern seaside China. The task was led by Hu Guirong, who turned into a tycoon in the instant noodle industry. After opening, the New South China Mall turned into the biggest shopping centre on the planet, outperforming the Golden Resources Mall. The expense of its development is assessed at around $1.3 billion.

Top 2: Dubai Mall (650000 m^2)

It is a shopping centre in Dubai and the world-famous shopping centre on the planet by all-out land territory. Situated in Dubai, United Arab Emirates, it is a piece of the 20-billion-dollar Downtown perplexing and incorporates 1200 shops. In 2011 it was the most visited expanding on earth, drawing in more than 54 million guests every year. Access to the shopping centre is given by means of Doha Street, remade as a twofold decker street in April 2009.

Twice postponed, Dubai Mall opened on November 4, 2008, with around 1000 retailers, denoting the world's second biggest ever shopping centre opening in retail history behind West Edmonton Mall. Anyway, it isn't the biggest in gross leasable space and is outperformed in that classification by a few shopping centres including the New South China Mall, which is the world's biggest, Golden Resources Mall, SM City North Edsa and SM Mall of Asia. The Dubai Aquarium and Underwater Zoo were structured by Peddle Thorp and are overseen by Emaar Entertainment. The aquarium, situated in the Dubai Mall, grandstands in excess of 300 types of marine

creatures, including sharks and beams.

Top 3: SM Tianjin (565000 m^2)

SM Supermalls, claimed by SM Prime Holdings, is a chain of shopping centres in the Philippines that, as of November 2018, has 72 shopping centres situated the nation over and around two dozen progressively planned to be open.

It additionally has 7 shopping centres in China, including SM Tianjin. SM Supermalls has turned out to be one of the greatest shopping centre administrators in Southeast Asia. Joined, the organization has about 9.24 million square meters of gross floor territory (GFA). It has 17230 inhabitants in the Philippines and 1867 occupants in China. It is one of the largest malls in the world.

A mall is a mall. Not so! Imagine a shopping and entertainment paradise that covers over 110 acres and attracts over 20 million visitors a year. Now, imagine this attraction sitting on the plains of Canada in the city of Edmonton, Alberta. If you have not visited this "shopping center", then you have missed seeing and experiencing one of the biggest malls on America—West Edmonton Mall. This mammoth package of tourist services attracts people from all over the world in record numbers. The West Edmonton Mall is not like most other malls: It is massive in size and excites the imagination. Sure, it has shops, shops, and more shops. In fact, it has more than 800 stores. But the mall has more than shops and shopping to attract visitors. Almost 40% of the mall's space is dedicated to attractions as well as a hotel and more than 100 food outlets, and it is all under one roof. It takes over 15000 employees to accomplish all of the administrative and operating duties to keep this giant enterprise ticking. The Fantasyland Hotel has 355 guest rooms, but 127 of these rooms have been specially "themed" and decorated to fulfill guests' desires for travel adventures. When it's time to take a break from shopping there are a number of things to do and see, including Galaxyland Amusement Park, World Waterpark, Ice Palace, Europa (miniature) golf course, Deep Sea Submarine Adventure, Dolphin Lagoon and Sea Life Caverns, a full-scale casino, a bowling emporium, three cinema complexes, and a replica of one of the ships of Christopher Columbus. Deciding what to do can be as difficult as deciding what to buy. Viewing the many animal attractions exhibiting more than 200 species of animals such as dolphins, fish, exotic birds and a colony of breeding penguins takes you back to nature. A ride on the Mindbender roller coaster will find you dropping 14 floors at over 70 mph, while the tranquility of the submarine ride will transport you to exotic coral reefs. Or, you can splash down into the water park that covers an area the size of five NFL football fields. The success of West Edmonton Mall and Mall of America as retailing and tourism magnets has set the stage for even bigger and better venues.

6. Live Entertainment

Visiting heritage and commercial attractions and participating in activities at these locations could easily be classified as entertainment. However, live entertainment opportunities fill a special need for travelers and others seeking additional leisure-time activities. The choices of live entertainment venues can run from the deafening crowds at hallmark sporting events such as the World Cup or the Super Bowl to the serene pleasures of the ballet.

6.1 Sporting Activities

Why sport?

Sport is a fundamental means of recharging the batteries, while holidays today are a key time for personal development and for breaking the daily routine. Obviously, participating in sports is much easier while on holiday.

Sport tourism is undergoing a significant boom in pace with social trends towards strengthening "taking care of yourself" and the "back to basics" vogue. At the same time, sport tourism has also sprung up as an aid to tourism development, a solution for local development and an economic opportunity.

Sports have drawn visitors to scheduled events from near and far for thousands of years. Over 3500 years ago, the Greeks initiated the idea of staging athletic competitions. The most famous of these competitions were the Olympic Games held in Olympia. The competitions began as part of their religious festivals and were staged in towns throughout Greece and Italy. The original competitions in Greece were organized as contests, but the Romans expanded the idea and staged them as games for public entertainment. Although the grand athletic competitions and festivals such as the classical Olympic Games faded and disappeared under Roman rule, the idea did not go away. Now, mega tourism sporting events such as the Olympics and FIFA World Cup Soccer that draw athletes and spectators from around the world offer unique opportunities for host countries and cities. Not only do they gain name recognition and top-of-the-mind awareness from being in the international media spotlight, but they also gain the opportunity for cross marketing other tourism venues. Specifically, the destination can also be promoted by hosting additional sport and cultural events, fairs or exhibitions, cultural festivals, or concerts staged in the new multipurpose facilities and congress centers initially constructed for a megaevent.

The idea of traveling for sports has continued to grow, and it has been suggested that, "there are three types of sport tourism: (a) active sport tourism where participants travel to take part in a sport; (b) event sport tourism where participants travel to watch a sport; and (c) nostalgia sport tourism where participants visit sports-related attractions such as halls of fame, famous stadia or sports-themed cruises". Modern-day professional and intercollegiate sporting events such as football, soccer, baseball, basketball and hockey draw millions of visitors each year to

regularly scheduled games and playoffs. Special sporting events such as the Super Bowl, the Stanley Cup Championship, the World Cup, the Pro Rodeo Championship, the Indianapolis 500, and the College World Series, to name just a few, attract international attention and vast numbers of spectators to host communities each year. These same sports are often played at local and regional levels and, although they may not draw the same crowds, they are just as important to the participants and spectators who are attracted to the excitement of the event. In addition to team sports, a wide array of sporting activities such as golf, tennis, swimming, hiking, biking, fishing, rock climbing and snowboarding/skiing round out the list of alternatives from which travelers can choose.

The National Basketball Association (NBA) was the growth sport of the 1980s, whereas the National Association for Stock Car Racing, better known as NASCAR, was the fastest-growing spectator sport in the United States during the 1990s. Which sport has taken over the title of fastest growing spectator sport of last decade? The answer is Professional Bull Riders (PBR). From 80000 during the founding year in 1994, attendance at PBR events has grown into the millions. And, the sport is expanding globally with events in Canada, Mexico, Brazil and Australia.

Tourists used to go to Alps for mountain scenery. The change in tastes and the development of centres in the alpine region thus paved the way for the subsequent growth of sports activities, such as climbing and skiing, which are so prominent today.

6.2 The Performing Arts

The performing arts "including plays, musicals, opera, ballet, orchestral concerts, singers, comedians, dancers, rock and pop groups" have been popular forms of entertainment for thousands of years. For some destinations, such as Branson, Missouri, they serve as primary tourism revenue generators; for other destinations, such as Las Vegas, Nevada and Vienna, Austria, they serve as one more ingredient in the menu of attractions and entertainment that the area can boast of to interest visitors to encourage them to extend their stay. Live entertainment has always been a draw for travelers. For some it may be the opportunity to select from a wide variety of plays in London's theater district; for others, it is a chance to attend a concert featuring the newest entertainment idol. For still others, it can be the opportunity to attend a country jam or an opera performance.

The classical performing arts include theater (live stage plays, not the movies), ballet, opera, concerts and the symphony. Contemporary performing arts include stand-up and improvisational comedy, rock concerts, and even the band that is playing in your favorite local "hot spot". Performing arts entertainment, especially the classical forms, are frequently offered in locations such as concert halls (the Lincoln Center in New York City, the Athens Concert Hall in Athens, Greece, and the

Forbidden City Concert Hall in Beijing, China) developed for the express purpose of showcasing the art form.

Theaters, concert halls and other large-seating-capacity facilities exist in almost all cities throughout the world and each, no matter how plain or impressive, serves as a draw for visitors. Some, such as the Sydney Opera House, are even renowned as landmarks. Many performing arts companies, whether a repertory acting group or symphony orchestra, have a season (a few months each year) when they stage productions and perform for the public. For example, the Desert Chorale is a classical choir that performs each summer in Santa Fe, adding to the entertainment options offered in that renowned arts city.

Think for a moment of all the performing arts productions you have enjoyed in the past year. Which were of the classical form and which would be considered contemporary? Maybe you even have experience as a participant in the performing arts? Band? Chorus? Local theater? If you traveled to enjoy any of these performances you can call yourself an arts tourist.

7. Medical Care

Medical tourism, where patients travel overseas for operations and various invasive therapies, has grown rapidly since the late 1990s, especially for cosmetic surgery. The main sources of such tourists are developed countries and the main destinations are in Asia. Conventional tourism has been a by-product of this growth, despite its tourist packaging, but the overall benefits to the tourism industry have been considerable. The rise of medical tourism emphasizes a number of contemporary themes including the privatization of health care in postindustrial economies, the growing dependence on technology, uneven access to health resources, the accelerated globalization of health care and tourism, rampant consumerism and cherishing the body beautiful.

Medical tourism is a recent example of niche tourism, with the rapid rise of international travel in search of cosmetic surgery and solutions to various medical conditions, benefiting health-care providers, local economies and the tourism industry. While medical tourism may be a new niche in the industry, tourism has always been associated with improved health and well-being, perhaps more usually perceived as occurring through entertainment, rest and relaxation rather than by substantial bodily changes. Indeed travelling for improved health is the most durable niche in the history of tourism. A long history of spa tourism dates back to antiquity, and in more recent centuries variants of a more general health tourism have included phenomena ranging from naturism and hiking/bushwalking to meditation and detoxification. In some respects medical tourism has evolved from all of these and taken on its own diversity, prompting Bookman (2007) to come up with such subcategories as pregnancy tourism, toothache tourism and detox tourism. There are many others.

When and where the term "medical tourism" itself originated is unknown.

It has become important for many reasons: ① disappointments with medical treatments at home; ②lack of access to health care at reasonable cost, in reasonable time or in a sympathetic context; ③inadequate insurance and income to pay for local health care; ④the rise of high-quality medical care in developing countries; ⑤uneven legal and ethical responses to complex health issues; ⑥ greater mobility; and ⑦perhaps, above all, a growing demand for cosmetic surgery that ties many other factors together. Sometimes, rather less positively, it has grown because of the impossibility of undertaking various procedures at home, and their availability overseas, which in the case of abortion, some forms of organ transplantation (transplant tourism) and stem cell therapy, even contraception and ultimately "death tourism", have raised ethical issues. In countries such as Malaysia, Mexico, Spain and the Philippines retirement provide a potential basis for a more comprehensive medical tourism. In other words medical tourism has grown as the outcome of changes in the institutional context of medical care, a more global economics of access to health (with "developing" countries undercutting the price structures of rich-world countries) and new attitudes to personal identity and medical care, enabled by developments in international communication, transport and tourism. Medical tourism is thus underpinned by diverse political, economic, social and cultural influences.

8. Summary

So many things to do and so little time sums up the delightful dilemma travelers face when selecting from the menu of attractions and entertainment options. How we choose to spend our leisure time while traveling can find us seeing and doing things ranging from the simple to the exotic. Sometimes we look for the comfort and convenience of the familiar, and at other times we seek new or unusual sights, sounds and activities.

The list of leisure-time alternatives from which visitors can choose can be conveniently classified into three broad categories: heritage attractions, commercial attractions and live entertainment. Each of these categories contains even more choices, ranging from museums and zoos to gaming and shopping, and the list goes on. Attraction and entertainment alternatives are limited only by our curiosity, imagination, ingenuity and resources.

Heritage attractions provide a unique two-way window that allows us to peer into the past for a fleeting glimpse of what the future may hold. Whereas heritage attractions meet our needs for self-fulfillment and education, commercial attractions can transport us to lands of make-believe for excitement and enjoyment. When live entertainment is added to the mix of other attraction and entertainment opportunities, travelers are faced with a broad menu of choices for filling their leisure time.

Whether our leisure-time choices are simply a sideline along the way or the main reason for a trip, attractions and entertainment add special spice and memories to our travels. Although the goals of providing visitors with self-fulfillment and enjoyment may be common threads that tie attractions and entertainment together, there are a variety of business decisions that make these operations challenging. They may be operated on either a for-profit or a not-for-profit basis, creating the need to look to different funding sources. They are typically affected by dramatic shifts in seasonal demand, creating the need for skillful marketing, management, and financial decisions for continued success.

Ⅳ Case Study

Archaeological Ruins of Liangzhu City

Located in the Yangtze River Basin on the southeast coast of the country, the archaeological ruins of Liangzhu (about 3300-2300 BC) reveal an early regional state with a unified belief system based on rice cultivation in Late Neolithic China. These ruins are an outstanding example of early urban civilization expressed in earthen monuments, urban planning, a water conservation system and a social hierarchy expressed in differentiated burials in cemeteries within the property.

Brief Synthesis

The Archaeological Ruins of Liangzhu City was the centre of power and belief of an early regional state in the Circum-Taihu Lake Area. It is located on a plain criss-crossed by river networks in the eastern foothills of the Tianmu Mountains in the Yangtze River Basin on the southeast coast of China. Figure 3.1 is the Liangzhu National Archaeological Site Park.

The property is composed of four areas: Area of Yaoshan Site; Area of High-dam at the Mouth of the Valley; Area of Low-dam on the Plain-Causeway in Front of the Mountains; and Area of City Site.

The Archaeological Ruins of Liangzhu City reveals an early regional state with rice-cultivating agriculture as its economic base, social differentiation and a unified belief system, which existed in the Late Neolithic Period in China. With a series of sites, including the City Site built during 3300-2300 BC, the Peripheral Water Conservancy System with complex functions and socially-graded cemeteries (including an altar), and the excavated objects represented by series of jade artefacts symbolizing the belief system, as well as its early age, the property represents the remarkable contributions made by the Yangtze River Basin to the origins of Chinese civilization. In addition, the pattern and functional zoning of the capital, together with the characteristics of the settlements of the Liangzhu culture and of the Outer City with the terraces, support strongly the value of the property.

Figure 3.1 Liangzhu National Archaeological Site Park

Criterion

The Archaeological Ruins of Liangzhu City, as the centre of power and belief of Liangzhu culture, is an outstanding testimony of an early regional state with rice-cultivating agriculture as its economic base, social differentiation and a unified belief system, which existed in the lower reaches of the Yangtze River in the Late Neolithic Period of China. It provides unparalleled evidence for concepts of cultural identity, social and political organization, and the development of society and culture in the late Neolithic and early Bronze Age in China and the region.

The Archaeological Ruins of Liangzhu illustrates the transition from small-scale Neolithic societies to a large integrated political unit with hierarchy, rituals and crafts. It includes outstanding examples of early urbanization expressed in earthen monuments, city and landscape planning, social hierarchy expressed in burial differentiations in cemeteries within the property, socio-cultural strategies for organization of space, and materialization of power. It represents the great achievement of prehistoric rice-cultivating civilization of China over 5000 years ago, and as an outstanding example of early urban civilization.

Integrity

The four component parts of the Archaeological Ruins of Liangzhu City include all the identified attributes necessary to convey its significance as an outstanding representation of a prehistoric early state and urban civilization in the Yangtze River Basin.

The property contains all material elements of the archaeological ruins, four main man-made elements, i. e. the City Site, the Peripheral Water Conservancy System, the socially-graded cemeteries (including an altar), and excavated objects represented by jade artifacts, as well as the natural topography that is directly linked to the function of the sites.

The buffer zone includes the historical environmental elements associated with the value of the property, such as mountains, isolated mounds, bodies of water and wetlands, but also includes scattered contemporaneous archaeological remains surrounding the ancient city, as well as the intrinsic association of value between different sites and their spatial layout and pattern.

The impact of urban development, construction and natural factors threatening the property have been properly addressed.

Authenticity

Sites in the four areas, including the City Site, the Peripheral Water Conservancy System, the socially-graded cemeteries (including an altar), preserved as archaeological sites, carry the authentic historical information of the heritage of the period 3300-2300 BC, including characteristics in site selection, space and environment, location and layout, contour of remains, materials and technologies, and historical function of the sites, as well as the internal connection between the overall layout of the property and individual elements, and the historical natural environment of the distribution region of the sites. The objects unearthed from the four areas represented by jade artifacts authentically preserve the shape, categories, decorative patterns, functions, materials and the complex processing technologies and exquisite craftsmanship of the artifacts. Together with the archaeological sites, they authentically and credibly demonstrate the degree of development of the rice-cultivating civilization in the lower reaches of the Yangtze River in the Neolithic Period and provide a panorama of Archaeological Ruins of Liangzhu City as an early regional urban civilization.

Protection and Management Requirements

Three components sites, Area of Yaoshan Site (01), Area of Causeway in Front of the Mountains (03-2), and Area of City Site (04) of the Archaeological Ruins of Liangzhu City, have obtained the highest-level national protection and are located in the Key Protection Subzone within the protection range of "Liangzhu Archaeological Site", a national priority protected site for the protection of cultural relics. The Area of High-dam at the Mouth of the Valley (02) and Area of the Low-dam on the Plain (03-1) were listed as Provincial Protected Sites of Zhejiang in 2017, and an application is being processed for listing them as national priority protected sites.

The property is owned by the state and is protected by relevant laws and regulations such as the Law of the People's Republic of China on the Protection of

Cultural Relics, Regulations for the Implementation of Law of the People's Republic of China on the Protection of Cultural Relics, and Administrative Regulations of Zhejiang Province on the Protection of Cultural Relics, and enjoys both national and provincial-level status in protection.

Special protection policies and regulations for the property have been formulated and improved, including Regulations for the Protection and Management of Liangzhu Archaeological Site of Hangzhou (revised in 2013), and a series of special regulations for heritage protection has been prepared, issued and implemented, including the Conservation Master Plan for the Liangzhu Archaeological Site (2008-2025) as a national priority protected site, and monitoring over the property and its surroundings is also strengthened.

All four areas of the Archaeological Ruins of Liangzhu City share the same buffer zone and are managed effectively in a uniform way by a common management authority—the Hangzhou Liangzhu Archaeological Administrative District Management Committee.

It has a clear system for division of work and responsibilities, complete functions, sufficient technical and management staff specializing in protection, sufficient resources of funds and complete facilities.

Various protection and management regulations will be strictly implemented, environmental capacity and development and construction activities in the property area will be effectively controlled, and negative impacts on the property from the pressures of various developments will be curbed; demands of stakeholders will be coordinated and taken into overall consideration, and the balance between the protection of the property and developments in tourism and urban construction will be kept, both rationally and effectively.

Research, interpretation and dissemination of the heritage value will be strengthened; the integrated function of the property, including cultural tourism and ecological protection, will be brought into play appropriately, and a sustainable and harmonious relationship between the protection of Archaeological Ruins of Liangzhu City and the development of Yuhang District and Hangzhou City will be maintained.

V Tips

25 New Tourist Attractions Worth Adding to Your Bucket List

Fondation Louis Vuitton, Paris

This must-see attraction floats like a cloud of glass above the treetops of the Bois de Boulogne. The Fondation Louis Vuitton, devoted to contemporary arts and culture from France and beyond and supported by the luxury fashion conglomerate LVMH, opened in October 2014. The building, designed by Frank Gehry, has galleries for its art collection (Daniel Buren, Rineke Dijkstra, Ellsworth Kelly), spaces for site-specific works and an auditorium for music and dance.

Canadian Museum for Human Rights, Winnipeg

Leave it to the Canadians to come up with an entire museum dedicated to human rights. Jazzing up the Winnipeg skyline with a swirly glass design culminating in a single gleaming spire, the 260000-square-foot ode to tolerance and hope opened in September 2014. It's the handiwork of architect Antoine Predock. Inside, you'll find thought-provoking exhibits encompassing the Holocaust, ethnic cleansing in Bosnia, and leaders like Nelson Mandela and Gloria Steinem.

Eiffel Tower, Paris

How do you update a 125-year-old landmark? For the Eiffel Tower, the answer came in the form of a glass floor from the 187-foot-high first-floor level. Visitors can now be transfixed by not only the city views unfurling all around them, but also those below them—in the latest example of a recent trend that includes the Grand Canyon's Skywalk and Chicago's Willis Tower. The first floor's $38 million renovation includes restaurants, solar panels, shops and a museum. But the highlight remains this new see-through floor. So next time you're at the Eiffel Tower, keep an eye out lest you trip over selfie-takers lying down on the glass.

Goods Line, Sydney

New York City's wildly successful High Line elevated park has set off a global chain reaction of inventive urban spaces reclaiming run-down zones. Case in point: Sydney's planned corridor from Ultimo (by the also-new Frank Gehry-designed business school at the University of Technology, Sydney) to Darling Harbour. The 800-foot-long North Section, to be revealed first, will feature cafés and a new Mary Ann Street amphitheater for outdoor events. Look for an early 2015 opening, in conjunction with the unveiling of the Gehry building.

Bombay Sapphire Distillery, Laverstoke, England

What the Guinness Storehouse is to Ireland's favorite stout is what the Thomas Heatherwick-designed Bombay Sapphire Distillery aspires to be for England's popular gin brand. The celebrated British starchitect constructed sinuous glass houses that seem to sprout from the walls of the historic paper mill he was tasked to revamp. It's a whimsically beautiful home for a product that, as some critics point out, is short on heritage (Bombay Sapphire gin only launched only in 1987). Still, the distillery is sure to be a hit with travelers who may not have otherwise ever discovered the village of Laverstoke.

Markthal Rotterdam, Netherlands

It's a building that appears to defy logic at first glance: a giant horseshoe-shaped arch in Rotterdam houses 228 apartments inside, and underneath, you'll find the

world's funkiest covered market. Officially unveiled in October 2014, the space beneath the 130-foot roof showcases 100 produce stalls and dozens of restaurants and shops, making it the city's hottest new gathering place. A massive 36000-square-foot mural by Arno Coenen and Iris Roskam called Cornucopia—with a rainbow of colorful fruits, vegetables and other food finds—covers the entire inner arch. The humble food market has never looked so cool.

Harvard Museum Extension, Cambridge, MA

Natural light pours into the dramatic new extension of Harvard's art museum complex, courtesy of a five-story glass atrium. Renzo Piano stripped the buildings housing the hallowed university's Fogg Museum, Busch-Reisinger Museum, and Arthur M. Sackler Museum of all post-1925 additions, and instead focused on preserving existing façades and adding airy new spaces for both viewing and studying art. It's a shiny new home for an age-old collection, showcasing everything from ancient Greek vases to sculpture by Rodin—and a work of art in itself.

Shanghai Tower

While Dubai's Burj Khalifa continues to hang on to the world's-tallest-building title (for now), there is a new behemoth on the block: at more than 2000 feet high, China's Shanghai Tower vies for second place. In the Pudong financial district, it towers over the Huangpu River with a 125-story spire; the twisting shape comes courtesy of U.S. architectural firm Gensler. Plans call for a mix of office and event space, high-end shops, and a sightseeing platform accessible by a speedy one-minute elevator ride.

Batman: The Ride, Six Flags Fiesta Texas, San Antonio, TX

Just when you thought the theme park wizards couldn't think of anything else: Six Flags Fiesta Texas in San Antonio is preparing to unleash a 120-foot Batman roller coaster, but this one in 4-D (and in time for summer 2015). What might that entail? Expect plenty of spinning around forward and backward in your seat as you navigate sheer drops and undulating tracks, all at 40 miles an hour and for 1000 gut-wrenching feet. This 4-D free-spin coaster will be one of a kind.

ICE Kraków Congress Centre, Poland

When the ICE kraków congress Centre opened in October 2014, it signified not only the debut of world-class performing space but a triumph over a bleak chapter in Poland's history. With the decimation of many of its concert spaces in World War II followed decades under Communist rule, Poland's rich cultural heritage had fallen by the wayside. This angular 2100-seat auditorium is part of a concerted revival effort.

Ⅵ Dialogue

(Sue is calling a tourist office to get some information about a family trip.)

Martin: Good morning. This is Burnham tourist office. Martin speaking.

Sue: Oh, hello. I saw a poster about free things to do in the area, and it said people should phone you for information. I'm coming to Burnham with my husband and two children for few days on June 27th, or possibly the 28th, and I'd like some ideas for things to do on the 29th.

Martin: Yes, of course. Let's start with a couple of events especially for children. The art gallery is holding an event called "Family Welcome" that day when there are activities and trails to use throughout the gallery.

Sue: That sounds interesting. What time does it start?

Martin: The gallery opens at 10:00, and the "Family Welcome" event runs from 10:30 until 14:00. The gallery stays open until 17:00, and several times during the day. They're going to show a short film that the gallery has produced. It demonstrates how ceramics are made, and there'll be equipment and materials for children to have a go themselves. Last time they ran the event there was a film about painting which went down very well with the children, and they're now working on one about sculpture.

Sue: I like the sound of that. And what other events happen in Burnham?

Martin: Well, do you all enjoy listening to music?

Sue: Oh, yes.

Martin: Well, there are several free concerts taking place at different times—one or two in the morning, the majority at lunchtime and a couple in the evening, and they range from pop music to Latin American music.

Sue: The Latin American music could be fun. What time is that?

Martin: It's being repeated several times, in different places. They're performing in the central library at 13:00, then at 16:00, it's in the City Museum, and in the evening at 19:30, there's a longer concert, in the theatre.

Sue: Right. I'll suggest that to the rest of the family.

Martin: Something else you might be interested in is the boat race along the river.

Sue: Oh, yes. Do tell me about that.

Martin: The race starts at Offord Marina to the north of Burnham, and goes as far as Summer Pool. The best place to watch it from is Charlesworth Bridge, though that does get rather crowded.

Sue: And who's taking part?

Martin: Well, local boat clubs, but the standard is very high. One of them came first in the West of England regional championship in May this year—it was the first time a team from Burnham has won. It means that next year they'll be representing the region in the national championship.

Sue: Now I've heard something about Paxton Nature Reserve. It's a good place for spotting unusual birds, isn't it?

Martin: That's right, throughout the year. There is a lake there, as well as a river, and they provide very attractive habitat. So it's a good idea to bring binoculars if you have them. And just at the moment you can see various flowers that are pretty unusual—the soil at Paxton isn't very common. They're looking good right now.

Sue: Right. My husband will be particularly interested in that.

Martin: Then there's going to be a talk and slide show about mushrooms—and you'll be able to go out and pick some afterwards and study the different varieties.

Sue: Uh. And is it possible for children to swim in the river?

Martin: Yes. Part of it has been fenced off to make it safe for children to swim in. It's very shallow, and there's lifeguard on duty whenever it's open. The lake is too deep, so swimming isn't allowed there.

Sue: OK. We must remember to bring their swimming things, in case we go to Paxton. How long does it take to get there by car from Burnham?

Martin: About 20 minutes, but parking is very limited, so it's usually much easier to go by bus and it takes about the same time.

Sue: Well, I'll discuss the options with the rest of the family. Thank you very much for all your help.

Martin: You're welcome.

Sue: Goodbye.

Martin: Bye.

Ⅶ Academic Thinking

Understanding Tourist Attraction Cooperation: An Application of Network Analysis to the Case of Shanghai, China

Author: Yong Yang

Journal: *Journal of Destination Marketing & Management*

Abstract:

This study explores the profile structure of tourist attraction cooperation from the perspectives of tourists and government by using web-based text data. Targets were tourist attractions in Shanghai rated grade 3A and above. The study collected travel notes published by tourists about their travel experiences on blog communities, as well as official news released by the Chinese government. Based on frequencies of occurrence and co-occurrence of information about tourist attractions in these travel notes and official news items, levels of cooperation between tourist attractions are analyzed. The results indicate a difference in the popularity of tourist attractions as portrayed in travel notes and official news. In addition, there are significant differences between the government's and tourists' preferences for tourist attraction cooperation. The profile structure of tourist attraction cooperation from the government perspective is not consistent with real cooperation structure as seen from the tourist's perspective. A number of policy implications for tourism development emerge and are presented.

理解旅游景点合作:网络分析在上海案例中的应用

这项研究使用基于网络的文本数据从游客和政府的角度探讨了旅游景点合作的概况结构。以上海3A级及以上的旅游景点为研究目标,该研究收集了游客发布在博客社区的旅行经历记录,以及中国政府发布的官方新闻。根据这些旅行记录和官方新闻中有关旅游景点的信息的出现和共现的频率,研究分析了旅游景点之间的合作水平。结果表明,在旅行记录和官方新闻中,旅游景点的受欢迎程度有所不同。此外,政府和游客在旅游景点合作方面的偏好也有很大差异。政府视角下的景区合作结构与游客视角下的景区合作结构不一致。出现并提出了一些对旅游业发展的政策影响。

Ⅷ Questions

扫码看答案

1. Why are attractions and entertainment important components of the tourism industry?
2. How does seasonality create marketing, management, and financial challenges for attraction and entertainment operators?
3. Explain the similarities and differences between heritage attractions and commercial attractions.
4. How have shopping malls been turned into tourism attractions?

Ⅸ Key Words and Terms

attractions	吸引物
botanical garden	植物园
festival	节日
Gross Gambling Revenues (GGR)	博彩业收入
heritage attractions	历史遗产景点

leisure activities	休闲活动
museum	博物馆
national park	国家公园
national reserve	国家保护区
national scenic trail	国家风景步道
recreational activities	娱乐活动
shopping tourism	购物旅游
sport tourism	体育旅游
world heritage site	世界遗产地

Single Choice Questions

Chapter 4
Tourism Service

I Chapter Introduction

The purpose of this chapter is to introduce the service management paradigm in the context of tourism. This is done via an explanation of the evolution from a product to a service management orientation and an evolutionary mapping of management thought. Then, an overview of relevant service management topics is provided followed by a case example of service management principles in action. We can know the latest knowledge about tourism services, and to contribute to the continuing improvement of services for all, with a stake in the success of this growing industry, whether they are staff, residents or tourists and guests. The quality of tourism services seems likely to become an ever more central factor for future managerial decisions.

II Chapter Objectives

1. Describe how services are different from goods.
2. Explain how a service is like a play.
3. Explain the different factors that affect a guest's service experience.
4. Explain how a person develops expectations of a service and how tourism organizations can meet or exceed these expectations.
5. Name and describe the five service quality dimensions.
6. Explain how a comparison of service expectations with the actual service encounter can give rise to three possible satisfaction levels.
7. Explain what tourism managers can do to ensure high-quality service.
8. Explain how negative "breaks from the script" should be handled in order to "turn a frown upside down" and create guest loyalty.
9. List the important aspects of a service guarantee.

Reading

1. The Unique Features of the Tourism Industry and Tourism Services

Tourism products are considered services and like all services are characterized by intangibility, heterogeneity, inseparability and perishability. These characteristics imply the increased involvement of consumers in the service process of production and consumption. In addition to the features related to their service nature, the particularities of the tourism industry named seasonality, globalization, low levels of loyalty, complexity (including multiple subsectors such as food and beverage, accommodation, transportation, recreation and travel), cross and income elasticity demand need to be taken into account before making any marketing decisions.

Seasonality in tourism has been defined as a temporal imbalance in the phenomenon of tourism, which may be expressed in terms of dimensions of such elements as number of visitors, expenditure of visitors, traffic on highways and other forms of transportation, employment and admission to attractions (Butler, 2001). Seasonality is considered a severe problem in tourism because it leads tourism firms to hire part time personnel, therefore limiting their ability to develop distinct capabilities. Moreover, the constant need to hire new seasonal employees leads to increased training and other costs associated with employee turnover. Thus, seasonality has been linked to low returns on investment, underutilization of facilities and limited access to capital (Butler, 2001). In some cases, 80% of tourism income occurs within a two-month period. Therefore, it has been suggested that destinations with extreme seasonality should develop policies to overcome extremes of seasonality while tourism enterprises should adopt marketing strategies to cope with the problem (Lundtorp, 2001).

Globalization in tourism means that tourism businesses have the ability to operate and market themselves not only locally but globally as well, while many of them have opted for a competitive strategy of internationalization. Nowadays, tourism firms consider the world as their operating environment and establish both global strategies and global market presence (Knowles, Diamantes, El Mourhabi, 2001). In tourism, globalization affects both the supply and the demand side in various ways. In the supply of tourism services, the most common trends refer to the development of large worldwide suppliers (e.g. transnational corporations such as Disney and Club Méditerranée) and intermediaries, which lead to oligopolies. Another development refers to the creation of virtual travel agencies, which jeopardize (owing to disintermediation) the traditional intermediate function of offline travel agencies (Tsiaotso, Rattan, 2010). On the demand side, globalization has been linked to decreasing costs of air travel, access to new and low-priced destinations, as well as relatively low social standards.

Moreover, tourism is characterized by low levels of customer loyalty. If developing loyalty in services is difficult (Tsiaotso, Wirt, 2012), then achieving loyalty in tourism is a feat. Because consumers search for new experiences by visiting various places and destinations all over the world, it is very difficult to develop loyalty, for example, in destinations or accommodation services. Therefore, the task here is to develop loyalty to global service brands so customers trust and purchase services from the same service providers (usually transnational corporations) no matter which destination they travel to.

Tourism is a complex industry because it is a compilation of various services such as accommodation, transportation, dining, recreation and travel. All these services comprise the tourism experience. Often these services are not offered by one provider who has control over them, but by different providers who might not communicate or collaborate with the remaining providers. Thus, a delayed flight might stigmatize the whole customer tourism experience, resulting in dissatisfaction not only with the particular service provider but with all the others as well (e. g. hotel and restaurants).

2. Evolution of the "Service" Discipline

By all accounts, the economic output of most developed countries today is dominated by services, with a generally accepted assumption that between 75%-80% of gross domestic product (GDP) is comprised of services (interesting that GDP is predominately comprised of services). This seems very large, until one reflects upon how and where they spend their money. The basic categories of services are government, tourism, retail trade, healthcare, transport, utilities, communications, finance, insurance and real-estate. Services were formerly named the "miscellaneous" (non-goods) economic category in the 19th century, but have now more appropriately been labelled the "new economy" and is dominant across much of the developed and developing world.

Much discourse has taken place over the differentiation of the terms "goods" and "services". Some (Kotler, 1997) suggest that nearly any business transaction would be either a purely tangible good, a tangible good with accompanying intangible service, a primarily intangible service with accompanying tangible good, or a purely intangible service. Others argue that the service and non-service distinction has become less meaningful and there are only industries, the service components of which are greater or less than those of other industries. Many years ago Marshall (1929) suggested that all industries provided some kind of service, although he pointed out that there was no specific literature which addressed the management of service.

As far back as 1940, Colin Clark stated that the economics of tertiary industry

had yet to be written. Fuchs attempts to demonstrate the rise of the "stepchild" of economic research which he calls the service (also referred to as the tertiary or residual) economy. Fuchs highlights the lack of any theoretical base regarding the management of services, and mentions two criteria that would lay the seed for future work in defining services theory. Firstly that services are delivered with "closeness" to the consumer, and secondly that services tend to be absent of a tangibility. Sibson (1971) identified the fundamental evolution of product to service economies, which, for the first time, emphasized the generalized knowledge, principles and concepts for the management of a professional services enterprise. He then made a number of observations:

(1) The economy of the developed world was moving rapidly from a production orientation to one that would soon be dominated by service enterprises.

(2) There was a genuine concern that such organizations would be unable to be managed using existing management theory and that most management methods and techniques used in organizations then evolved to meet the needs of manufacturing/production oriented enterprises.

(3) He suggested that no literature dealing with the characteristics, questions and problems of managing services enterprises had ever been published (with the exception of some articles and books dealing with administration and detailed operational questions rather than a broad management view).

(4) Finally, that there would not be a suitable workforce available to fill positions in this sector (accurate premonition).

The current service management discipline is often attributed to a seminal paper (Shostack, 1977) in which the author called for services marketing to "break free" from product marketing. Shostack, a senior vice president of Marketing at Citibank, came to realize that the marketing paradigms taught at university did not adequately apply to what customers "buy" at banks.

More recently, a series of articles and books by Virgo and Lush have questioned this call to "break free", proposing the need for all marketing and management to break free of the manufacturing/production orientation, by adopting instead a service orientation (focused on value creation).

The original call for services to "break free" from goods included a movement by service management scholars to find a way to make service "distinct" or unique from more traditional management. As such, a number of generally accepted characteristics were touted as "unique" to service. While these characteristics may no longer be accepted as "unique" it is important to be familiar with these concepts because they are still relevant to service management. The four most commonly cited "distinctive features" of services are:

(1) Intangibility—services cannot be seen, felt, tasted or touched; they are

performances rather than objects.

(2) Inseparability—goods are often produced, sold and then consumed, whereas services are usually produced and consumed at the same time.

(3) Heterogeneity—people play a critical role in service delivery; service and people are generally inextricably linked; this creates variability between service providers and customers which makes managing service so difficult.

(4) Perishability—services cannot be stored; once a service is gone, it can never be sold again (e.g. airline seat, a dinner reservation).

3. Service Encounters

3.1 Service Encounter / Customer Contact Employees

Given the fundamental premise that service is often provided in an interaction between employees and customers, it is important to be aware of some of the important issues around the "moment of truth" in service, or what is called the service encounter. A service encounter can be defined as the interaction between a tourist and the service provider. The outcomes of service encounters thus depend on the skills, knowledge, personality, behaviour and performance of these employees. If successful, effective service encounters can lead to many favorable outcomes, including satisfaction, loyalty and positive word-of-mouth recommendation. It is therefore imperative that tourism firms understand how to manage these critical service encounters.

At the heart of service management is the unavoidable fact that a significant proportion of tourism experiences are delivered by people (tourism employees, managers, owners). The unfortunate irony about this fact is that many customer-contact employees are the youngest and least trained of employees. Although many services have become more reliant on technology (vending machines, airline self-check in), person-to-person interactions still predominate in most tourism businesses. The employees who deliver the service obviously have a direct influence on tourists, as of course do owners, managers, and other stakeholders who indirectly contribute to the service. Moreover, other people in the service environment at the time-of-service delivery, including other tourists, also play a part. The personal appearance, attitudes and behavior of all involved, directly or indirectly, have an influence on a tourist's perception of services.

From the tourist's perspective, the most immediate evidence of service quality is the service encounter itself. Interactions with service employees are the experiences that tourists are most likely to remember, and employees who are uncomfortable in dealing with tourists or who lack the training and expertise to meet expectations can cause tourists to retain unpleasant memories of a service experience. Service employees are thus the primary resource through which service businesses can gain a competitive advantage (Lovelock, Wirtz, 2004).

A number of management approaches have been suggested which can help tourism businesses manage or control service encounters. Examples of these include:

(1) Scripts—where service providers follow predetermined statements, such as "would you like fries with that?"

(2) Role-play training—putting employees into mock service situations to assist them in correctly dealing with a range of circumstances.

(3) Clearly defined service processes—a more general approach than scripts, but with clear expectations of steps of service.

(4) Engrained service culture—embedding the importance of customers into the fabric of the organization (more on this below).

(5) Effective recruitment / Human resource management—ensuring that the right people are employed and that individual development continues throughout the term of employment.

Customer-contact employees have been given many labels, including "boundary spanners" "gatekeepers" and "image-makers" (Bowen, Schneider, 1985). They are a tourism organization's primary interface with customers and, as such, are often perceived by the customer as the product. Bowen and Schneider (1985) insist that employees not only create and deliver the service, but also are the entire image of the organization. Within tourism businesses, service is performed for a customer by a service person (e.g. a waiter, front desk receptionist, a tour guide). From the customer's point of view, service is essentially the performance of the staff who serve as the public face of the organization or in some cases, the destination. It should be noted that most services do have a tangible aspect which must also be acceptable to the customer, and it is this package of tangible and intangible aspects that define a tourist's experience.

Bowen and Ford (2002) argue that managing the service employee is different to managing employees located in positions with little or no customer contact. There are six basic differences:

(1) Service employees must be both task and interactive capable, because customers are present in the service "factory" (producing and engaging simultaneously).

(2) Attitudes and behaviours are more critical than technical skills for service employees (and skills can be taught more easily than attitude).

(3) Formal mechanisms for employee control cannot be used with service employees. Instead, a service culture and climate must be in evidence to fill gaps which form as the result of unexpected or unplanned customer-interactions or circumstances.

(4) Emotions play a role with service employees, as observable facial and body displays create impressions, and emotional displays by service providers can have

positive/negative effects on customers. Therefore, service employees, to be most effective, must be skilled to understand which emotions are appropriate in different circumstances (empathy when something has gone wrong, excited when a customer is, etc.).

(5) Service employees must be trained to deal with role-related conflict. For example, if a customer is unhappy with a service standard, he might become angry with the service provider, even though the employee was doing his/her job as expected by the organization.

(6) Service employees are expected to be "part-time marketers". This implies that service employees are expected to fully understand their firm's offerings and demonstrate enthusiasm for them. This can be enhanced through the concept known as "internal marketing". Here, a firm's products and service should first be marketed to its employees so that they are in the best position to "sell" when interacting with customers.

3.2 Quality

In the case of tourism, quality and hospitality are two words that are inseparable. When thinking about a high-quality experience in any tourism service, whether a restaurant meal, a hotel stay, an airline flight, or a guided tour, most people think of friendly, helpful personnel who treat them with concern and kindness. The concept of quality with its important hospitality component is the focus of this chapter.

As the tourism marketplace becomes more competitive, quality becomes more crucial for continued financial success. Consumers are more critical and demanding today than they have ever been. Simply providing guests average service is not good enough in this competitive environment. In a market full of tourism suppliers, a company needs to offer more and better service because guests can always take their business elsewhere. For example, for hotel operators, "Service quality and customer satisfaction have gradually been recognized as key factors used to gain competitive advantage and customer retention".

Virtually every survey of restaurant guests tells a similar story. If a property (hotel or a restaurant) has great service, the guests will come back even if the food is mediocre. Reverse the situation and the opposite occurs: Great food with bad service, and guests will most likely not return.

As we have already suggested, different travelers have different needs and wants. What is "high quality" to one may be perceived as entirely unacceptable to another. Think of Mexican food. Some restaurant patrons believe that high-quality Mexican food must make you perspire and set your tongue on fire.

3.3 Definitions of Quality

In the manufacturing sector the concept of quality is widely accepted. The basis is technical specifications for components, dimensions and performances. The statistical

measurement of a run of products for divergence from specifications such as advocated by Shewart (1931) laid a foundation for the evaluation of the costs of defects as an answer to the question "how much quality is enough?" Feigen Baum(1956) developed the notion of total quality control starting with the design of the product and ending only when the product has been placed in the hands of a customer who remains satisfied.

Garvin (1988) has remarked that "despite the interest of managers, quality remains a term that is easily misunderstood…Scholars in four disciplines—philosophy, economics, marketing and operations management have…each viewed it from a different vantage point". Thus, even in the case of manufactured goods, the management of quality is problematic. Part of the problem arises from the differing views of its meaning and significance taken between the various functions of one company as a consequence of their task cultures and traditions.

Transcendent quality varies between individuals and over time, and can be understood in the common phrase "I know it when I see it". An approach relying on the measurable features of the product, an expert view of quality, leads to design specification and technical drawings. User-based quality, while in part based on individual judgement, is also the basis of consumer legislation which introduced the test of merchantability, requiring goods sold commercially to be fit for their purpose: The classic test was that a bucket should not leak. Manufacturing quality is concerned to minimize deviations from the standards set in technical specifications.

3.4 Service Encounters—Moments of Truth

The tourism industry is one of close customer contact, and every interaction between a service employee and a customer becomes a service encounter. Both tourism customers and tourism suppliers personnel bring to each encounter expectations about what will occur during the interaction. As customers and suppliers, we learn what to expect in tourism encounters from past experiences and from the experiences of others that we observe. In a sense, we all perform an important role in a service encounter "play". As customers or suppliers, we both have role expectations of each other that dictate appropriate behavior for each party.

In Table 4.1, we extend this theater metaphor for services a little further. Most tourism services have a backstage area referred to as "back-of-the-house" that the audiences (guests) do not usually see. Managers of these services must be careful in their choices of props and sets onstage, those service areas guests experience referred to as "front-of-the-house". Services even have two types of employees, backstage hands, those who work behind the scenes to ensure a smooth running "show" and front stage actors, those employees who directly interact with guests.

Table 4.1 Services as theater: Everyone has a role

Service Terminology	Theater Terminology
Employee	Cast
Customer	Audience
Physical facilities	the set
Uniform	Costume
Front stage	Those areas that the audience see
Backstage	Those areas that the audience seldom see
Manager	Director
Service encounter	Performance
Personal front/"character"	Face/role that cast assumes when front stage (allowed to "break character" when backstage)

Source: Grove S J, Fisk R P. The dramaturgy of services exchange: An analytical framework for services marketing in Emerging Perspectives on Services Marketing, Chicago, January, 1983[C]. American Marketing Association,1983.

Although we can think of service encounters as little plays that involve service scripts, we all realize that they do not involve a rigid, pre-rehearsed set of lines. After all, a stay at Accor brand Motel 6 in the United States or Formula 1 in Europe is not expected to be as well rehearsed and performed as a Broadway production.

Much of what customers notice and judge during a service is the contact they have with the service staff who deliver the technical features of the service. Czepiel, Solomon and Surprenant, in an important edited collection of research which has not received as much attention as it merits, call this the "service encounter". Normann referred to the points of interaction in a service episode as "moments of truth", a phrase which Carlzon (1987) had adopted from the consultant for the title of his perceptive book reflecting on his experiences managing the Scandinavian tour operator Vingressor and its parent airline, SAS. Both Carlzon and Normann have demonstrated that each of the moments of truth is an occurrence used by customers to judge the overall quality of the service and the organization. In complex services, such as undertaking a journey or going on a holiday, it is not just the main organization's staff who provide services to clients; subcontracting organizations also have direct contact with the client, raising further issues for managers dealing with partners in the service chain.

The concept of "moments of truth" and the issues surrounding service experiences and service encounters between clients and staff are discussed throughout this book.

4. Human Resources: the Key to High-Quality Service

A wide range of skills from entry-level dishwashers to senior executives are

needed in every service organization. Effectively and efficiently managing these human resources is the cornerstone of success for every organization from entrepreneurial tour companies to large multinational lodging chains.

Everyone wants to hire a winner and create a "sustainable competitive advantage". In large organizations, the human resources department is a means to achieve these goals. In very small firms, this responsibility is usually shared among the immediate supervisor and other management personnel. Some organizations have even found it to be cost effective to contract out or "outsource" some of these activities. For example, many airlines, convention centers, stadiums and theme parks contract with outside firms to perform cleaning and security services.

With labor costs exceeding 70% of operating costs in many service organizations, it is easy to identify and quantify the value of employees in terms of cost. However, employees are more than just the cost of doing business—they are also organizational assets that management is obligated to safeguard and develop.

Guests will perceive, judge and value their experiences based on the culmination of dozens, even hundreds of one-on-one service encounters over the course of a visit. The demand for organizational excellence translates into:

(1) Encouraging employee participation and commitment to delivering value at every level.

(2) Developing and expanding employee commitment, capacity and innovation.

(3) Creating a workplace environment where everyone is motivated to excel and is accountable for organizational success.

One of the primary functions of human resource departments in today's service environment is to implement best practices through effective recruitment, selection, training, retention and team-building programs.

4.1 Bringing Employees into the Organization

When new employees report for work the first day, the manner in which their supervisor and other employees welcome them may have a lasting impact on their future performance. Orientation or on-boarding is a process designed to help new employees become acquainted with the organization and understand the expectations the organization and their supervisor have for them. This process is sometimes referred to as the socialization process. Employees want to know what is expected of them in the way of performance. In most large organizations, someone from the human resources department will give new employees general information about the organization, including policies, benefits and procedures.

4.2 Working with Organized Labor

Labor unions are common in most industrialized countries. Understanding the importance of these unions and learning to work with them or avoid having to work with them is critical to every organization whether they are unionized or nonunionized. An important aspect of human resource management involves employees and employers having agreements and understandings about a wide array of matters affecting working conditions and the accomplishment of the organization's work. Among these, for example, are how work is to be assigned, how jobs are to be filled, how employees are to be disciplined and rewarded, and how disagreements are to be handled.

4.3 Setting the Stage for Peak Performance

Performance management begins during the orientation process of the first few weeks of employment, which are the most tenuous and susceptible to turnover. Even with well-written job descriptions and realistic job previews, new employees bring many preconceived notions with them about a job that can be easily shattered as they collide with on-the-job realities. In addition, new employees may often be subjected to a little "good-natured" teasing from co-workers as they settle in to daily routines.

When the right employees have been hired, comprehensive orientation programs can help to alleviate these potential new hire stumbling blocks, setting the stage for successful organizational integration. However, thinking that successful organizational entry can be achieved simply through orientation is short-sighted, since it is only the beginning to organizational assimilation and personal development.

4.4 Achieving and Maintaining Peak Performance

Think about the different supervisors you have worked for. Were they achievement oriented or task oriented? Did their orientation toward getting the job done make a difference in how you worked or how you enjoyed your job? As you think about answering these questions, it becomes clear that supervisors, those first-line managers who are responsible for day-to-day operations, have a huge impact on employees and customers. However you answered these questions, the most effective supervisors gained the cooperation of others.

5. Anticipating and Meeting Guest Needs

5.1 Customer Participation in Services

A complicating factor is that passengers have differing expectations of the service.

Customers' expectations and requests that exceed the firm's ability to perform account for 74% of the reported communications difficulties. This implies that even if the system is working at optimal efficiency, employees can expect to face a large number of communications difficulties. (Nyquist, Bitner and Booms, 1985)

The authors went on to identify nine service situations likely to cause problems for staff, summarized in Table 4.2.

Table 4.2 Difficulties in dealing with customers

Difficulties in dealing with customers
(1) unreasonable demands
(2) demands against policies
(3) unacceptable treatment of employees
(4) drunkenness
(5) breaking social norms
(6) special needs customers (psychological, language or medical difficulties)
(7) unavailable services
(8) unacceptably slow performances
(9) unacceptable services

Based on Nyquist, Bitner and Booms (1985)

The foregoing discussion of service design has given additional emphasis to the role of contact staff in the satisfaction of clients. A complex service such as that provided during air travel or in a hotel is often designed to be delivered by several teams of people, each with specialized but separated skills such as check-in or in-flight service. The service management model proposed by George and Kelly discussed above therefore has to be enlarged to accommodate issues involved in the coordination and management of work teams. Many organizations have implemented programs to help staff understand the ways in which their particular role contributes to the overall success of the enterprise. Lockwood et al. (1992) have described how one hotel puts on a program called "Together we care". They comment, "The company realized that, although together they might have cared, individually nobody gave a damn!" The significance of this has been underlined by Bitner, Booms and Tetreault(1990):

Many times interaction is the service from the customers' point of view yet front line employees are not trained to understand customers and do not have the freedom and discretion needed to relate to customers in ways that ensure effective service.

In addition to understanding the customers' needs and expectations, hospitality and tourism managers must be able to hire the right people and train them well. To delight guests, tourism employees must have a positive service attitude; they must have the necessary abilities to learn and perform jobs well; and they must be flexible enough to meet different customers' needs and expectations. Employees with a genuine service orientation will try to anticipate customers' needs even before customers realize the needs or ask for such services. Management must decide on proper training for employees and set standards and policies that result in high quality and high satisfaction.

5.2 Building Service Teams

In addition to individual efforts, employees must work together as a team. If you have worked in any tourism industry job, you already know that delivering good service is a team effort. Imagine two different restaurants: One features servers who have a "that is not my table" attitude; the other has servers who constantly help each other out by refilling water at any table needing it and by delivering meals to any table when the meals are ready to come out of the kitchen.

Allowing employees to think as they serve and building teams are not easy managerial tasks, but the rewards are worth the efforts. Recognizing individual efforts that lead to team success promotes employee involvement and commitment. When employees understand organizational goals and how to measure their performance in accomplishing these goals, the foundation for improving service delivery has been laid. Understanding the importance of their individual and team efforts leads to organizational success.

Some companies allow employees to make decisions using their own best judgment. Other firms train employees to handle a wide variety of customer scripts and problem situations. Put this all together and more in hotel companies such as Joie de Vivre Hospitality and Four Seasons, and you discover the benefits of focusing on employees that range from lower employee turnover (less than half of industry standards) to intense customer loyalty.

The Shangri-La Hotels and Resorts is a Hong Kong (China)-based company, inspired by the legendary land featured in James Hilton's 1933 novel, *Lost Horizon*. The name Shangri-La encapsulates the serenity and service for which their hotels and resorts are renowned worldwide.

As immigration and multiculturalism become more common across the globe, tourism service suppliers will depend on diversity training and education to meet team building as well as guest needs. Managing employees with similarities and differences in language, culture, education and religion can create a competitive advantage as we deal more effectively with staff and guests.

5.3 Service Mistakes

As illustrated in the chapter opener, although management and employees may want to delight guests in each and every service encounter, problems can occur. Fortunately, most consumers are willing to forgive "service mistakes" or service failure, when appropriate responses to them occur. What constitutes a service failure that can result in a guest being dissatisfied? In simple terms, a mistake occurs when the customers' expectations are not met—when a customer's "service script" is broken. We have learned that customers' script expectations develop from word-of-mouth and marketing communications, from personal needs and from past experiences. When customers experience an unexpected change from their expected script, we call this a "break from the script".

The first type of break is a positive change from what the customer expects. For example, a particularly cheerful and efficient front desk clerk who provides a

suggestion for a good, inexpensive place to dine that evening might be perceived as a pleasant change from the expected script—a "positive break" from the script. Positive breaks lead to highly memorable and highly satisfying service encounters that guests enjoy recounting to friends.

5.4 Mistakes Happen

Researchers have found that common negative breaks from the script occur from ①failures in the core service (a broken-down mattress in a hotel room; an overdone cold steak; or a bus that breaks down mid-tour); ②unwillingness to accommodate a customer's special need or request (to locate a disabled guest on the ground floor of a hotel in a handicapped accessible room, to modify an entrée to fit a patron's special dietary needs); ③unsolicited tourism employee actions (inattention, rudeness, or thievery on the part of an employee). What was the negative break from the script the Johnsons faced in the chapter opener?

So, the bad news is that mistakes are inevitable in tourism businesses. The good news is that, with proper handling, a negative break from the guest's script can be reversed and turned into an extra-satisfying, memorable service encounter. Keep in mind that satisfied guests represent potential future flows of revenues and profits, whereas dissatisfied guests represent future losses because they fail to return and they pass negative word-of-mouth comments on to their friends.

5.5 Be a Can-Do Problem Solver

Most service unreliability is rooted in poorly designed service processes, inattention to detail and simple carelessness. The tourism service team members need to have a "do-it-right-the-first-time" spirit. All team members, managers and front-line employees should constantly search for fail points—steps in the process that are vulnerable to failure. What can be done then to try to retain the customers? Thankfully, there are several things.

When a customer complaint or a service employee somehow senses that a service mistake has occurred, what happens next is critical to customer satisfaction. If the problem is ignored, the customer is likely to be furious and subsequently spread negative comments about the company. If the problem is handled, but not to the customer's complete satisfaction, the customer is still likely to be dissatisfied and also speak ill of their experience.

To solve problems, employees must know problems exist. Therefore, managers must encourage customers to voice their problems immediately so that employees can solve them. Because most guests are hesitant about voicing complaints, employees should also be trained to recognize problem situations so that they can fix the problems. And the problem solution needs to occur immediately.

"Making things right" for most customers simply involves doing a few simple things. Customers want acknowledgment that the problem exists. They also like to be told why the problem arose in the first place. Next, they want a sincere apology. Finally, customers want to be made "whole" again. In other words, they want some form of compensation that will lessen the cost of the problem to them. They need to be compensated for any bother or annoyance they perceived or experienced because of the problem. Which of these steps did Mike use in the chapter opener to make things right for the Johnsons?

Correcting the immediate mistake and satisfying the customers are a great start to creating a truly service-oriented organization, but there is still more to do. Steps should be taken to make sure that the problem does not recur. This requires figuring out why the mistake happened and making operational or training changes so that it does not happen again. These changes could be very simple or creative. In addition, customer co-participation, being actively involved in the resolution process, may be an effective recovery strategy for service companies as it could: influence satisfaction with the recovery process, encourage repurchase intentions, and be more cost effective than what a company would be prepared to offer.

6. Service Guarantees

One way to instill more confidence in guests regarding quality of service is by guaranteeing it. You are probably familiar with guarantees for hard goods. So how can a tourism service provider guarantee service quality? By using a customer satisfaction guarantee that has five important features forming the basis for a service guarantee:

(1) The guarantee should be unconditional with regard to the elements that are under the control of management and the employees. Airlines and other transportation providers cannot control the weather, but they can control most other aspects of your flight or ride experience.

(2) The service guarantee should be easy to understand and communicate to guests. It should be brief and worded very simply. Fine print and legal language should not be used to confuse the customer.

(3) The guarantee should be meaningful, guaranteeing an important quality aspect to guests. For example, if speed of service (responsiveness) is an important element of quality to lunchtime restaurant patrons, the restaurant might use the following guarantee "Your meal in just 5 minutes or it's free!"

(4) The guarantee should be easy to collect. The customer should not have to "jump through hoops" to collect, and no guilt should be heaped on the guest for asking for the guaranteed restitution.

(5) Compensation should be appropriate. How does management decide what is appropriate compensation for a service failure? Management needs to consider not only the price of the service to the customer in money, but also the seriousness of the failure in inconvenience or other bother. Finally, but probably most important, what does the customer think is fair given the problem?

Service guarantees provide assurances to both service personnel and customers that the organization is focused on delivering quality service. When these guarantees are supported with training programs and process reviews focused on continuous improvement; what should be the ultimate goal of every tourism organization—delighted customers, repeat visits and increased profitability—can be achieved. In pre-purchase situations, research has shown that customers perceive a higher quality for hotels offering unconditional guarantees, significantly lowering customers' perceived risk. It has also been shown that service guarantees, both conditional and unconditional, could be an effective tool to encourage customers to complain about their dissatisfaction allowing employees to apply appropriate service recovery strategies.

Service guarantees come in many different forms. Some are in the form of a commitment. For example, management at the Best Rest Inn in Boise, Idaho, uses its welcome sign, "We delight every guest, every day, one guest at a time" as a statement of its service commitment. The Hampton Inn chain uses the slogan "Get what you expect—guaranteed!"

Others are more direct and detailed. For example, Holiday Inn calls its service guarantee its Hospitality Promise. The promise is prominently displayed in each guest room. It reads, "Making your stay a complete success is our goal."

7. Emerging Issues and a Future Focused Agenda for the Field

There is no doubt that increased interest, deeper understanding and the ongoing growth of service management, particularly in the context of tourism, will continue. To ensure this growth, more and more university programs are now embedding variations of service marketing and management into their core curriculum, viewing this subject on par with other business core disciplines such as accounting, finance and human resource management.

Listed below are a list of current "hot" topics in service management and marketing. Some have been established in the literature for a while now, but continue to be of interest in the academic and practice communities, others are emerging.

(1) Multiculturalism and Globalization—improved understanding about how service management will be affected by globalization and multiculturalism, particularly on employee-customer interactions in service recovery and service encounters.

(2) Experience Management—Pine and Gilmore (1998) advocate customer experience as critical to tourism; creating and managing tourism experiences will gain further emphasis in the tourism and service management literature.

(3) Social Psychology / Social Identity—the role of group dynamics in the provision of service.

(4) Service Speed / Efficiency—continued challenges in understanding the

conflicts between staffing levels, ever-tightening margins / cost control and consumer demands for service speed.

(5) Self Service Technologies (SST/e-service)—on going study of SST in terms of customer satisfaction; comparing consumer attitudes against traditional service methods.

(6) Intra-organizational Practices (and Employee-customer-firm performance linkages)— continued examination into the impacts of various workplace practices on customer perceptions and financial performance.

(7) Emotions—the extent to which stress and emotions play a role in customer and employee interactions and their impact on service, customer satisfaction, service failure and recovery.

(8) Loyalty—drivers of customer loyalty and the effectiveness of loyalty programs.

(9) Generational Issues—gaining an improved understanding about how new generations (particularly Generation Y) will differ as customers and employees.

(10) Customer Feedback—improved ways to gain more accurate and timely feedback from customers which provides effective information for the business with minimal intrusion on the customers.

Ⅳ Case Study

Cactus Jacks Restaurants—Queensland, Australia

Always open-minded to new ways to improve the business, the owner of Cactus Jacks, an Australian casual theme restaurant chain, learned about the balanced score card as applied to tourism businesses via a 2006 financial review magazine article written by the author of this review. The benefits of implementing a balanced score card type of system was highlighted in this article, principally for the purposes of:

(1) identifying the important drivers of success;

(2) clarifying standards of customer experience;

(3) measuring the performance of the business based on non-financial measures; and paying staff bonuses based on key metrics additional to financial performance.

Step one was to clarify the strategic drivers of the business. These were determined to be:

(1) financial performance—principally driven by revenue growth and profitability;

(2) customer satisfaction and loyalty-based on the entire customer experience including food, service, value and ambiance;

(3) employee attitudes—a system to identify and focus on critical issues about employee well-being and workplace practices;

(4) individual performance—of supervisors and managers.

Over the course of the first 12 months, work was undertaken in consultation with management and staff to create a diagnostic system which would effectively measure the key strategic drivers listed above. This was designed to help the owner identify and gauge the long-term performance of the business.

The summary below provides further information about the way in which the balanced score card was set up for this particular business, and highlights some of the key issues related to each:

(1) Financial performance. A matrix was created which was modeled on the company budgets for sales and profits. Weightings were then allocated to each criteria based on the importance given to that area by the owner and the company leadership team.

(2) Customer perceptions. A detailed and complex customized Customer Experience Evaluation Program (similar to what is often called a Mystery Shopper Program) was created. The first step in this process was a detailed mapping of the customer experience standards for the business (one of the benefits of this type of program is that it forces the business to clarify these standards in great details). Once the standards were created, and some pilot tests run on the questionnaire, a regular series of visits were undertaken during every 6-month period by highly trained evaluators. The results of each key service criteria were then tabulated and scored, with detailed reports which outline opportunities and provide scores for each aspect of each visit. Each report and the corresponding scores were emailed to the corporate office and the respective management teams for review. This information was used to (a) improve the business; (b) let the corporate office gain an in-depth perspective about satisfaction and standards adherence; and (c) inform the management remuneration program.

(3) Employee perceptions. A customized organizational engagement survey was developed, which integrated service climate factors coupled with other related measures such as staff turnover intentions, internal service quality, employee engagement and perceptions of owner commitment to excellence. The survey was administered every 6 months with scores continually assessed for improvement and opportunities to improve. Managers met in teams to strategic ways to improve various aspects of the survey results to ensure continuous work was done to improve the way employees perceive their workplace.

(4) Intangibles. Each member of staff was given a comprehensive appraisal of their performance by their respective supervisors as well as an overall effectiveness rating by the managers and company owner, and a point score allocated.

As a result of this program, major changes have occurred in this company. The entire team began to rally around the exact performance measures which the owner identified as important drivers for success. By focusing on customers, employees, training and individual performance ("What gets measured gets managed!"), sales and profits naturally flowed. The team has been able to share in small wins, work more closely in teams trying to make their targets and feel as though they could share in the successes of the business.

Rather than driving success through financial measures only, the balanced score card measurement system has altered the focus to the important drivers of success and have helped take Cactus Jacks to a higher plane and protect its long-term viability.

 V Tips

Service Failure and Recovery

No business can satisfy every customer every time. But the likelihood of failure in services is significantly magnified because of the human element! When we refer to the human element, we do not only mean that service employees can make errors. Customers can at times be dissatisfied even if the service is provided correctly and appropriately! (According to the firm's definition of correct and appropriate!) This can be due to many reasons, such as customers' expectations being misaligned with the businesses service offering or due to the customers' being in a poor state of mind (for a review of customer misbehavior, see Harris and Reynolds, 2004).

Regardless who is to blame for a service failure or a perceived service failure, it is vital for service firms to make every effort to retain their customers. It is often suggested that it costs as five times as much to attract a new customer as it does to retain an existing one.

Adding to the challenge of service failure is the fact that many customers will simply not complain (Voorhees, Brady and Horowitz, 2006). This is because it is often too time consuming to do so, or that they do not see it as likely that the firm will take notice. In addition, complaining can be unpleasant and stressful (more so in some cultures than others). It is therefore critical for service managers to: ① encourage customers to voice their complaints; ② take immediate action wherever possible to return aggrieved customers into satisfied ones.

Customers who do complain often do so for one of four main reasons:

(1) to obtain some kind of compensation (or to have the service performed again);

(2) to release anger;

(3) to help improve the service organization;

(4) concern for others.

There are a number of conceptual frameworks and theories which are used to understand and measure customer perceptions of service recovery efforts. Because consumers generally perceived some kind of inequity in response to service failure, a frequently applied framework in research about service recovery is known as justice theory. This theory consists of three dimensions, distributive justice, procedural justice and interactional justice. Distributive justice refers to the way in which a firm assigns resources to rectify and compensate for a service failure (e.g. refunding money, future discounts). Procedural justice refers to the methods a firm uses to deal with complaints (speed, access, flexibility). Interactional justice includes perceptions about the extent of empathy, courtesy, sensitivity and caring shown by employees after a service failure. This framework represents a useful tool for service managers to consider when addressing service failure policies and procedures.

Top performing service firms, aware of the potential harm of service failures—but also understanding the potential benefits of rectifying service failures—take extraordinary measures to train staff in how to identify service failures and how to handle customer complaints.

Ⅵ Dialogue

Travel Agency Plans a Trip

(Customer's conversation about the travel arrangements and the services provided by travel agents during a trip around the world.)

Mark: Welcome! How can I help you?

Customer: I would like a short holiday somewhere.

Mark: I recommend one of these destinations. Let's look at this pamphlet, shall we?

Customer: Sounds good.

Mark: How does Vietnam sound?

Customer: That sounds interesting. Can you please tell me about the food, the culture, the activities, the destinations?

Mark: Full noodle soup is very popular, rice wine with pickle snake is a traditional drink. Tourists enjoy diving and snorkeling. Hanoi is one of the top honeymoon destinations for newlyweds.

Customer: Great! Let's make a plan.

Mark: Thank you. This will be your itinerary. Day 1: Ho Chi Minh City, visit museums. Day 2: Hanoi, visit historic sites. Day 3: Hoi An beaches and spas.

Customer: How much will it be?

Mark: The package comes to $500.

Customer: Can I pay with my credit card?

Mark: Of course.

Customer: Here is my credit card.

Mark: Thank you. Here is your ticket. Enjoy!

Ⅶ Academic Thinking

1. The Concept of Smart Tourism in the Context of Tourism Information Services

Author: Yunpeng Li, Clark Hu, Chao Huang, Liqiong Duan

Journal: *Tourism Management*

Abstract:

Smart tourism has become increasingly popular in China. Different types of events and activities have been classified as smart tourism, leading to the misuse of the term. What, then, is smart tourism? How to define it? Although researchers have defined the term, there has not been any consensus on a widely accepted interpretation. The definition provided by this study emphasizes smart tourism as an individual tourist support system within the context of information services and an all-encompassing technology. This paper compares the characteristics of both traditional tourist information services and those incorporated in smart tourism. Based on the concepts, recommendations are provided and future research/industrial directions are discussed. For the Chinese tourism market, smart tourism represents a new direction implying a significant influence on tourist destinations, enterprises, and also tourists themselves.

旅游信息服务背景下的智慧旅游理念

智慧旅游在中国日益普及。不同类型的事件和活动被归类为智慧旅游，导致了该术语的误用。那么，什么是智慧旅游？如何定义？尽管研究人员已经定义了这个术语，但对一个广泛接受的解释还没有任何共识。本研究提出的定义强调智慧旅游是一种信息服务背景下的个体旅游支持系统，是一种无所不包的技术。本文比较了传统旅游信息服务和智慧旅游信息服务的特点。基于这些概念，提出了建议，并讨论了未来的研究/产业方向。对于中国旅游市场来说，智慧旅游是一个新的发展方向，对旅游目的地、旅游企业和游客自身都有重要影响。

2. Tourism Service Quality Begins at the Airport

Author: Roberto Rendeiro Martín-Cejas

Journal: *Tourism Management*

Abstract:

This work analyses the level of service of Gran Canaria airport facilities as an approximation to evaluate the service quality given to tourism. Through a linear programming model we will determine the level of service established in a check-in

service at this airport. The relevance of this parameter is related to the leisure time available for tourists in the airport terminal building. Therefore, it gives us an indirect measure of their perceived satisfaction of the service.

旅游服务质量从机场开始

本研究以大加那利机场设施的服务水准作为评估旅游服务品质的近似方法。通过线性规划模型,我们将确定在该机场的登机服务中建立的服务水平。该参数的相关性与机场航站楼内可供游客休闲的时间有关。因此,它给了我们一种间接的衡量他们对服务满意度的方法。

3. An Exploratory Study into Managing Value Creation in Tourism Service Firms: Understanding Value Creation Phases at the Intersection of the Tourism Service Firm and Their Customers

Author: Aron O'Cass, Phyra Sok

Journal: *Tourism Management*

Abstract:

To satisfy customers, managers of tourism services need to understand their customers' value requirements and then develop a unique service value offering based on those requirements. This understanding underpins their effort to provide superior value to customers and deliver the proposed services through employees. Problematically, previous work on value creation (i.e. customer value) has focused separately on either the firm or customer. This theoretical separation does not allow investigation of whether there may be discrepancies between what value firms offer and what value customers perceive they have received. We bring tourism service firms (manager and employee) and customers together and examine the nature of a tourism service provider's value proposition, its contribution to the value offering, and subsequent impact on customers' perceived-value-in-use. We focus on the important role that employees play as boundary spanning workers in the value creation phases, linking the tourism service provider and customer.

旅游服务企业价值创造管理初探:基于旅游服务企业与顾客交汇处价值创造阶段的认识

为了满足顾客,旅游服务管理者需要了解顾客的价值需求,然后根据这些需求开发出独特的服务价值。根据这些需求开发出卓越的价值,并通过员工的服务实现顾客所需要的价值。问题是:以前关于价值创造(即客户价值)的工作分别关注公司和客户。这种理论上的分离不允许调查公司提供的价值和客户认为他们已经获得的价值之间可能存在差异。我们把旅游服务公司(经理和员工)和客户放在一起,研究旅游服务提供商的价值主张的性质,它对价值提供的贡献,以及随后对客户感知的使用价值的影响。我们关注员工在价值创造阶段扮演的重要角色,即跨越员工的边界,将旅游服务供应商和客户联系起来。

Ⅷ Questions:

1. Describe how services are different from goods.
2. Define quality using the many meanings the word can have.
3. How are expectations of a tourism service formed?

Ⅸ Key Words and Terms

service encounter	服务接触
service expectation	服务期望
service guarantee	服务保证
service recovery	服务补救
service script	服务脚本
learning organization	学习型组织
market share	市场份额
marketing communication	营销沟通
perceived quality	感知质量

Ⅹ Single Choice Questions

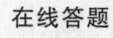

Chapter 5
Marketing for Tourism

I Chapter Introduction

The world tourism industry is confronted with challenges of fierce global competition, dynamic technological evolution and increasingly demanding customers. All these changes together with economic, social, political and environmental developments require all tourism firms to embrace marketing in order to respond and compete in an effective way. With the increase of outbound and inbound tourists, the role of tourism market is becoming more and more prominent. The chapter has an international focus, which is especially important in this era of increasing globalization. Business markets have become internationalized—domestic companies are expanding overseas as foreign companies seek to enter Chinese tourism markets—therefore, it is crucial that today's students be exposed to business and cultural examples from other parts of the world.

II Chapter Objectives

1. Help you master the basic concepts and practices of modern hospitality marketing in an enjoyable and practical way.
2. Understanding of the marketing theories and concepts.
3. Give you a thorough understanding of theories of marketing for tourism.
4. Describe the marketing environment.
5. Describe tourism marketing strategies.
6. Allow you to analyze future situations and make the proper decisions based on the methods of forecasting tourism market.
7. Provided practices and applications to give you examples of how we currently apply the concepts to industry situations.
8. Describe marketing highlights, written cases and other features to make

learning about marketing interesting and enjoyable.

Ⅲ Reading

1. Introduction to Tourism Marketing

1.1 What Is Hospitality and Tourism Marketing?

In the hotel industry, marketing and sales are often regarded as the same. No wonder the sales department is one of the most prominent departments in the hotel. The sales manager provides travel to potential customers and entertains them in the hotel's restaurants. Therefore, the sales function is highly visible, and most of the marketing functions in the non-promotion field occur in the closed door. In fact, sales is just a marketing function, often not the most important. Advertising and sales are part of the promotional element of the marketing mix. Other marketing mix elements include product, price and distribution. Marketing also includes research, information systems and planning. The fourP framework requires marketing professionals to decide on products and their characteristics, set prices, decide how to distribute products and choose ways to promote them.

Marketing means "hit the target". "The goal of marketing is to make sales redundant," says Peter Drucker, a leading management thinker. "Its purpose is to fully understand and understand customers, make products or services suitable for them and sell by themselves."

1.2 Marketing in the Hospitality Industry

1.2.1 Importance of Marketing

As we have seen, the hospitality industry is one of the world's major industries. Marketing has assumed an increasingly important role in the restaurant sector of the hospitality industry. We must understand our customers and develop a service delivery system to deliver a product they want at a price they will view as being fair. And do all this while still making a profit. In other ways marketing is ever changing and is changing very rapidly. Social media has given the customers a powerful voice; dashboards track comments customers are making about our products on social media; millennials are replacing baby boomers as the most important travel segment, and their wants are very different than the boomers.

1.2.2 Tourism Marketing

The two main industries that comprise the activities we call tourism are the hospitality and travel industries. Thus, throughout this book we refer to the hospitality and travel industries. Successful hospitality marketing is highly dependent on the entire travel industry. Meeting planners choose destinations based on the cost of getting to the destinations, the value of the hotels, the quality of restaurants, and evening activities for their attendees.

1.2.3 Definition of Marketing

Marketing must be understood in the sense of satisfying customers' needs. If the marketer understands customers' needs; develops products that provide superior customer value; prices, distributes and promotes them effectively, these products will sell easily. Here is our definition of marketing: Marketing is the process by which companies create value for customers and build strong customer relationships in order to capture value from the customers in return.

1.2.4 The Marketing Process

Figure 5.1 presents a simple five-step model of the marketing process. In the first four steps, companies work to understand consumers, create customer value, and build strong customer relationships. In the final step, companies reap the rewards of creating superior customer value. By creating value for customers, they in turn capture value from customers in the form of sales, profits and long-term customer equity.

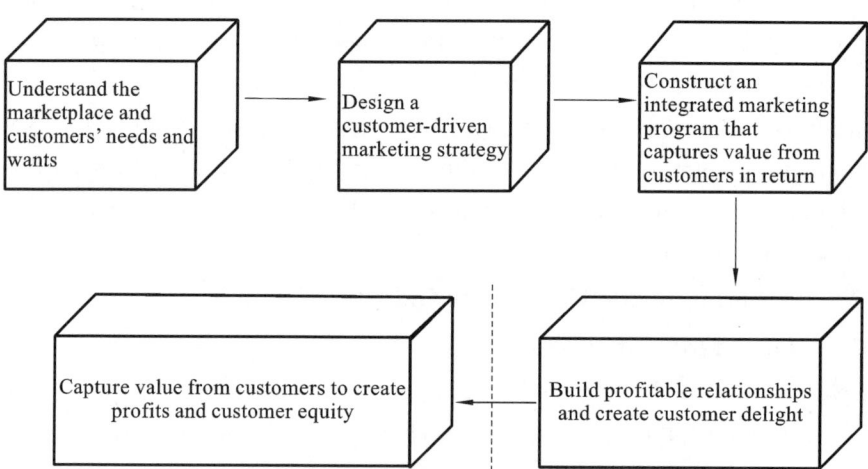

Figure 5.1　A simple model of the marketing process

1.3　Understanding the Marketplace and Customers' Needs

As a first step, marketers need to understand customers' needs and wants and the marketplace within which they operate. We now examine five core customer and marketplace concepts: ①needs, wants and demands; ②marketing offerings (tangible products, services and experiences); ③ value and satisfaction; ④ exchanges and relationships; ⑤markets.

1.3.1　Customers' Needs, Wants and Demands

(1) Needs. The most basic concept underlying marketing is that of human needs. A human need is a state of felt deprivation. Included are the basic physical needs for food, clothing, warmth and safety, as well as social needs for belonging, affection,

fun and relaxation.

(2) Wants. Human wants are the form human needs take as they are shaped by culture and individual personality. Wants are how people communicate their needs. Many sellers often confuse wants with needs. A manufacturer of drill bits may think that customers need a drill bit, but what the customer really needs is a hole. These sellers suffer from "marketing myopia". They are so taken with their products that they focus only on existing wants and lose sight of underlying customers' needs. They forget that a physical product is only a tool to solve a consumers problem. These sellers get into trouble if a new product comes along that serves the need better or cheaper. The customer will then have the same need but want the new product.

(3) Demands. People have almost unlimited wants, but limited resources. They choose products that produce the most satisfaction for their money. When backed by buying power, wants become demands.

1.3.2 Market Offerings: Tangible Products, Services and Experiences

Consumers' needs and wants are fulfilled through a market offering: a product that is some combination of tangible, services, information or experiential product components. We often associate the word product with a tangible product or one that has physical properties (e.g. the hotel room or the steak we receive in a restaurant). In the hospitality industry, the intangible products, including customer services and experiences, are more important than the tangible products. Managers of resorts realize that their guests will leave with memories of their stay. They try to create experiences that will generate pleasant memories. Delivery of memorable experiences lies at the core of the experience economy (Fiore and Jeoung, 2007; Pine and Gilmore, 1999) and tourism creates experiences (Buhalis and O'Connor, 2006; Ihamaki, 2012; Ooi, 2010).

Customer Value

Customer value is the difference between the benefits that the customer gains from owning and/or using a product and the costs of obtaining the product. Costs can be both monetary and non-monetary. One of the biggest non-monetary costs for hospitality customers is time. New electronic forms of registration through smartphones will make the hotel registration redundant. One of the challenges for hotel managers will be replace the welcoming reception guests received from front desk clerks with another form of welcoming, perhaps through a lobby ambassador.

1.4 Designing Customer Value-Driven Marketing Strategy

Once it fully understands consumers and the marketplace, marketing management can design a customer-driven marketing strategy. We define marketing management as the art and science of choosing target markets and building profitable relationships with them. The marketing manager's aim is to find, attract, keep and grow target customers by creating, delivering and communicating superior customer

value. To design a winning marketing strategy, the marketing manager must answer two important questions: What customers will we serve? (What's our target market?) How can we serve these customers best? (what's our value proposition?)

1.4.1 The Production Concept

The production concept is one of the oldest philosophies guiding sellers. The production concept holds that consumers will favor products that are available and highly affordable, and therefore management should focus on production and distribution efficiency. The problem with the production concept is that management may become so focused on production systems that they forget the customer.

1.4.2 The Product Concept

The product concept, like the production concept, has an inward focus. The product concept holds that consumers will favor products that offer the most in quality, performance and innovative features. Under this concept, marketing strategy focuses on making continuous product improvements.

Product quality and improvement are important parts of most marketing strategies. However, focusing only on the company's products can lead to marketing myopia. Consumers are trying to satisfy needs and might turn to entirely different products to better satisfy those needs, such as bed and breakfast (B&Bs) instead of hotels or fast-food outlets in student centers instead of cafeterias.

1.4.3 The Selling Concept

The selling concept holds that consumers will not buy enough of the organization's products unless the organization undertakes a large selling and promotion effort. The aim of a selling focus is to get every possible sale, not to worry about satisfaction after the sale or the revenue contribution of the sale.

1.4.4 The Marketing Concept

The marketing concept is a more recent business philosophy and one that has been adopted in the hospitality industry. The marketing concept holds that achieving organizational goals depends on determining the needs and wants of target markets and delivering the desired satisfaction more effectively and efficiently than competitors.

The marketing concept starts with a well-defined market, focuses on customers' needs, and integrates all the marketing activities that affect customers. It meets the organizational goals by creating long-term customer relationships based on customer value and satisfaction. As Herb Kelleher, former CEO of Southwest Airlines, stated, "We don't have a marketing department, we have a customer department." (Figure 5.2).

1.4.5 The Societal Marketing Concept

The societal marketing concept questions whether the pure marketing concept overlooks possible conflicts between consumer short-run wants and consumer long-run

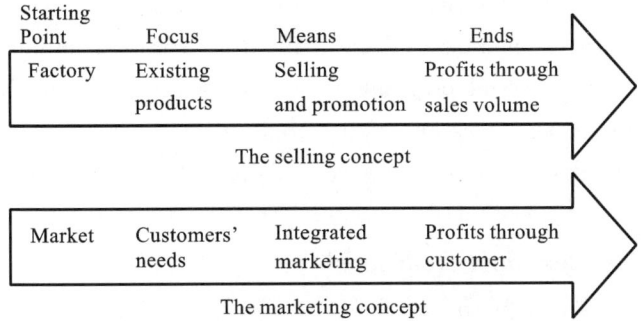

Figure 5.2 The selling and the marketing concept

welfare. Is a firm that satisfies the immediate needs and wants of target markets always doing what's best for its consumers in the long run? The societal marketing concept holds that marketing strategy should deliver value to customers in a way that maintains or improves both the consumers' and society's well-being. It calls for sustainable marketing, socially and environmentally responsible marketing that meets the present needs of consumers and businesses while also preserving or enhancing the ability of future generations to meet their needs(Figure 5.3).

Figure 5.3 Three considerations underlying the societal marketing concept

Source: Kotler P, Armstrong G. Principles of Marketing[M]. 16th ed. New York: Pearson Education, Inc.

1.5 Preparing an Integrated Marketing Plan

The company's marketing strategy outlines which customers the company will serve and how it will create value for these customers. Next, the marketer develops an integrated marketing program that will actually deliver the intended value to target customers. The marketing program builds customer relationships by transforming the marketing strategy into action. It consists of the firm's marketing mix, the set of marketing tools the firm uses to implement its marketing strategy.

The major marketing mix tools are classified into four broad groups, called the four P of marketing: product, price, place and promotion. To deliver on its value proposition, the firm must first create a need-satisfying market offering (product). It must decide how much it will charge for the offer (price) and how it will make the offer available to target consumers (place). Finally, it must communicate with target customers about the offer and persuade them of its merits (promotion). The firm must blend all of these marketing mix tools into a comprehensive, integrated marketing program that communicates and delivers the intended value to chosen customers.

1.6 Building Customer Relationships

The first three steps in the marketing process—understanding the marketplace and customers' needs, designing a customer value-driven marketing strategy, and constructing a marketing program—all lead up to the fourth and most important step: building and managing profitable customer relationships. We first discuss the basics of customer relationship management. Then, we examine how companies go about engaging customers on a deeper level in this age of digital and social marketing.

1.6.1 Customer Relationship Management

Customer relationship management (CRM) is perhaps the most important concept of modern marketing. In the broadest sense, CRM is the overall process of building and maintaining profitable customer relationships by delivering superior customer value and satisfaction. It deals with all aspects of acquiring, engaging and growing customers.

The key to build lasting customer relationships is to create superior customer value and satisfaction. Satisfied customers are more likely to be loyal customers and give the company a larger share of their business. Beyond offering consistently high value and satisfaction, marketers can use specific marketing tools to develop stronger bonds with customers.

1.6.2 Engaging Customers

Significant changes are occurring in the nature of customer brand relationships. Today's digital technologies—the Internet and the surge in online, mobile and social media—have profoundly changed the ways that people on the planet relate to one another. In turn, these events have had a huge impact on how companies and brands connect with customers, and how customers connect with and influence each other's brand behaviors.

1.7 Capturing Value from Customers

The final step involves capturing value in return in the form of current and future sales, market share and profits. By creating superior customer value, the firm creates highly satisfied customers who stay loyal and buy more. This, in turn, means greater long-run returns for the firm. Here, we discuss the outcomes of creating customer value: customer loyalty and retention, share of market, share of customer and customer equity.

1.7.1 Customer Loyalty and Retention

Good CRM creates customer delight. In turn, delighted customers remain loyal and talk favorably to others about the company and its products. Studies show big differences in the loyalty of customers who are less satisfied, somewhat satisfied, and completely satisfied. Even a slight drop from complete satisfaction can create an enormous drop in loyalty. Thus, the aim of CRM is to create not only customer satisfaction but also customer delight.

1.7.2 Growing Share of Customer

Beyond simply retaining good customers to capture customer lifetime value, good CRM can help marketers increase their share of customers—the share they get of the customer's purchasing in their product categories. We can now see the importance of not only acquiring customers but also keeping and growing them. One marketing consultant puts it this way: "The only value your company will ever create is the value that comes from customers—the ones you have now and the ones you will have in the future. Without customers, you don't have a business."

1.7.3 Building Customer Equity

We can now see the importance of not only acquiring customers but also keeping and growing them. The value of a company comes from the value of its current and future customers. CRM takes a long-term view. Companies want to not only create profitable customers but also "own" them for life, earn a greater share of their purchases, and capture their customer lifetime value. The ultimate aim of CRM is to produce high customer equity. Customer equity is the total combined customer lifetime values of all of the company's current and potential customers. Therefore, it's a measure of the future value of the company's customer base.

1.7.4 Building the Right Relationships with the Right Customers

The company can classify customers according to their potential profitability and manage its relationships with them accordingly. One classification scheme defines four relationship groups based on potential profitability and projected loyalty: strangers, butterflies, true friends and barnacles (Figure 5.4).

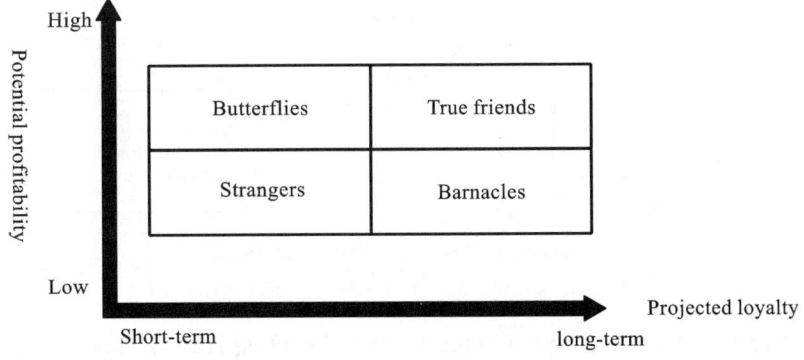

Figure 5.4 Customer relationship groups

Source: Kotler P, Armstrong G. Principles of Marketing [M]. 16th ed. New York: Pearson Education, Inc.

Each group requires a different relationship management strategy. For example, "strangers" show low potential profitability and little projected loyalty. There is little fit between the company's offerings and their needs. The relationship management strategy for these customers is simple: Don't invest anything in them.

"Butterflies" are potentially profitable but not loyal. There is a good fit between the company's offerings and their needs. However, like real butterflies we can enjoy them for only a short while and then they're gone.

"True friends" are both profitable and loyal. There is a strong fit between their needs and the company's offerings. The firm wants to make continuous relationship investments to delight these customers and nurture, retain and grow them. It wants to turn true friends into "true believers" those who come back regularly and tell others about their good experiences with the company.

"Barnacles" are highly loyal but not very profitable. There is a limited fit between their needs and the company's offerings.

2. Service Characteristics of Hospitality and Tourism Marketing

2.1 The Service Culture

One of the most important tasks of a hospitality business is to develop the service side of the business, specifically, a strong service culture. The service culture focuses on serving and satisfying the customer. Creation of a service culture has to start with top management and flow down.

2.2 Characteristics of Service Marketing

Service marketers must understand the four characteristics of services: intangibility, inseparability, variability and perishability (Figure 5.5).

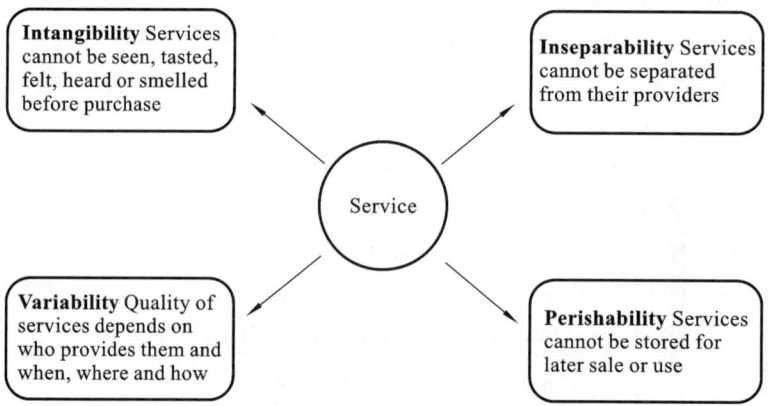

Figure 5.5　Four service characteristics

Source: Kotler P, Bowen J T, Makens J C. Marketing for Hospitality and Tourism[M]. New York: Pearson, 2009.

2.3 Service Management Concepts for the Hospitality Industry

2.3.1 The Service Profit Chain

In a service business, the customer and the frontline service employee interact to create the service. Effective interaction, in turn, depends on the skills of frontline service employees and on the support processes backing these employees. Thus, successful service companies focus their attention on both their customers and their employees. They understand the service profit chain, which links service firm profits with employee and customer satisfaction. This chain consists of the following five links:

(1) Internal service quality: superior employee selection and training, a quality work environment and strong support for those dealing with customers, which results in…

(2) Satisfied and productive service employees: more satisfied, loyal and hard-working employees, which results in …

(3) Greater service value: more effective and efficient customer value creation and service-delivery, which results in …

(4) Satisfied and loyal customers: satisfied customers who remain loyal, repeat purchase, and refer other customers, which results in …

(5) Healthy service profits and growth: superior service firm performance. Therefore, reaching service profits and growth goals begin with taking care of those who take care of customers.

2.3.2 Three Types of Marketing

Service marketing requires more than just traditional external marketing using the 4 P shows that service marketing along with external marketing also requires both internal marketing and interactive marketing.

Internal marketing means that the service firm must effectively train and motivate its customer-contact employees and all the supporting service people to work as a team to provide customer satisfaction.

Interactive marketing means that perceived service quality depends heavily on the quality of the buyer-seller interaction during the service encounter.

Today as competition and costs increase and as productivity and quality decrease, more marketing sophistication is needed. Hospitality companies face the task of increasing three major marketing areas: their service differentiation, service quality and service productivity.

2.4 Management Strategies for Service Businesses

2.4.1 Managing Service Differentiation

Service marketers often complain about the difficulty of differentiating their services from those of competitors. To the extent that customers view the services of different providers as similar, they care less about the provider than the price. Service companies can differentiate their service delivery in three ways: through people, physical environment and process. The company can distinguish itself by having more able and reliable customer-contact people than its competitors, or it can develop a

superior physical environment in which the service product is delivered. It can design a superior delivery process. Finally, service companies can also differentiate their images through symbols and branding. For example, a familiar symbol would be McDonald's golden arches, and familiar brands include Hilton, Shangri-La and Sofitel.

2.4.2 Managing Service Quality

One of the major ways that a service firm can differentiate itself is by delivering consistently higher quality than its competitors. With hospitality products, quality is measured by how well customer expectations are met. The key is to exceed the customers' service quality expectations.

Studies of well-managed service companies show that they share a number of common virtues regarding service quality. First, top service companies are "customer obsessed". They have a philosophy of satisfying customers' needs, which wins enduring customer loyalty. Second, well-managed service companies have a history of top management commitment to quality. Third, the best service providers set high service quality standards. Fourth, the top service firms watch service performance closely, both their own and that of competitors. They use methods such as comparison shopping, customer surveys, suggestions and complaint forms. Good service companies also communicate their concerns about service quality to employees and provide performance feedback.

2.4.3 Managing Service Productivity

With their costs rising rapidly, service firms are under great pressure to increase service productivity. They can do so in several ways. They can train current employees better or hire new ones who will work harder or more skillfully. Or they can increase the quantity of their service by giving up some quality. The provider can "industrialize the service" by adding equipment and standardizing production. Finally, a service provider can harness the power of technology.

2.4.4 Resolving Customer Complaints

Many service companies have invested heavily to develop streamlined and efficient service-delivery systems. They want to ensure that customers will receive consistently high-quality service in every service encounter. Unlike product manufacturers, who can adjust their machinery and inputs until everything is perfect, service quality always varies, depending on the interactions between employees and customers. Companies should take steps not only to provide good service every time but also to recover from service mistakes.

2.4.5 Managing Employees as Part of the Product

In the hospitality industry employees are a critical part of the product and marketing mix. This means that the human resources and marketing departments must work closely together. In restaurants without a human resources department, the restaurant manager serves as the human resource manager. The manager must hire friendly and capable employees and formulate policies that support positive relations between employees and guests. Even minor details related to personnel policy can have a significant effect on the product's quality.

In a well-run hospitality organization, there are two customers, the paying customers and the employees. The task of training and motivating employees to provide good customer service is called internal marketing. In the hospitality industry, it is not enough to have a marketing department focused on traditional marketing to a targeted external market. The job of the marketing department includes encouraging everyone in the organization to practice customer-oriented thinking.

2.4.6 Managing Perceived Risk

Customers who buy hospitality products experience some anxiety because they cannot experience the product beforehand. This is one of the reasons customers rely on user-generated content on sites such as Yelp, TripAdvisor and other social media they use. These sources are deemed to be credible sources.

One way of combating concern is to encourage the client to try the hotel or restaurant in a low-risk situation. Hotels and resorts offer familiarization trips to meeting planners and travel agents. Airlines often offer complimentary flight tickets because they are also interested in creating business. Hotels provide rooms, food, beverage and entertainment at no cost to the prospective client in the hope that this exposure will encourage him or her to recommend the hotel. Familiarization trips reduce a product's intangibility by letting the intermediary customer experience the hotel beforehand.

2.4.7 Managing Capacity and Demand

Managers have two major options for matching capacity with demand: change capacity or change demand. For example, airlines use dynamic capacity management to adjust capacity to match demand. The airlines swap small aircraft for larger aircraft on flights that are selling out faster than normal. The smaller aircraft are assigned to flights that are expected to have low load factors.

3. Analysis of Consumer Buying Behavior

3.1 Consumer Markets and Consumer Buying Behavior

3.1.1 A Model of Consumer Behavior

Today's marketplace has become very competitive with thousands of hotels and restaurants. In addition, during recent years the hospitality and travel industries have undergone globalization. To win this battle, they invest in research that will reveal what customers want to buy, which locations they prefer, which amenities are important to them, how they buy and why they buy.

This is the central question: How do consumers respond to the various marketing stimuli that a company might use? The company that really understands how consumers will respond to different product features, prices and advertising appeals has a great advantage over its competitors. As a result, researchers from companies and universities are constantly studying the relationship between marketing stimuli and consumer response. Their starting point is the model of buyer behavior shown in Figure 5.6. This figure shows that marketing and other stimuli enter the consumer's "black box" and produce certain responses. Marketers must determine what is in the buyer's black box.

On the left side of Figure 5.6, the marketing stimuli consist of the 4 P: product, price, place and promotion. Other stimuli include major forces and events in the buyer's environment: economic, technological, political and cultural. All these stimuli enter the buyer's black box, where they are turned into the set of observable buyer responses shown on the right: product choice, brand choice, dealer choice, purchase timing and purchase amount.

Marketers must understand how the stimuli are changed into responses inside the consumer's black box. The black box has two parts. First, a buyer's characteristics influence how he or she perceives and reacts to the stimuli. Second, the buyer's decision process itself affects outcomes.

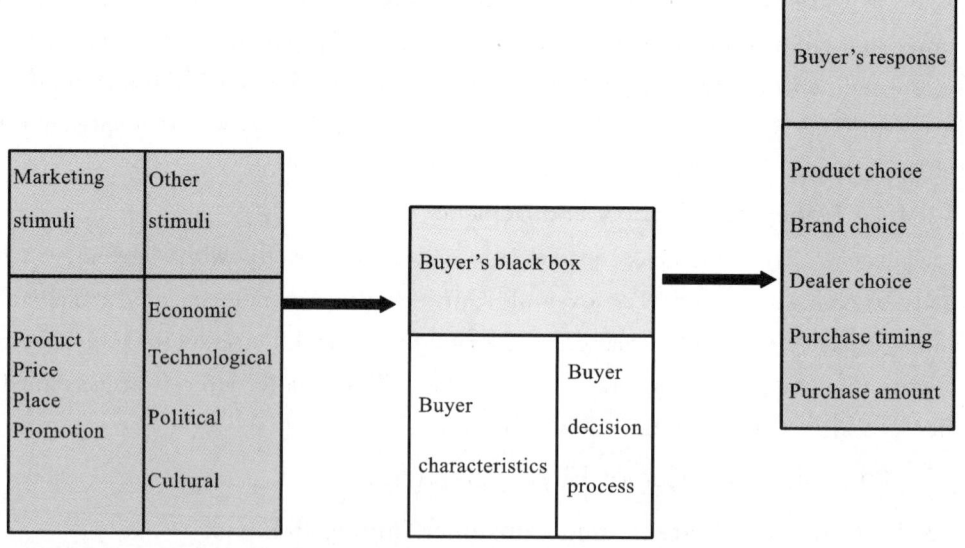

Figure 5.6　Model of buyer behavior

3.1.2　Personal Characteristics Affecting Consumer Behavior

(1) Cultural Factors.

Cultural factors exert the broadest and deepest influence on consumer behavior. We examine the role played by the buyer's culture, subculture and social class.

(2) Social Factors.

Consumer behavior is also influenced by social factors, including the consumers' groups, family, social roles and status.

(3) Personal Factors.

A buyer's decisions are also influenced by personal characteristics, such as age and life-cycle stage, occupation, economic situation, lifestyle, personality and self-concept.

(4) Psychological Factors.

A person's buying choices are also influenced by four major psychological factors: motivation, perception, learning, beliefs and attitudes.

3.1.3 The Buyer Decision Process

We are now ready to look at how consumers make buying decisions. Figure 5.7 shows that the buyer decision process consists of five stages: need recognition, information search, evaluation of alternatives, purchase decision and post-purchase behavior. This model emphasizes that the buying process starts long before and continues long after the actual purchase. It encourages the marketer to focus on the entire buying process rather than just the purchase decision.

The model appears to imply that consumers pass through all five stages with every purchase they make. But in more routine purchases, consumers skip or reverse some of these stages. A customer in a bar purchasing a glass of beer may go right to the purchase decision, skipping information search and evaluation. This is referred to as an automatic response loop. The dream of every marketer is to have customers develop an automatic response to purchase its products. However, this does not typically happen. The model in Figure 5.7 shows the considerations that arise when a consumer faces a new and complex purchase situation.

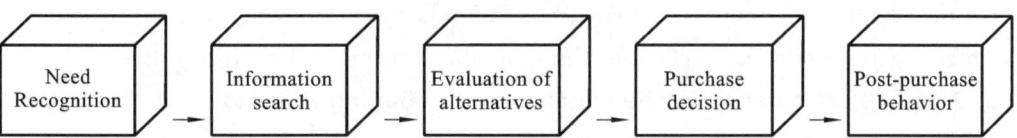

Figure 5.7 Buyer decision process

3.2 Organizational Buyer Behavior

3.2.1 The Organizational Buying Process

(1) Market Structure and Demand.

Organizational demand is derived demand; it comes ultimately from the demand for consumer goods or services. It is derived or a function of the businesses that supply the hospitality and travel industry with meetings, special events and other functions.

A business purchase usually involves more decision makers and a more professional purchasing effort. Corporations that frequently use hotels for meetings may hire their own meeting planners. Professional meeting planners receive training in negotiating skills. They belong to associations such as Meeting Planners International (MPI), which educates its members in the latest negotiating techniques. A corporate travel agent's job is to find the best airfares, rental car rates and hotel rates. Therefore, hotels must have well-trained salespeople to deal with well-trained buyers, creating thousands of jobs for salespeople. Additionally, once the meeting is sold, the account is turned over to a convention service manager who works with the meeting planner to make sure the event is produced according to the meeting planner's expectations. Outside the hotel, jobs relating to meetings include corporate meeting planners, association meeting planners, independent meeting planners, convention and visitor bureau salespeople.

(2) Types of Decisions and the Decision Process.

Organizational buyers usually face more complex buying decisions than consumer buyers. Their purchases often involve large sums of money, complex technical features (room sizes, room setups, breakout rooms, audiovisual equipment, and the like), economic considerations, and interactions among many people at all levels of the organization. The organizational buying process tends to be more formalized than the consumer process and a more professional purchasing effort. The more complex the purchase, the more likely it is that several people will participate in the decision-making process.

Finally, in the organizational buying process, buyer and seller are often very dependent on each other. Sale is a consultative process. The hospitality organization's staff develops interesting and creative menus, theme parties and coffee breaks. The staff works with meeting planners to solve problems and works. They also have a close working relationship with their corporate and association customers to find customized solutions to satisfy their needs. Hotels and catering firms retain customers by meeting their current needs and thinking ahead to meet their future needs.

3.2.2 Participants in the Organizational Buying Process

The decision-making unit of a buying organization, sometimes called the buying center, is defined as "all those individuals and groups who participate in the purchasing decision-making process, who share common goals and the risks arising from the decisions".

The buying center includes all members of the organization who play any of the six roles in the purchase-decision process:

(1) Users. Users are those who use the product or service. They often provide recommendations to those directly involved in the purchase decision, either directly or through user-generated comments on websites.

(2) Influencers. Influencers directly influence the buying decision but do not make the final decision themselves. They often help define specifications and provide information for evaluating alternatives. Past presidents of trade associations may exert

influence in the choice of a meeting location.

(3) Deciders. Deciders select product requirements and suppliers.

(4) Approvers. Approvers authorize the proposed actions of deciders or buyers.

(5) Buyers. Buyers have formal authority for selecting suppliers and arranging the terms of purchase. Buyers may help shape product specifications and play a major role in selecting vendors and negotiating.

(6) Gatekeepers. Gatekeepers have the power to prevent sellers of information from reaching members of the buying center.

3.2.3 Major Influences on Organizational Buyers

(1) Environmental Factors.

Organizational buyers are heavily influenced by the current and expected economic environment. Factors such as the level of primary demand, the economic outlook and the cost are important. In a recession, companies cut their travel budgets, whereas in good times, travel budgets are usually increased.

(2) Organizational Factors.

Each organization has specific objectives, policies, procedures, organizational structures and systems related to buying. The hospitality marketer has to be familiar with them and must know the following: How many people are involved in the buying decision? Who are they? What are the evaluation criteria? What are the company's policies and constraints on the buyers?

(3) Interpersonal Factors.

The buying center usually includes several participants, with differing levels of interest, authority and persuasiveness. Hospitality marketers are unlikely to know the group dynamics that take place during the buying decision process. Salespeople commonly learn the personalities and interpersonal factors that shape the organizational environment and provide useful insight into group dynamics.

(4) Individual Factors.

Each participant in the buying decision process has personal motivations, perceptions and preferences. Buyers definitely exhibit different buying styles. Hospitality marketers must know their customers and adapt their tactics to known environmental, organizational, interpersonal and individual influences.

3.2.4 Organizational Buying Decisions

Organizational buyers do not buy goods and services for personal consumption. They buy hospitality products to provide training, to reward employees and distributors, and to provide lodging for their employees. Eight stages of the organizational buying process have been identified and are called buyphases. This model is called buygrid framework. The eight steps for the typical new-task buying situation are as follows:

(1) Problem Recognition.

The buying process begins when someone in the company recognizes a problem or need that can be met by acquiring a good or a service. Problem recognition can occur because of internal or external stimuli. Internally, a new product may create the need for a series of meetings to explain the product to the sales force.

(2) General Need Description.

Having recognized a need, the buyer goes on to determine the requirements of the product and to formulate a general need description.

(3) Product Specification.

Once the general requirements have been determined, the specific requirements for the meeting can be developed. Salespersons must be prepared to answer their prospective client's questions about their hotel's capabilities to fulfill the product specification.

(4) Supplier Search.

The buyer now conducts a supplier search to identify the most appropriate choice.

(5) Proposal Solicitations.

Once the meeting planner has drawn up a short list of suppliers, qualified hotels are invited to submit proposals.

(6) Supplier Selection.

In this stage, members of the buying center review the proposals and move toward supplier selection.

(7) Order-Routine Specification.

The buyer now writes the final order with the chosen hotels, listing the technical order-routine specifications of the meeting.

(8) Performance Review.

The buyer does a post-purchase performance review of the product.

4. Analysis of Tourism Marketing Environment

4.1 The Company's Micro-environment

Marketing management's job is to build relationships with customers by creating customer value and satisfaction. This requires working closely with the company's micro-environment. These actors are shown in Figure 5.8. They include supplier, market intermediaries, customers and publics that combine to make up the company's value delivery system.

4.1.1 The Company

Marketing managers must work closely with top management and the various company departments. The finance department is concerned with finding and using funds required to carry out the company's plans. The accounting department has to measure revenues and costs to help marketing know how well it is achieving its

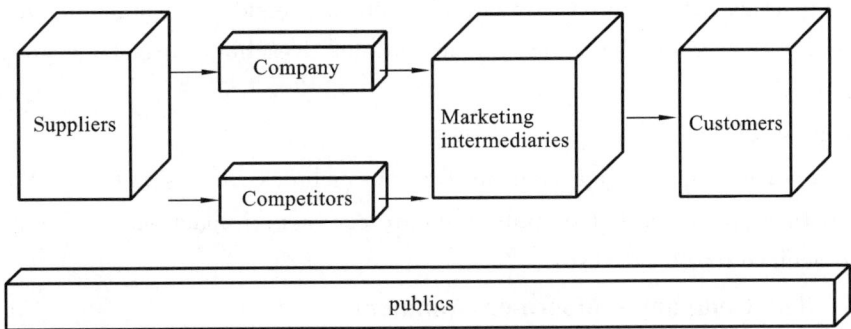

Figure 5.8　Major actors in the company's micro-environment

objectives. Housekeeping is responsible for delivering clean rooms sold by the sales department. Top management sets the company's mission, objectives, broad strategies and policies. Marketing decisions must be made within the strategies and plans made by top management.

4.1.2　Existing Competitors

We include competitors in both the micro-environment and macro-environment. Existing customers are part of the micro-environment. Every company faces a broad range of existing competitors. The marketing concept holds that a successful company must satisfy the needs and wants of consumers better than its competitors. It must also adapt to the strategies of other companies serving the same target markets. Companies must gain strategic advantage by strongly positioning their products in the minds of consumers.

4.1.3　Suppliers

Suppliers are firms and individuals that provide the resources needed by the company to produce its goods and services. Trends and developments affecting suppliers can, in turn, seriously affect a company's marketing plan.

4.1.4　Marketing Intermediaries

Marketing intermediaries help the company promote, sell and distribute its goods to the final buyers. Intermediaries are business firms that help hospitality companies find customers or make sales. They include travel agents, wholesale tour operators, hotel representatives and online travel agencies (OTAs), such as Expedia, Travelocity and Orbitz. The OTAs bundle airfare with hotel rooms, creating value for the customers.

4.1.5　Customers

The hospitality company needs to study five types of general customer markets closely. Consumer markets consist of individuals and households that purchase hospitality services for leisure activities, medical needs and gatherings such as reunions, weddings or funerals. Business markets buy hospitality services to facilitate their business. This can be individual rooms for travelers representing the company or for group meetings the company or organization may conduct. Companies have sales meetings and associations have annual conventions. Resellers purchase a product and then resell it.

4.1.6 Publics

The company's marketing environment also includes various publics. A public is any group that has an actual or potential interest in or impact on an organization's ability to achieve its objectives.

4.2 The Company's Macro-environment

The company and all of the other actors operate in a larger macro-environment of forces. Figure 5.9 shows the seven major forces in the company's macro-environment. In the remaining sections of this chapter, we examine these forces and show how they affect marketing plans.

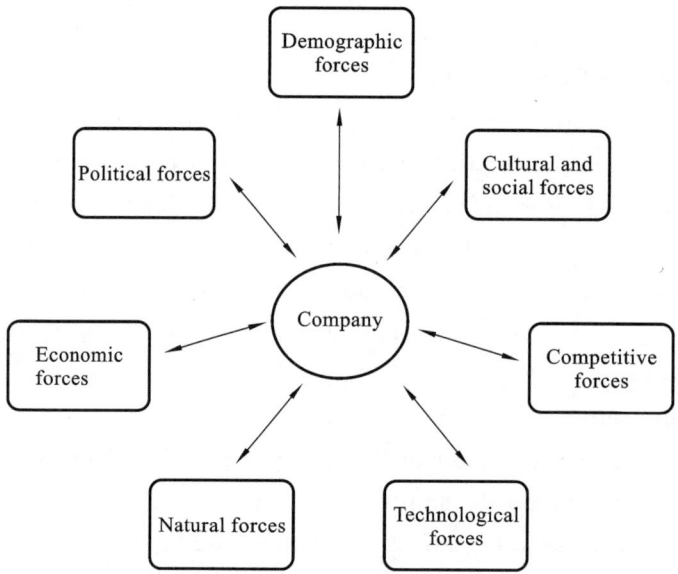

Figure 5.9　Major forces in the company's macro-environment

4.2.1 Competitors

We consider future competitors as part of the macro-environment. The entrance of future competitors is often difficult to predict and can have a major effect on existing businesses.

Two forces that affect competition are the ability of companies to enter and exit markets. Entry barriers prevent firms from getting into a business, and barriers to exit prevent them from leaving. Hotels have moderately high barriers of entry, due to the costs of building a hotel and the scarcity of good locations. High barriers to exit from the industry present a different set of competitive problems. The large capital investment required to build a hotel becomes a sunk cost. As a result, hotels that cannot meet all of their debt payments, taxes and other fixed costs, but can produce enough gross profit to partially offset these fixed costs, may operate at a loss rather than close their doors. Thus when hotel demand plummets, room supply remains the same. With fewer customers bidding for the same number of hotel rooms in a marketplace, competition becomes intense.

The hotel's competitive environment is affected by another factor: Most hotels are planned during upswings in the business cycle when there is not enough supply to meet demand. But it can take four years or more from the planning stages to the opening of a hotel. By that time the economic cycle may have turned down. Sadly, new hotels often open their doors during a recessionary period. So at a period when existing hotels are struggling to fill their rooms, it is not uncommon for competitors to enter the market.

4.2.2 Demographic Environment

Demography is the study of human populations in terms of size, density, location, age, gender, race, occupation and other statistics. The demographic environment is of major interest to marketers because it involves people, and people make up markets. The world population is growing at an explosive rate. It now exceeds 6.6 billion people and will grow to 8.5 billion by 2030. The world's large and highly diverse population poses both opportunities and challenges.

Changes in the world demographic environment have major implications for business. For example, consider China. More than a quarter century ago, to curb its skyrocketing population, the Chinese government passed regulations limiting families to one child each. As a result, Chinese children have been showered with attention and luxuries under what's known as the "six-pocket syndromes". As many as six adults—two parents and four doting grandparents—may be indulging the whims of an only child. These children, now ranging in age from newborns to mid-twenties, are affecting markets for everything including restaurants and travels. Parents with only child at home spend about 40 percent of their income on their cherished child.

4.2.3 Economic Environment

Markets require buying power as well as people. The economic environment consists of factors that affect consumer purchasing power and spending patterns. Nations vary greatly in their levels and distribution of income. Some countries have subsistence economies: They consume most of their own agricultural and industrial output. These countries offer few market opportunities. At the other extreme are industrial economies, which constitute rich markets for many different kinds of goods. Marketers must pay close attention to major trends and consumer-spending patterns both across and within their world markets.

4.2.4 Technological Environment

The most dramatic force shaping our destiny is technology, which has given us wireless access to the Internet. This has made it possible for individuals to have

interactions with others involving both audio and visual connections using programs such as Skype and FreeConference.com. Many organizations now accept a document that has been signed, scanned, and emailed instead of a hard copy of the original document. The end result is that speed at which business is occurring has increased dramatically. Sites like LinkedIn and Facebook allow us to keep track of both our business and personal networks.

4.2.5 Political Environment

Marketing decisions are strongly affected by developments in the political environment. This environment consists of laws, government agencies and pressure groups that influence and limit the activities of various organizations and individuals in society.

4.2.6 Cultural Environment

The cultural environment includes institutions and other forces that affect society's basic values, perceptions, preferences and behaviors. As a collective entity, a society shapes the basic beliefs and values of its members.

A practice widely followed in China and Singapore (and that has also spread to Japan, Vietnam and Korea), Fengshui means wind and water. Practitioners of Fengshui, or geomancers, recommend the most favorable conditions for any venture, particularly the placement of office buildings and the arrangement of desks, doors, and other items. The Hyatt Hotel in Singapore was designed without Fengshui in mind and had to be redesigned to boost business.

4.2.7 Natural Environment

The natural environment involves the natural resources that are needed as inputs by marketers or that are affected by marketing activities. Environmental concerns have grown steadily during the past three decades. In many cities around the world, air and water pollution have reached dangerous levels.

5. Developing the Hospitality and Tourism Marketing Value-driven Strategy and Mix

5.1 Designing and Managing Products and Brands: Building Customer Value

We define the term product as follows: A product is anything that can be offered to a market for attention, acquisition, use or consumption that might satisfy a want or need. It includes physical objects, services, places, organizations and ideas.

5.1.1 Product Levels

Hospitality managers need to think about the product on four levels: the core product, the facilitating product, the supporting product and the augmented product.

5.1.2 Branding Strategy

Building Strong Brands

A brand is a name, term, sign, symbol, design or a combination of these elements that is intended to identify the goods or services of a seller and differentiate them from competitors.

Branding is the process of endowing products and services with the power of a brand. It's all about creating differences between products. This process must be carefully developed and managed. In this section, we examine the key strategies for building and managing brands (Table 5.1).

Table 5.1　Marketing advantages of strong brands

Marketing advantages of strong brands
Improved perceptions of product performance
Greater loyalty
Less vulnerability to competitive marketing actions
Less vulnerability to marketing crises
Larger margins
More inelastic consumer response to price increases
More elastic consumer response to price decreases
Greater cooperation and support from suppliers
Greater support from marketing intermediaries
Increased marketing communications effectiveness
Brand extension opportunities

5.1.3　The New-product Development

A company can obtain new products in two ways. One is through acquisition—by buying a whole company or a license to use someone else's product. The other is through the company's own new-product development efforts. To create successful new products, a company must understand its consumers, markets and competitors and develop products that deliver superior value to customers. It must carry out strong new-product planning and set up a systematic, customer-driven new-product development process for finding and growing new products. Figure 5.10 shows the eight major steps in this process.

(1) Idea Generation.

New-product development starts with idea generation—the systematic search for new-product ideas. A company typically generates hundreds of ideas, even thousands, to find a few good ones. Major sources of new-product ideas include internal sources and external sources such as customers, competitors and distributors and suppliers.

(2) Idea Screening.

The purpose of idea generation is to create a large number of ideas. The purpose of screening is to spot good ideas and drop poor ones as quickly as possible.

(3) Concept Development and Testing.

Surviving ideas must now be developed into product concepts. It is important to distinguish between a product idea, a product concept and a product image. A product

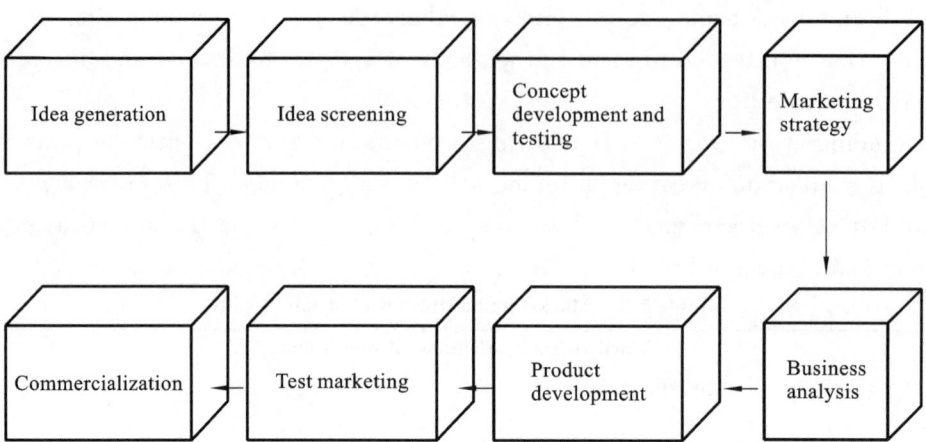

Figure 5.10 Major stages in new-product development

idea envisions a possible product that company managers might offer to the market. A product concept is a detailed version of the idea stated in meaningful consumer terms. A product image is the way that consumers picture an actual or potential product.

(4) Marketing Strategy.

The next step is marketing strategy development: designing an initial marketing strategy for introducing the product into the market. The marketing strategy statement consists of three parts. The first part describes the target market, the planned product positioning, and the sales, market share and profit goals for the first few years. The second part of the marketing strategy statement outlines the product's planned price, distribution and marketing budget for the first year. The third part of the marketing strategy statement describes the planned long-run sales, profit goals and marketing mix strategy.

(5) Business Analysis.

Once management decides on the product concept and marketing strategy, it can evaluate the business attractiveness of the proposal. Business analysis involves a review of the sales, costs and profit projections to determine whether they satisfy the company's objectives. If they do, the product can move to the product development stage.

(6) Product Development.

If the product concept passes the business test, it moves into product development and into a prototype. Up to now it existed only as a word description, a drawing or mockup. The company develops one or more physical versions of the product concept. Restaurants can develop prototypes of menu items and run them as specials; hotels build guest room prototypes. It hopes to find a prototype that meets the following criteria:①Consumers perceive it as having the key features described in the product concept statement;②It performs safely under normal use;③It can be produced for the budgeted costs.

(7) Test Marketing.

If the product passes functional and consumer tests, the next step is market testing in which the product and marketing program are introduced into realistic market settings.

Market testing allows the marketer to gain experience in marketing the product, to find potential problems, and to learn where more information is needed before the company goes to the great expense of full introduction. Market testing evaluates the product and the entire marketing program in real market situations. The product and its positioning strategy, advertising, distribution, pricing, branding, packaging and budget levels are evaluated during market testing. Market testing results can be used to make better sales and profit forecasts.

(8) Commercialization.

Market testing gives management the information it needs to make a final decision about whether to launch a new product. If the company goes ahead with commercialization, it will face high costs. It may have to spend several million dollars for advertising and sales promotion alone in the first year.

5.1.4 Product Life Cycle

After launching a new product, management wants the product to enjoy a long and lucrative life. Although the product is not expected to sell forever, managers want to earn enough profit to compensate for the effort and risk. To maximize profits, a product's marketing strategy is normally reformulated several times. Strategy changes are often the result of changing market and environmental conditions as the product moves through the product life cycle (PLC).

(1) Product development begins when the company finds and develops a new-product idea. During product development, sales are zero and the company's investment costs add up.

(2) Introduction is a period of slow sales growth as the product is being introduced into the market. Profits are nonexistent at this stage because of the heavy expenses of product introduction.

(3) Growth is a period of rapid market acceptance and increasing profits.

(4) Maturity is a period of slowdown in sales growth because the product has achieved acceptance by most of its potential buyers. Although sales are still high, profits level off or decline because of increased marketing outlays to defend the product against competition.

(5) Decline is the period when sales fall off quickly and profits drop.

5.2 Pricing: Understanding and Capturing Customer Value

Price is the only marketing mix element that produces revenue. All others represent cost. Some experts rate pricing and price competition as the number-one problem facing marketing executives. Pricing is the least understood of the marketing

variables, yet pricing is controllable in an unregulated market. Pricing changes are often a quick fix made without proper analysis. The most common mistakes include pricing that is too cost oriented, prices that are not revised to reflect market changes, pricing that does not take the rest of the marketing mix into account, and prices that are not varied enough for different product items and market segments. A pricing mistake can lead to a business failure, even when all other elements of the business are sound. Every manager should understand the basics of pricing.

Simply defined, price is the amount of money charged for a good or service. More broadly, price is the sum of the values consumers exchange for the benefits of having or using the product or service.

5.2.1 Factors to Consider When Setting Prices

Internal and external company factors affect a company's pricing decisions. Figure 5.11 illustrates these. Internal factors include the company's marketing objectives, marketing mix strategy, costs and organizational considerations. External factors include nature of the market, demand competition and other environmental elements.

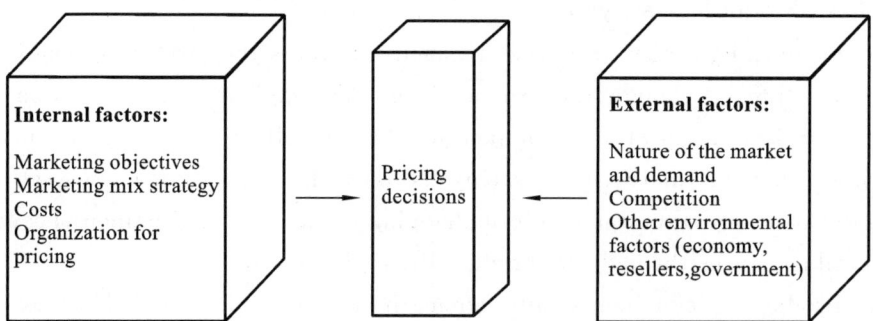

Figure 5.11　Factors affecting price decisions

5.2.2 General Pricing Approaches

The price the company charges is somewhere between one that is too low to produce a profit and one that is too high to produce sufficient demand. Product costs set a floor for the price; consumer perceptions of the product's value set the ceiling. The company must consider competitors' prices and other external and internal factors to find the best price between these two extremes.

Companies set prices by selecting a general pricing approach that includes one or more of these sets of factors. We look at the following approaches: the cost-based approach (cost-plus pricing, BE analysis and target profit pricing), the value-based approach (perceived-value pricing) and the competition-based approach (going rate).

(1) Cost-based Pricing.

The simplest pricing method is cost-plus pricing, adding a standard markup to the cost of the product.

(2) Break-even Analysis and Target Profit Pricing.

Another cost-oriented pricing approach is BE pricing, in which the firm tries to determine the price at which it will break even. Some firms use a variation of BE pricing called target profit pricing, which targets a certain ROI.

(3) Value-based Pricing.

An increasing number of companies are basing their prices on the products' perceived value. Value-based pricing uses the buyers' perceptions of value, not the sellers' cost, as the key to pricing. Value-based pricing means that the marketer cannot design a product and marketing program and then set the price. Price is considered along with other marketing mix variables before the marketing program is set.

(4) Competition-based Pricing.

A strategy of going-rate pricing is the establishment of price based largely on those of competitors, with less attention paid to costs or demand.

5.2.3 Psychological Pricing

Psychological pricing considers the psychology of prices, not simply the economics.

5.3 Distribution Channels Delivering Customer Value

5.3.1 Nature and Importance of Distribution Systems

If we view properties as the heart of a hotel company, distribution systems can be viewed as the company's circulatory system. Distribution systems provide a steady flow of customers. A well-managed distribution system can make the difference between a market-share leader and a company struggling for survival. Many hospitality companies are making greater use of the marketing channels available to them.

Competition, a global marketplace, electronic distribution techniques and a perishable product have increased the importance of distribution. Innovative ways of approaching new and existing markets are needed. Globalization has meant that many hotel companies must choose foreign partners to help them market or distribute their products.

5.3.2 Hospitality Distribution Channels

The largest number of reservations, 33 percent, comes to a hotel through brand. com. Brand. com is a term used for the brands reservation system. For example, for Hilton it would be www.hilton.com. About 24 percent come from direct bookings, and 13 percent come from the calls into the central reservation office (CRO). Twenty-nine percent come from third parties: online travel agencies and global distribution systems. The cost of these different channels varies greatly. The least expensive way is when the guest makes a reservation through the brand's website. However, when a hotel has rooms to fill, OTAs can help sell the rooms. A revenue manager has to

manage the channels, knowing when to open and close different channels.

5.4 Promoting Products: Public Relations and Sales Promotions

5.4.1 Public Relations

Public relations, perhaps the most misunderstood part of marketing communications, can be the most effective tools. Definitions for public relations differ widely. We think that this definition by Hilton best fits the hospitality industry: "The process by which we create a positive image and customer preference through third-party endorsement."

Public relations (PR) is an important marketing tool that until recently was treated as a marketing stepchild. PR is moving into an explosive growth stage.

5.4.2 Major Activities of PR Departments

(1) Press Relations.

The aim of press relations is to place newsworthy information into the news media to attract attention to a person, product or service.

(2) Product Publicity.

Product publicity involves various efforts to publicize specific products. Special events such as food festivals, redesigned products such as a newly renovated hotel and products that are popular because of current trends, such as nonfat desserts, are all potential candidates for publicity.

(3) New Products.

New products are the lifeblood of any industry, including tourism/hospitality.

(4) Corporate Communication.

Corporate communication covers internal and external communications and promotes understanding of the organization.

Ⅳ Case Study

Disney

Few companies have been able to connect with their audience as well as Disney has. From its founding by brothers Walt and Roy Disney in 1923, the Disney brand has always been synonymous with trust, fun and quality entertainment for the entire family. Walt Disney was interested in bringing laughter to people.

Today, Disney consists of five business segments: Studio Entertainment, which creates films, recording labels and theatrical performances; Parks and Resorts, which focuses on Disney's 11 theme parks, cruise lines and other travel-related assets; Consumer Products, which sells all Disney-branded products; Media Networks, which includes Disney's television networks such as ESPN, ABC and the Disney Channel; and Interactive.

Disney's greatest challenge today is keeping a 90-year-old brand relevant and current with its core audience while staying true to its heritage and core brand values. Disney was faced with showing respect to its heritage, while at the same time maintaining it relevancy through innovation.

Internally, to achieve quality and recognition, Disney has focused on the Disney Difference, which stems from one of Walt Disney's most recognizable quotes: "Whatever you do, do it well." He said if you do, people will come back and bring others to show them how well you do it.

Disney works hard to connect with its customers on many levels and through every single detail. For example, at Disney World, "cast members" or employees are trained to be "assertively friendly" and greet visitors by waving big Mickey Mouse hands, hand out maps to adults and stickers to kids, and clean up the park so diligently that it's difficult to find a piece of garbage anywhere.

Every detail matters, right down to the behavior of custodial workers who are trained by Disney's animators to take their simple broom and bucket of water and quietly "paint" a Goofy or Mickey Mouse in water on the pavement. It's a moment of magic for guests that lasts just a minute before it evaporates in the hot sun.

Disney's broad range of businesses allows the company to connect with its audience in multiple ways, efficiently and economically. Hannah Montana provides an excellent example. The company took a tween-targeted television show and moved it across several divisions to become a significant franchise for the company, including millions of CD sales, video games, popular consumer products, box office movies, concerts around the world, and ongoing live performances at international Disneyland resorts in China, India and Russia.

Perhaps the most anticipated new product of 2013 was the Disney Infinity gaming platform, which crossed all Disney boundaries. Disney Infinity allowed consumers to play with many of the Disney characters at the same time, interacting and working together on different adventures. For example, Andy from *Toy Story* might join forces with Captain Jack Sparrow from *Pirates of the Caribbean* and several monsters from Monsters, Inc. to fight villains from outer space.

With so many brands, characters and businesses, Disney uses technology to ensure that a customer's experience is consistent across every platform. The company connects with its consumers in innovative ways through email, blogs and its website. It was one of the first companies to begin regular podcasts of its television shows as well as to post news about its products and interviews with Disney's employees, staff and park officials. Disney's website provides insight into its movie trailers, television clips, Broadway shows and virtual theme park experiences.

Disney's marketing campaign in recent years has focused on how it helps make unforgettable family memories. The campaign, "Let the Memories Begin" features

real guests throughout Disney enjoying different rides and magical experiences. Disney realized that each and every day it is making memories for its guests.

According to internal studies, Disney estimates that consumers spend 13 billion hours "immersed" with the Disney brand each year. Consumers around the world spend 10 billion hours watching programs on the Disney Channel, 800 million hours at Disney's resorts and theme parks, and 1.2 billion hours watching a Disney movie—at home, in the theater or on their computer. Today, Disney is the 10th most powerful brand in the world, and its revenues topped $59.43 billion in 2018.

V Tips

1. The Digital Age: Online, Mobile and Social Media Marketing

Digital and social media marketing involves using digital marketing tools such as websites, social media, mobile ads and Apps, online video, email, blogs and other digital platforms that engage consumers anywhere, anytime via their computers, smartphones, tablets, Internet ready TVs and other digital devices. These days, it seems that every company is reaching out to customers with multiple websites, newsy tweets and Facebook pages, viral ads and videos posted on emails, and mobile Apps that solve consumer problems and help them shop Mobile marketing is perhaps the fastest-growing digital marketing platform. Twenty-nine percent of smartphone owners use their phones for shopping-related activities—browsing product information through Apps or the mobile web, reading online product reviews, finding and redeeming coupons and more.

2. Sustainable Marketing

Marketers are reexamining their relationships with social values and responsibilities and with the very Earth that sustains us. As the worldwide consumerism and environmentalism movements mature, today's marketers are being called on to develop sustainable marketing practices. Corporate ethics and social responsibility have become hot topics for almost every business. And few companies can ignore the renewed and very demanding environmental movement. Every company action can affect customer relationships. Today's customers expect companies to deliver value in a socially and environmentally responsible way.

3. Buzz Marketing

Buzz marketing involves enlisting or even creating opinion leaders to serve as "brand ambassadors," who spread the word about a company's products. Many companies now create brand ambassador programs in an attempt to turn influential but everyday customers into brand evangelists. A recent study found that such programs can increase the effectiveness of word-of-mouth marketing efforts by as much as fifty percent. For example, JetBlue's CrewBlue program employs real customers to create buzz on college campuses.

Ⅵ Dialogue

(Tom is tour guide. This is Lulu and Lucy's first visit to the Great Wall.)

Tom: Good morning. I am Tom, your tour guide. Welcome to our tour group. Today we are going to visit the Great Wall. If you have any need during the trip, I am at your service.

Lulu: I have heard so much about the Great Wall, and today I am very happy that I can visit this marvelous piece in person.

Lucy: So do I. I did a lot of research before I came to China. And the Great Wall is one of the most popular tourist attractions in China. And I cannot wait to visit.

Tom: I am glad that you all are interested in the Great Wall. Here are your tickets. Please put your tickets away. When we leave, you can go to the customers' service center near the exit to get a souvenir by the ticket.

Lulu & Lucy: OK. Thank you.

Tom: The Great Wall of China is also known in China as the Great Wall of 10000 Li. The first major wall was built during Qin Dynasty. This wall was not constructed as a single endeavor, but rather was created by combining several regional walls built by the Warring States.

Lulu: Oh. It is very impressive. I have a question that the Great Wall is built for protect another state to attack or for other reason?

Tom: During the Qin Dynasty, the wall was built to protect the kingdom from raids by the Mongolian nomadic tribes. The primary purpose of the wall in Ming Dynasty was to ensure that semi-nomadic people outside of the wall could not across with their horses or return easily with the stolen properties. And next we will have one hour for free activities; you can go anywhere to have some photographs as memory. We will need to gather in the exit one hour later. Thanks again for joining our tour group. I hope all of you had a good time today. See you next time.

Ⅶ Academic Thinking

Electronic Word-of-mouth in Hospitality and Tourism Management

Author: Stephen W. Litvina, Ronald E. Goldsmith, Bing Pan

Journal: *Tourism Management*

Abstract:

Interpersonal influence and word-of-mouth (WOM) are ranked the most important information source when a consumer is making a purchase decision. These influences are especially important in the hospitality and tourism industry, whose intangible products are difficult to evaluate prior to their consumption. When WOM becomes digital, the large-scale, anonymous, ephemeral nature of the Internet induces new ways of capturing, analyzing, interpreting and managing the influence that one consumer may have on another.

酒店和旅游管理的网络口碑

在消费者进行购买决策时,人际影响和口碑是最重要的信息来源。这些影响在酒店业和旅游业尤其重要,因为酒店业和旅游业的无形产品在消费前很难评估。当网络口碑变得数字化时,互联网的大规模、匿名性和短暂性会催生新的方式来捕捉、分析、解释和管理一个消费者可能对另一个消费者的影响。本文描述了在线人际影响,或网络口碑,作为一种潜在的成本效益的手段营销酒店和旅游,并讨论了一些营销人员面临的新生的技术和道德问题,因为他们寻求利用新兴的网络口碑技术。

Ⅷ Questions

1. Many managers view the purpose of business as making a profit, whereas some view the purpose as being able to create and maintain a customer. Explain how these alternative viewpoints could affect a company's interactions with its customers. If a manager views the purpose as being able to create and maintain a customer, does this mean that the manager is not concerned with profits?

2. Talk with persons who travel for business. Ask them if they can choose their own hotel and airlines when they travel for their company. If they can choose their own hotels and airlines, ask if they have any restrictions or guidelines. If they are not able to choose their own hotels and airlines, ask if they have any input into where they stay. How would this information help you market travel products to their organization?

Ⅸ Key Words and Terms

advertising	广告活动
brand	品牌
branding	品牌活动
brand equity	品牌资产

buzz marketing	蜂鸣营销
counseling	咨询
cost-plus pricing	成本加成定价
customer value	客户价值
demand	要求
demography	人口统计学
digital and social media marketing	数字和社交媒体营销
economic environment	经济环境
hospitality industry	酒店业
human need	人类的需要
human want	人类的需求
interactive marketing	互动营销
internal marketing	内部营销
marketing mix	营销组合
marketing	市场营销
marketing intermediaries	营销中介
micromarketing	微观营销
millennials	千禧一代
Online Travel Agency (OTA)	在线旅行社
order-routine specification	常规订购方式说明
performance review	绩效评估
press relations	媒体关系
price	价格
political environment	政治环境
product idea	产品理念
product concept	产品概念
product image	产品形象
product development	产品开发
promotion mix	促销组合
public	公共的
public relations	公共关系
relationship marketing	关系营销
return on marketing investment (or marketing ROI)	营销投资回报率
sales promotion	促销活动
strategic planning	战略规划

supplier	供应商
survey research	调查研究
sustainable tourism	可持续旅游
tourism	旅游业
value chain	价值链
value-based pricing	基于价值定价

Single Choice Questions

Chapter 6
Cultural Tourism

Chapter Introduction

　　Cultural tourism has changed dramatically since it was first recognized as part of the array of available tourism experiences in the late 1970s and early 1980s. It was recognized as a distinct product category only in the late 1970s when tourism marketers and tourism researchers realized that some people travelled specifically to gain a deeper understanding of the culture or heritage of a destination. This chapter introduces conceptual, theoretical and management dimensions of culture tourism. We highlight a range of theoretical models that try to frame cultural tourism, bringing together definitions of culture and tourism and illustrating the constant strain between the terms and acknowledging various "higher order" means of exploring culture inevitable commodification of culture that emerges when discussing cultural tourism. This chapter also looks at the general concept of products, examines the idea of products as tourist attractions, discusses the need to commodify and standardize product offering. Different academic discourses are applied to explore how producers and consumers of tourism might collaborate to co-create meanings, values and experiences related to cultural tourism. While the tourism industry works on a goods-dominant logic, both service dominant logic and consumer theory are used. It is possible to create a theoretical foundation to add to the embryonic field of tourism and leisure research, which is attempting to understand the co-creation of experience. As customers are to be fully involved in defining experience environments, cultural tourism managers need to engage customers in communication processes in the planning of those environments, some of the core concepts and applications of cultural heritage management. This chapter also presents an overview of cultural heritage management by discussing a number of principles, grouped into four broad themes: core concepts, sustainability, stakeholders and tourism.

Ⅱ Chapter Objectives

1. Consider different definitions of culture.
2. Explain what is cultural tourism products.
3. Explain the three levels of cultural tourism products.
4. Explain the functions of cultural tourism products.
5. Describe benefits of standardizing, modifying and commodifying cultural tourism.
6. Illustrate the principles of protecting cultural heritage.
7. Explain the three types of cultural tourism destinations.
8. Explain cultural heritage site typology and characteristics.

Ⅲ Reading

1. Defining Cultural Tourism

Cultural tourism is one of the oldest forms of special interest tourism, and yet, remains one of the more misunderstood types. People have been travelling for what we now call cultural tourism reasons since the days of the ancient Romans visiting ancient Greece and ancient Egypt or Chinese scholars making journeys to beautiful landscapes. At the same time, places and activities that we now label as representing cultural tourism products were not identified as such until recently. Instead, visiting historic sites, cultural landmarks, attending special events and festivals, watching street performances or visiting museums were seen as part of a broader lexicon of sightseeing activities that formed part of the total tourism experience.

1.1 Cultural Tourism

Early tourism-related definitions place cultural tourism within a broader framework of tourism and tourism management theory or as a form of special interest tourism. For example, the United Nations World Tourism Organization (UNWTO) defines cultural tourism as: The movement of persons to cultural attractions in cities in countries other than their normal place of residence, with the intention to gather new information and experiences to satisfy their cultural needs and all movements of persons to specific cultural attractions, such as heritage sites, artistic and cultural manifestations, arts and drama to cities outside their normal country of residence.

Organizations such as the UNWTO (2006a) and the Canadian Tourism Commission describe cultural tourism on the basis of the desire to learn about a destination's cultural heritage as a significant travel motive. Building on this idea, a third group of definitions adopts an experiential approach that argues motivation alone does not encapsulate the full magnitude of this sector. Instead, cultural tourism involves some meaningful experience with the unique social fabric, heritage and special character of places or as a quest or search for greater understanding. The US National Endowment for the Arts, for example, defines it as "travel directed toward experiencing the arts, heritage and special character of a place".

The UNWTO (2006a) suggests cultural tourism represents movements of people motivated by cultural intents such as study tours, performing arts, festivals, cultural events, visits to sites and monuments, as well as travel for pilgrimages. Whyte, Hood and White (2012), for example, indicate the Canadian Tourism Commission definition includes performing arts (theatre, dance, music), visual arts and crafts, festivals, museums and cultural centres, historic sites and interpretive centers, while the US National Endowment for the Arts specifies museums, historic sites, dance, music, theatre, book and other festivals, historic buildings, arts and crafts fairs, neighborhoods and landscapes. Indeed, it is common to define cultural tourism by activity, using definitions that read something like "cultural tourism includes visits to …" The Australian State of Victoria, for example, defines cultural tourists as "those who attended a theatre performance, a concert or other performing arts, a cultural festival, fair or event; or visited a museum, art gallery, art, craft workshop or studios, or a history or heritage site while on their trip to Australia" (TV 2013).

1.2 Conceptualizing Cultural Tourism—a Thematic Approach

1.2.1 Tourism

The word "tourism" is a noun and the word "cultural" is an adjective used to modify it. As such, it is vital to recognize that, above all else, cultural tourism is a form of tourism and not a form of cultural management. The decision to embark on cultural tourism must be based on sound tourism reasons first and cultural management reasons second. And, equally as important, cultural tourism products must be managed as products. This point needs to be appreciated more by some members of the cultural management community, particularly those who resist the tourismification of cultural assets that are already attracting tourists.

1.2.2 The Use of Cultural Assets

While recognizing this activity is a form of tourism, one can never forget that its principal building blocks are a community's or a nation's cultural heritage assets. ICOMOS (International Council on Monuments and Sites) defines heritage as a broad concept that includes tangible assets, such as natural and cultural environments, the encompassing of landscapes, historic places, sites and built environments, as well as intangible assets such as collections, past and continuing cultural practices, knowledge and living experiences. In recent years, the concept has also been expanded to include a wide array of contemporary and heritage arts that express something

unique about a group's or an individual's world view. These assets are identified, performed, safeguarded, handed down and conserved for their intrinsic values or significance to a community rather than for their extrinsic use values as tourism attractions. In fact, the tourism potential of assets is rarely considered when they are first identified as significant to a community. One of the paradoxes of cultural tourism is that, while the decision to enter this sector must be driven by tourism considerations, the assets it utilizes are managed by the principles of cultural management (CM) within which arts management (AM) and cultural heritage management (CHM) are subcategories. That is, contemporary arts, tangible and intangible heritage from which cultural assets spring can be subject to the professional management principles and practices of heritage site managers, arts administrators, gallery and museum curators, and more. In addition, many cultural assets may serve a multitude of user groups, including tourists but also including local schoolchildren, traditional owners and other local residents. These groups may value the asset for different reasons and seek different benefits from its use, making the presentation task more difficult. These competing approaches can be a source of friction between tourism, arts and CHM interests. Throughout the book, a distinction is made between a cultural asset/item and a cultural tourism product. On one hand, a cultural asset/item represents the uncommodified or raw asset that is identified for its intrinsic values. A cultural tourism product, on the other hand, represents an asset that has been transformed or commodified specifically for tourism consumption.

1.2.3 The Tourist

Tourists are non-local residents travelling primarily for fun, recreation, escape or to spend time with family and friends. They have limited and, usually, fixed time budgets. Most are looking to be entertained, while only a small number are looking for deeper learning experiences. Most also have a limited knowledge of a destination's cultural heritage and living culture. As such, they are a fundamentally different user group than local residents, with completely different needs and wants. Products that suit their needs may be inimical with the needs of local residents. The type, quality and veracity of information received prior to arrival will shape their expectations and also their expected behavior while visiting. A vast array of information gatekeepers will set expectations, a task that has become more complicated with the social media revolution. Some of these sources are reliable, but many others may not be, and instead promote behaviors that are incompatible with the desires of asset managers. Successful cultural tourism products must be shaped with this type of visitor in mind, as they are likely to be the majority. An umbrella product class: overview the maturation of the field has also seen the fracturing of the cultural tourism concept into a series of increasingly small sub-genres of allegedly discrete activities or product types. Each is identified as being unique and each is then positioned as having special management challenges and opportunities. Whereas once we talked about cultural tourism, today attempts have been made to disaggregate many products, activities and experiences that fall under the broad umbrella of cultural tourism, such as arts and crafts workshops, fringe festivals, purchasing souvenirs of folk arts, gastronomy tours, industrial heritage museums, agricultural heritage parks, cultural activities that are part of mega events (e. g. the London 2012 Cultural Olympiad) and many more.

2. Cultural Tourism Products

The concept of a tourism product is complex as it involves elements of service, hospitality, free choice, consumer involvement and consumption of experiences that must be actualized in some way.

Identifying the core product and the core audience is vital in the sustainable development of cultural tourism. Defining the core product facilitates a range of marketing tactics that can communicate an effective message about the key attributes of the attraction, stimulate some to visit and also discourage others from visiting. It sets expectations of the type of experience to be gained, modulates demand by discouraging peak season use, and controls visitor's actions while at the attraction. In addition responsible marketing must take into account the needs of the host population, which may be quite different from those of tourists.

The tangible product represents the second level. It represents the physical manifestation of the core product that facilitates the need satisfaction. In short, it is the physical product or service that is purchased. It is the historic fort that is entered, the battlefield site that is visited, the museum that is seen, the cultural tour that is joined, or the festival that is attended. The tangible product is not the core experience provided. It is the means by which the core need can be satisfied. This concept is difficult for many people to appreciate for most people are so attuned to purchasing tangible products that they do not think about the deeper needs being satisfied. Indeed, one of the powerful features of cultural tourism is that its tangible products subliminally signal an expected experience so effectively that people will respond to the product without thinking about why. A fort signals history and struggle, an art gallery signals beauty, ruins signal the deep past and so on.

Tourism is the quintessential example of a sector that must adopt a marketing approach to products, for it sells dreams. People participate in cultural and heritage tourism to have an inner need satisfied, regardless of whether the person is seeking a deep or shallow experience. People do not go to Civil War battlefield sites to look at an empty field with a monument. Rather they go to gain an appreciation of American history, to visit hallowed ground, to honor the memory of those soldiers who fought

and died, to connect to their own cultural roots, to marvel at the incredible waste of war and loss of life, or even to try to imagine how they would react if they were placed in a similar circumstance. Sometimes the motive is more banal, as shown in Ramsey and Everitt's study of visitors to archeological sites in Belize, where the primary reason was focused on an enjoyable sightseeing day trip.

Thinking of cultural assets as products means they also need to be managed the same way as any other product. The most suitable way to do this is to adopt a marketing approach to asset management. Doing so provides a number of benefits, whereas the failure to do so presents a number of threats to the sustainability of the asset. Marketing involves more than sales. It is an overarching management philosophy that seeks to link consumers and products to provide appropriate experiences that satisfy both the needs of visitors and help the organization achieve its long-term financial and non-financial objectives. Non-financial objectives, such as conservation, preservation, education and the creation of awareness of the cultural or heritage significance are often more important than financial goals, especially given that many cultural tourism products are owned by government agencies, trusts or other not-for-profit organizations.

Not all cultural tourists are the same. So too must it be recognized that not all cultural tourism products are the same. Some will be of great interest to the visitor and will draw visitors from great distances. Others will be of limited interest, while many more will have little or no appeal to tourists. Tourism theory recognizes that a clear hierarchy of attractions exists in most destinations and that this hierarchy is defined by the degree of compulsion felt to visit them. The more powerful the demand generation capacity of the attraction, the greater its ability to draw visitors from far away. Lesser attractions may provide activities for visitors while at a destination, but do little to draw them to it. Attractions can, therefore, be an intrinsic part of a trip and a major motivator for selecting a destination, or they can be an optional, discretionary activity engaged in while at a destination.

Cultural tourism attractions do not exist in isolation from the destination's other tourism products, possible activities and overall destination image. Instead, they represent part of the product mix found in most destinations. As such, the decision to visit involves more than simply choosing which of many temples or historic buildings to visit. It also involves a more basic decision whether to include any cultural site in the itinerary or to participate in something else. Cultural attractions, thus, need to offer something special that moves them up the choice set. Attractions or activities that are seen to be common, boring or otherwise not appealing, will not be visited.

Moreover, the issue of serial monotony must also be considered, for after a while, similar attractions all begin to look the same. While tourists may be interested in sampling some cultural features, their interest in having the same type of experience over and over again is limited unless they are purposeful cultural tourists. Visiting one or two cathedrals or taking part in one historical walk may be appealing but the point of diminishing returns is reached quickly after that. While local custodians and asset managers may be aware of the subtleties of their places that make them unique, most tourists are not.

Whether or not the destination is associated with cultural tourism will influence both the volume and type of visitor. Cultural products located in places with a compatible destination image have a greater chance of succeeding while those located in destinations with incompatible images will struggle. The relationship between products, destination image and tourist interest is shown in Figure 6.1.

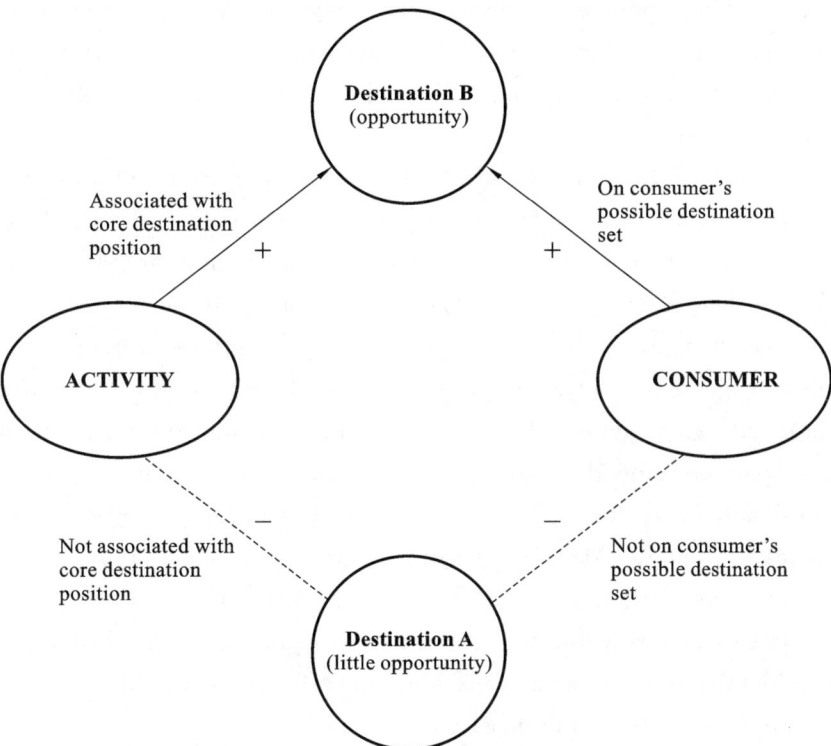

Figure 6.1 Compatibility with destination image

Destinations invest heavily to create a desired image that will appeal to their target markets. The image conveys a number of messages about the type of experience tourists can expect when visiting and, just as importantly, defining what they will not experience. Products that complement the image tend to receive preferential treatment in marketing campaigns, while those that are inimical to it receive far less attention. At the same time, tourists look for destinations that can satisfy their needs. Again, the image portrayed will help place the destination on a possible choice set list, while a perception of an incompatible image will result in the destination being overlooked.

The combination of the consumer's predisposition to seek destinations that are compatible with his or her desired experiences, and the destination's propensity to promote activities that reflect its overall desired image, benefits those products that are congruent with both while also creating equally powerful barriers for those that satisfy neither. A place like Hong Kong has a clear image as a sophisticated urban destination. It supports this image through the promotion of shopping, dining, sightseeing and festivals. Tourists thinking about an urban holiday would place Hong Kong on their choice set. Few people realize, though, that it also contains ten percent of the world's identified soft coral species and that some businesses offer diving tours to see these corals. Why? Such nature-based experiences are not compatible with its urban image and, because of that urban image, few tourists would consider Hong Kong when thinking about a nature-based holiday. Thus, local operators offering such experiences face the dual challenge of offering a product that does not support the destination's image and operating in a destination that tourists simply do not see as a nature-based option.

Much the same situation occurs in cultural tourism. Some destinations have a clear image and market perception that is compatible with cultural products, while others do not. Melbourne and Edinburgh, for example, are seen as festival destinations. Other cities that are not will struggle to develop major festivals as attractions. London and New York are theatre capitals. Other places have incompatible images. Las Vegas is seen as a gambling capital whose only cultural association is with stage shows. In other cases, the image is confused. Macau is now the world's largest casino destination and also one that happens to have a World Heritage designated core that reflects 500 years of Portuguese colonial settlement and the emergence of a unique Macanese culture. After a few years trying to please two completely different markets after the 2006 WHS(World Heritage Site) inscription, Macau's heritage image is losing the battle with its gambling image. Gambling is more visible in residential areas (e. g. slot machines in coffee shops or "Mochas") as well as those areas designated for casino mega-resorts.

The origins of the debate over the consumption of tourism experiences can be traced to tourism sociologists who were active in the 1960s. They felt people were no longer experiencing reality in their lives and instead they were being presented with a series of pseudo-events. Mass tourism was seen as being a prime example of how life had become overpowered by contrived experiences. Tourists were portrayed as being passive onlookers who were isolated from the host environment and local residents. Some felt they were victims of an all-powerful tourism industry who forced them to stay in tourist ghettos and who controlled their experiences. Others felt that tourists preferred to be ghettoized, choosing to disregard the real world around them. The end result was contrived tourism experiences that surrounded the visitor in a thicket of unreality.

This work led Erik Cohen (1972) to explore tourist behavior from the perspective of "strangeness" by looking at the extent, variety and degree of change tourists seek are capable of seeking when they travel. He argued the degree to which strangeness prevails in the tourist's activities determines the nature of the tourism experience as well as the effects he or she has on the host society. While all tourists are, to some extent, strangers in the host community, different tourists have different abilities to engage with that strangeness. Some travel explicitly to engage themselves as fully as possible in the alien environment, while most want to experience the novelty of a destination but from the safety of their own environmental bubble. The environmental bubble is essentially a social or cultural safety blanket that surrounds the tourist with the known or familiar, enabling the person to sample the unfamiliar, while not being overwhelmed by it. Different tourists have different abilities to cope with strangeness and therefore require different sized environmental bubbles.

In essence, then, he argued that tourists seek strangeness only to the extent that it remains non-threatening. Tourists would choose different destinations if threat levels exceeded their comfort zones alternatively, would have to use the environmental bubble to reduce strangeness to an acceptable level. The environmental bubble within a cultural tourism context tends to address intellectual and emotional risk factors rather than physical concerns.

The process of tourism product development involves some form of strangeness reduction or environmental bubble creation that provides a number of benefits for the tourist, the tourism industry and the asset itself. Reducing strangeness enhances touristic enjoyment, certainty about the experience, the ability to place the experience within a known cultural context and, ultimately, to provide greater confidence in the product being consumed. The tourism industry and the attraction itself benefit by the standardization, modification and commodification of its products to achieve efficiency in operations management, to reduce costs, and to provide some certainty of experience. Importantly, strangeness reduction broadens the market base, making it more accessible to a large number of consumers.

Minimal strangeness reduction may involve nothing more than signage or directional arrows. The provision of multilingual guides who can place the assets in context represents a stronger form of strangeness reduction. The creation of purpose-built spaces, such as museums, where the visitor can experience the society's past and form a sense of its cultural identity represents an even greater form of strangeness reduction. Purpose-built cultural theme parks, in particular, represent an extreme example of environmental bubble formation to reassure the more timid, pleasure-seeking tourists by creating themed spaces offering a safe, controlled and controllable environment. Hughes (1998) also observes the arts industries have standardized their product in order to satisfy consumers' demands and enable effective signification to the

consumers. Similarly, museums combine consumption activities with personal experiences that appeal to a larger number of people from different backgrounds.

The key here is fitness for purpose. The level of commodification must match the type of experience to be provided, the needs of the visitor, and the legitimate interests of stakeholders. It also involves balancing authenticity with practical product delivery concerns. Ashley et al. (2005) note maintaining sufficient authenticity in a cultural product that is packaged for tourists is one of the biggest challenges facing the sector. They comment that lack of authenticity can lead to tacky or mundane products and embarrassed or bored guests. But, at the same time, being too "authentic" may not comply with tourist requirements for safety, accessibility and tight scheduling. They suggest, further, more authentic products are most feasible on a small scale, while higher volumes require standardization. In addition, heritage site managers and museum spokespeople discuss an extra ethical obligation they face, whereby they must balance edutainment with authenticity. While theme parks may be able to be a little more flexible with the truth, museums have a professional obligation to present materials in a factual, culturally appropriate and culturally sensitive manner. Theme parks aimed at providing a more superficial experience to the casual and incidental cultural tourist, for example, may employ costumed actors to perform certain roles. However, museums can not do that.

3. Cultural Heritage Management and Practice (with Special Reference to World Heritage)

CHM and AM are subcategories of CM. CHM is the systematic care taken to maintain the cultural values of heritage assets for the enjoyment of present and future generations. As such, it is both a management philosophy and a management process. CHM, or cultural resource management, as it is known in North America, is now a global phenomenon, governed by a series of internationally recognized codes and charters. Most countries have embedded these principles into formal heritage protection legislation or accepted heritage management policies.

3.1 Cultural Heritage Management

Tourism is recognized increasingly as a user of heritage, placing greater pressure on all stakeholders to collaborate. The term "cultural heritage management" is used commonly in most jurisdictions, except in the United States, where the terms "cultural resource management" and sometimes "heritage resource stewardship" are used. The use of the word "heritage" instead of "resources" signifies subtle but important differences in meaning. "Resources" imply that the asset being considered has an economic, extrinsic or use value that can be exploited. "Heritage" is a much broader term that recognizes the non-economic, intrinsic and social values of the asset in question. In doing so, it acknowledges further a legacy with certain obligations and responsibilities.

The main goal of CHM is to conserve a representative sample of our tangible and intangible heritage for future generations. This issue is important for two reasons.

First, the speed with which the world is changing is so fast that much of our heritage is at risk of being lost either through its physical destruction or the loss of knowledge. CHM seeks to establish a formal system to identify and conserve this heritage for the future. Equally important, the use of the term "representative sample" acknowledges that not everything can or should be conserved, only the best or most representative of all that has gone before.

People have always produced different kinds of traditions and physical remains, each of which is unique to its era and some of which is non-renewable. There will never be another genuine wreck of the Titanic, Egyptian pyramid, Angkor Watt or peat bog Iron Age burial. They were created under a special set of social, cultural and economic circumstances, which are impossible to replicate. Where a cultural heritage asset is recognized as being of high cultural significance, then it is imperative to maintain it for future generations to observe and understand. While we may not run out of heritage, we may lose certain types altogether or be overwhelmed by others in a way that gives a lop-sided view of a culture or historical period.

Second, what is to be conserved, though, is broad. The focus is often on conserving iconic cultural assets, but a truly representative sample must also include more mundane examples that represent normal daily life, values or traditions. Here, age is less important than knowing the full story, for that it is vital to conserve a representative sample of contemporary assets that are evocative of early twenty-first century life as it will become tomorrow's heritage (for instance, designer handbags and the first smartphones).

Conservation has a different connotation than preservation. While preservation implies keeping something safe from harm or loss, often by hiding it away, conservation implies the wise use of resources. A key element of CHM then is to make conserved heritage accessible physically and intellectually for use, enjoyment and education. As such, cultural heritage managers are expected to plan for a heritage asset's presentation and interpretation as an important part of its ongoing conservation and management. English Heritage (2011) argues that making cultural assets accessible is part of a virtuous cycle of heritage management (Figure 6.2). By enabling people to access heritage, they can then understand its meaning, which in turn, helps them to appreciate its value and why it should be cared for, which in turn helps people enjoy it. And the circle continues.

Good presentation of objects/places means their intrinsic cultural values are interpreted in such a way that all kinds of visitors can understand them. However,

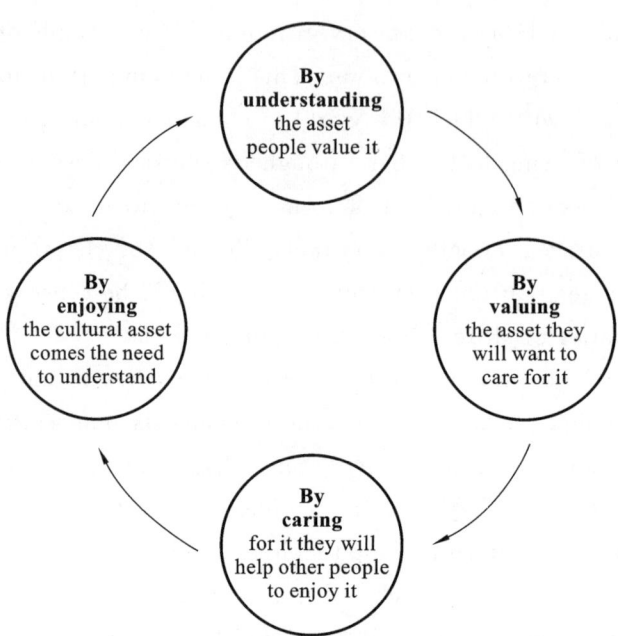

Figure 6.2 The virtuous cycle of cultural heritage management

two critical caveats must be appreciated. First, making things accessible does not necessarily mean free and open access to all. Access must be managed carefully to ensure that the tangible values of the asset are not damaged or the intangible values compromised. Second, a balance between education and entertainment must be achieved. Museums, for example, are predicated on mainly educational objectives, while some heritage theme parks that also see themselves as having a conservation role may focus more on entertainment.

3.1.1 Heritage Varies in Scale, Complexity and Management Challenges

When most non-heritage professionals think of heritage, they tend to think of heritage places, routes and objects, such as old buildings, historic sites, archeological sites and other physical remains. However, intangible heritage, cultural landscapes and traditions that embody such things as folklore, storytelling, practices associated with worship, festivals and other cultural expressions are an equally important element. Different types of cultural tourists want to experience different types of heritage. The casual and incidental cultural tourist and, to a lesser extent, the sightseeing cultural tourist are most interested in consuming tangible heritage experiences. The purposeful and serendipitous cultural tourists, and sometimes the sightseeing cultural tourists, are looking for a more back of house experience and value intangible heritage the most.

Assets can vary in scale and complexity, creating their own unique management challenges. For example, tangible heritage can be as small as a snuffbox collection or near global in scale, as in the case of the Transatlantic Slave Route or the built heritage that comprises the Silk Road. Likewise intangible assets can be as complex as the folklore of 20 ethnic groups in a region or as small as a favorite story told by a storyteller. Importantly as well, the tangible and intangible are intrinsically linked, for the intangible often gives meaning to the tangible, and the tangible often embodies intangible practices.

The conferring of heritage designation represents a form of contemporary recognition of the intrinsic values of these assets and also implies an obligation to manage them for future generations. In some cases, the task is relatively easy, as in the case of museum displays of small items. In other cases, though, the task is incredibly complex, infused with domestic politics and transnational legislation. Whether minority or indigenous cultural heritage is deemed worthy of conserving is an innately political process, while how best to preserve it may lead to conflict between stakeholders. Ideally, tradition bearers should collaborate with archivists, academics or musicologists to contextualize cultural objects in their care or when documenting "living" heritage. Custodians, tradition bearers and local communities should also seek to establish control of the management of particular cultural heritage places and objects, which are closely associated with their intangible heritage by establishing their own site registers, museums and keeping places. How transnational heritage assets are managed may depend on each country's heritage protection legislation, the understanding of the asset's cultural significance, political goodwill, and the way in which human resources can be organized to oversee the implementation of any conservation policy decided upon.

3.1.2 Cultural Heritage Management: an Evolving Framework Influenced by Local Conditions

The practice of CHM is still a relatively new phenomenon—its rules, guidelines and protocols are still evolving. It has been observed that jurisdictions tend to follow a five-phase development comprising inventory, development of initial legislation, increased professionalism, emergence of stakeholder consultation, review and integration of prior practices before maturity is established. This is basically a process where public sector agencies gradually implement more principles and practices to enhance CHM in any particular jurisdiction. It coincides often with the community's desire to conserve heritage, followed by a deeper involvement in decision-making and management. These five phases are shown in Table 6.1 along with supporting sub-indicators of their implementation with the final phase allowing for more integration with other planning and management efforts and a review to enhance particular aspects of the earlier phases.

Table 6.1 Cultural heritage management's evolving framework

Phase	Key features
Inventory	• Growing community interest • Documentation • Evolution from amateurs to professionals conducting work
Initial legislation	• First generation legislation to guide identification and protection of heritage assets • Focus on tangible not intangible heritage • Creation of government heritage agencies • Little integration with other government agencies or laws
Increased professionalism	• Formation of heritage IGOs and NGOs • Formalization of codes of ethics, conservation principles in charters, etc. • Development of related heritage professions (public and private)
Stakeholder consultation	• Emergence of wide array of stakeholders • Areas of conflict identified • More attention paid to community interests
Review	• New understanding of responsibilities • New or revised legislation • More integrated planning and practice • Greater awareness of intangible heritage • Recognition of other users • New paradigm in place • Maturity

Jurisdictions first become involved in this activity when academics, community leaders and politicians begin to recognize the intrinsic value of heritage and see the need to conserve it. This stage often occurs reactively, out of the awareness that important heritage values are being lost. The first step, then, involves nascent attempts to document assets and is often driven by keen amateurs or a small group of heritage professionals. Once the scope of a jurisdiction's assets is recognized, the second stage involves invoking some form of legislation to recognize and conserve them. It may also involve systematically cataloguing the work of enthusiasts and then engaging them further. The creation of formal heritage departments or the establishment of heritage units in other government departments often accompanies this action. Although inventorying of heritage places and cataloguing of objects are important, overemphasis on these actions can mean that long-term conservation objectives are not addressed. Problems can also occur in a heritage planning process when conflicts over use of a cultural asset by different user groups are not anticipated or avoided. CHM must become a process that is both professional and systematic to deal with a diverse range of concerns.

Hence, the next phase reflects increased professionalism in the sector and greater acceptance of this within the local political system. Formal codes of practice and conservation charters are adopted, with countries typically becoming signatories to international charters. Formalizing the management process, rather than just enacting legislation to protect tangible assets, leads to greater professionalism in how assets are identified, how their values are assessed, and how they are managed in the long term. It is at this stage that a wide array of public and private sector heritage professionals, ranging from architects to consulting archaeologists, enter the sector. Similarly, it is often at this stage that universities begin to offer specialist heritage-oriented degree programs. Much of the expertise in these areas only existed in developed Western countries until UNESCO and ICCROM (International Centre for the Study of the Preservation and Restoration of Cultural Property) established the Asian Academy Heritage Management Network in 2005 to encourage more courses and training programs in Asia.

The fourth and fifth stages reflect even greater sophistication of the field. In the fourth stage, instead of being imposed by outsiders, an increased awareness of the involvement of key stakeholders as interested parties and managers or co-managers of assets begins to emerge. More attention is paid to community concerns. Existing legislation has to be modified and a more integrative approach to management needs to be adopted. The fifth and last step recognizes the dynamic nature of heritage management where current practice is reviewed and revised as necessary to ensure that a broader societal good is served. The evolution of specific CHM actions, therefore, coincides with the more general societal and political evolution of the value of culture and ways of managing it. As a result, it is almost impossible to impose the final two evolutionary stages successfully in jurisdictions that have just begun to appreciate the need to conserve their heritage and in which CHM has few links with other stakeholders.

A series of international codes, conventions and charters has been developed by a variety of agencies to ensure jurisdictions adhere to similar principles for the identification and management of heritage. These codes define core heritage philosophy and in doing so influence legislation and subsequent management protocols. Some of the agencies involved in heritage management include:

(1) UNESCO: United Nations Educational, Scientific and Cultural Organization (which began the international focus on heritage with the Convention on the Protection of Cultural Property in the Event of Armed Conflict, 1954);

(2) ICOMOS: International Council on Monuments and Sites (an international

professional organization of heritage professionals concerned mainly with the conservation of tangible heritage assets);

(3) IUCN: International Union for Conservation of Nature;

(4) IATF: Inter-Agency Task Force (for improving risk-preparedness for World Heritage places—a more recent development);

(5) ICCROM: International Centre for the Study of the Preservation and Restoration of Cultural Property (established in Italy by UNESCO in the early 1960s);

(6) ICOM: International Council of Museums (an international professional organization of heritage professionals concerned mainly with museums).

The use of, or adherence to international standards and principles is increasing. One example of such a set of standards is the *Venice Charter* devised during the Second Congress of the Architects and Technicians of Historic Monuments in Venice in 1964 and adopted when the International Council on Monuments and Sites formed in 1965. It has not been amended much over the years, although two new principles were added in 2003. Recently, it has been used in combination with other charters or declarations. The key features of the *Venice Charter* spell out the principles behind best practice (as it was understood at the time) and a set of standard definitions of terms for the conservation and restoration of monuments and sites, particularly in relation to:

(1) historic buildings (extended now to groups of buildings);

(2) conservation (restrictions on modification);

(3) restoration with authenticity in mind (no reconstruction);

(4) archaeological investigation to be professionalized;

(5) documentation (any action should be documented systematically and a public record kept).

Other international organizations besides ICOMOS have charters that form the basis of constitutions (e. g. ICOM's Code of Ethics was adopted in 1986; ICOM 2014a). The influence these articles have at the local level can guide the professionalism phase in the development of CHM in each member State (Party) chapter of these international organizations. How well they use these charters and codes in debates over the direction of heritage management and tourism development also varies.

What makes a difference in every jurisdiction is how much general support these codes and charters have from the public sector agencies and how much these documents provide support for the views of professional heritage managers. The phase of increased stakeholder consultation (Table 6.1) is extremely important in the development of every CHM tradition, because this is where heritage professionals first have their views challenged by the community and learn how to share power (if they have any) with them over the cultural assets being managed.

3.2 Management Challenges

The management of cultural heritage assets can be complicated by a number of exogenous factors. To begin, it is much easier to achieve consensus when there is a single overriding agency responsible for the entire site, but becomes increasingly difficult where there are multiple agencies or where no single formal agency exists. Land tenure arrangements also complicate the management challenge. The Hadrian's Wall WHS in the UK is, perhaps, an exceptional case. Here, the majority of the site is in private ownership, as is most of the buffer zone around it. According to its most recent management plan (UNESCO, 2007), a considerable number of bodies own and manage approximately 10 percent of the site specifically for conservation and access, while the rest consists of medium to large estates, owner occupied farms and residential and commercial lots in urban areas. A number of trusts have some involvement in the site, along with eight local authorities, English Heritage and other groups. Tourism and economic development roles, plus a large number of central government agencies and departments all share some responsibility for site management, creating a significant management challenge to address the needs of multiple stakeholders with differing levels of influence and often holding competing views.

Revenue generation and allocation are issues that receive less attention. Heritage assets rarely receive much of the revenue generated from tourism. If the asset is run by government agencies, income goes into "consolidated revenues" in much the same way as income or sales tax. It is then redistributed at the government's will for whatever purposes it sees fit. Income from tourism sites is seen as a profit generator, where the income generated exceeds the expenses incurred. If it is a public asset that is managed by a private firm under a management contract, then the firm normally agrees to pay a flat fee or a percentage of sales back to the lead agency and retain excess income. In some cases, sites are licensed to private firms, as happens in some developing economies.

3.3 World Heritage

World Heritage represents a unique form of cultural heritage. WHS are recognized as having outstanding universal value to humanity. Designation is prized, for it represents an "International Top Tourism Brand" that places destinations among the pantheon of other world-class destinations. It is for this reason that designation can act as a focal point for national marketing campaigns. While tourism is often the motive behind the pursuit of World Heritage status, tourism potential is not one of the criteria used to identify prospective sites. This duality creates a range of challenges.

The "Convention Concerning the Protection of the World's Cultural and Natural

Heritage", more commonly referred to as the "World Heritage Convention" was approved by UNESCO in 1972 and adopted formally in 1976. The objectives of the Convention are to encourage the identification, protection and preservation of cultural heritage properties which "because of their exceptional qualities, can be considered to be of 'Outstanding Universal Value' and as such worthy of special protection against the dangers which increasingly threaten them". It achieves this goal by encouraging countries to sign the Convention, nominate sites for inclusion, establish management plans and set up reporting systems for sites, assist countries to safeguard WHS by providing technical assistance and professional training, provide emergency assistance for WHS in immediate danger, support public awareness-building activities, encourage participation of the local population in the preservation of their cultural and natural heritage, and promote international cooperation in the conservation of our world's cultural and natural heritage. Over the years, the convention has stayed close to its original promise, although it has been modified from time to time. For example, new heritage categories such as cultural landscapes have been added, revisions have been made to national and international guidelines, changes to the implementation guidelines were introduced, and more emphasis was placed on partnerships with a broader range of stakeholders.

4. Operational Management of Cultural and Heritage Sites

History, culture and religion constitute significant elements of tourism. Millions of tourists in any one year visit historic centers, temples and places of unique cultural value. Many of these major cultural attractions are located in close proximity to, or within, large urban centers. In general terms, this could be considered as "mass tourism", which reflects the high numbers of visitors to cultural and heritage sites; often for little more than a short stay or brief excursion. This pattern of visitation creates pressures that need to be managed effectively, taking into consideration the visitor's experience and the capacity of local systems to support such pressures. These two areas are explored below. The constraints of space preclude detailed analysis of the varied forms of cultural tourism and associated sites; to an extent this is well illustrated by the cases encompassed within this text. The approach taken is to focus more on those generic aspects of operational management that may vary according to the type, or more appropriately perhaps, the site, of cultural attraction. In the process, the aim is to highlight key issues and potential management responses.

4.1 Site Typology and Characteristics

Any typology of cultural tourism destinations or attractions will be both diverse and potentially very extensive depending on the degree of categorization used and the level of detail required. However, in this context, a broad approach is adopted based on three general categories, namely, historic towns and cities, ancient and historic sites and festivals. In terms of tourism, the operational management of these sites has

to address similar opportunities and challenges, but their significance will vary according to the characteristics specific to a particular category and thus the management planning and development of the site will vary in approach.

4.1.1 Historic Towns and Cities

Tourists are attracted to historic towns and cities for diverse reasons; for example, the built heritage, cultural traditions and events, and the urban amenities. Furthermore, a city may offer widespread attractions and create new ones through urban regeneration to promote tourism and encourage the wider dispersal of tourists. This is well illustrated by Barcelona's Port Vell, where a former "harbor arm" has been transformed into a tourist destination. Each year they receive a large proportion of the world's tourist flows. These visitor destinations are often densely populated, the home of vibrant communities and centers of activity and transport hubs. Major cities may have the infrastructure to absorb high-volume tourism, coupled with transport systems generally able to deliver people into the heart or other parts of the city. Conversely, in small historic towns a concentration of tourists can lead to environmental management problems such as congestion, noise and pollution. Tourist flows into these areas can impact on the general day-to-day functions, creating conflicts between tourism and the dynamics of the city, threatening both tourism development and the socioeconomic structure of the settlement. Thus, tourism may engender conflicts between visitors and the local population and impact on urban management capability and urban structure. The management of these conflicts becomes of the utmost importance to ensure the conservation of these sites along with their socioeconomic development, in which tourism can play as significant role.

4.1.2 Archaeological Sites, Monuments and Temples

This type of cultural tourism attraction evidences a diverse range of sites. They may be isolated (e. g. Stonehenge) or within a wider site (e. g. the Acropolis in Athens or Temple Mayor in Mexico), in private or public ownership, and may or may not charge an entrance fee. Visitor numbers vary with their importance and historical recognition as well as in terms of scale and accessibility.

4.1.3 Festivals

Festivals are characterized by the arrival of visitors in a defined period, generally in a restricted area, to participate in an event of a particular nature. They range in scale from a local community gala drawing relatively few visitors, through concerts and theatre festivals, to religious events such as the Maria festival in Coto Doñana, and art festivals, e. g. Biennale, Cannes, which may attract many thousands of visitors. They can be one-off events or more regular, e. g. annual. The staging of festivals needs to be compatible with site preservation and protection and with respect for the aesthetic, historical and scientific integrity of the place by following existing regulations for the site or establishing and applying site-specific regulations.

4.2 The Visitor's Experience

Visitor's satisfaction depends on a diverse range of factors, from the site of interest and the quality of services provided to the facilities available and, indeed, the number of visitors. The visitor's experience and satisfaction also depend on personal expectations and the anticipated outcomes of the visit. As such, there are potentially variable visitor's needs and requirements, which create different management opportunities; for example, the management of a particular site on the basis of their philosophy and objectives may decide to satisfy the expectations of some particular categories of visitors, while denying satisfying other groups' expectations. Hence, a knowledge and understanding of visitor's profiles, preferences and needs is invaluable in the setting of objectives for the infrastructure, staffing needs and education and interpretation programs of the site. These aspects, along with the characteristics and assets of the site, will influence the visitor's experience. While the expectations of the visitor are often related to the importance of the site, there are several more widely applicable factors that are generic to all cultural attractions, such as management planning and development, access and assets; all of which can contribute to enriching the visitor's experience or fall short of his or her expectations. Furthermore, the general condition of the site and thus maintenance and cleanliness of the site, facilities and services will contribute to perceptions of the site's management and organization, and to making the visit a more enjoyable experience. The adoption of best practice in these areas is axiomatic. Therefore, the operational aspects attended to here are heritage interpretation and education, facilities and services, followed by a consideration of wider, more general factors.

4.2.1 Heritage Interpretation and Education

Heritage interpretation and education programs are an important part of any visitor management plan. These programs should communicate particular themes and ideas that accord with the aims of the general visitor management plan. To evaluate the success of visitor interpretation and education programs, visitor surveys should be conducted periodically to assess visitor satisfaction and provide input for readjusting the visitor management plan.

To be highly effective, a variety of media for site interpretation and education should be chosen with the intention of International Cultural Tourism: management, implications and cases making the visit as enjoyable and informative as possible. Due consideration should be given to the needs of different categories of visitor, e. g. scholars, schoolchildren and the general public, as well as providing information in different languages according to the provenance of the major visitor markets. Signage should be complementary to interpretation, possibly integrated at times where appropriate. It should be well designed and positioned with clear panels (possibly using internationally recognized symbols and colors) and, as necessary, in more than one language. Outdoor panels should also be specifically designed to be weather and vandal resistant. Due consideration should be given to people with special needs in terms of physical access to and around the site, as well as to information and with respect to potential difficulties.

Major cultural attractions often have a reception and visitor orientation center designed to introduce the visitors to the site, its significance, major aspects and so forth; and what it offers to visitors in terms of experiencing the site. This is usually the first and main point of visitor contact and thus it is vital that staff are polite, informed and willing to help visitors. Special exhibits can add value to a visit, enhancing the visitor's experience and their understanding of the attraction. Thus, an exhibit should attract the visitor's attention, avoid tediousness and emphasize the most interesting aspects. Special exhibits for less able persons, for example, poorly sighted and blind people, should be created with more attention to narration to inform and aid their understanding. Complementary to the above methods is the availability of guides who can enrich the visitor's experience (or conversely make a visit boring and tedious); thus, their knowledge and skills are very important. For this reason they need to be carefully selected, trained, motivated, monitored and regularly evaluated. Guided tours should also be specifically orientated to the needs of different groups, e.g. scholars, school children and members of local history societies.

4.2.2 Facilities and Services

It is essential for any site receiving significant numbers of visitors to address their needs through the provision of the necessary facilities and services. The planning and development of facilities and services needs to be well thought through, as undue "commercialization" will detract from the conservation and presentation of the site features and overall aesthetics. The conservation of the historic fabric and character and authenticity of the site (the locale) are thus seen as influences on visitors' expectations. Operational plans should therefore aim to anticipate and preempt problems. In many cases these services, such as hospitality operations, provide invaluable revenue flows; therefore, to maximize the benefits they should be of good quality with attentive customer services. Within this context, the management should adopt and promote environmentally friendly practices and encourage visitors to act accordingly. Thus, there should be a clear environmental policy and environmental management system in place, an approach that could also be part of the marketing strategy.

4.2.3 Wider Factors

All sites attractive to cultural tourists, irrespective of type of location, will be influenced by the degree of access, the quality of the surroundings and the general environment. These wider factors should be carefully considered by the management

team and, as necessary, through liaison with the appropriate authorities. Accessibility should be carefully planned to avoid traffic and pollution problems in areas around the site, ensuring comfortable access but with due regard to the impact of infrastructural development on the visual amenity of the location. The use of well-planned "park and ride" facilities may be advantageous in avoiding congestion around the site, on major routes or in urban centers. Such an approach may help to ameliorate traffic problems during peak visitor periods, at which point members of the local community may become annoyed by the extensive International Cultural Tourism: managements, implications and cases presence of visitors using "their resources", potentially leading to hostility towards visitors. The volume and diversity of visitors that many sites attract require attention to be paid to the quantity and type of accommodation and hospitality services available, the actual and potential demand with regard to the capacity of the locale and environment and, overall, the visual impact. Attention must be paid to public amenities such as toilets, drinking water, environmental health and safety, and emergency medical services. Consideration should be given to availability and capacity levels in the context of visitor numbers and duration of stay and in the case of litter disposal, for example, strategically positioned collection points, which are not unduly invasive.

4.3 Problems Arising From Visitors to the Site

The actual and potential problems arising from visitors can be broadly categorized into the following three areas. However, it should be noted that despite such problems, it is generally recognized that tourism also has a positive impact on the local economy and employment.

4.3.1 Urban Management Capability

One of the most common problems around or at cultural sites attracting many visitors arriving by car or coach is traffic, congestion and associated problems, e.g. noise and air pollution. Furthermore, the local infrastructure and amenities may not have the capacity to deal with high visitor numbers, such as found during peak periods. This can lead to dysfunction of those systems, creating environmental problems and conflicts with local users that can be especially evident with events attracting many people. This can also lead to associated problems such as litter and damage to the physical environment and overload on public amenities. Allied with this is the impact on the visual amenity of historic towns and the setting of individual sites through the uncontrolled development of tourism services and facilities that may be visually intrusive. This may lead to the alteration of urban fabric and the architectural character of a site or historic town or city, damaging in this way the identity of the locale—the sense of place.

Conversely, a tourism development policy may lead to improvement in infrastructure and services to deal with increased numbers of people due to tourist arrivals.

4.3.2 The Site

Too many visitors at any one time can lead to queues at access points or bottlenecks at interpretation displays, overwhelm exhibitions, and block the flow of visitors or the view of smaller groups or individuals, thereby negatively influencing the visitor's experience. Visitors cause wear and tear on buildings and monuments through intensive use and are also associated with vandalism, leading to further damage of the site and environment, and overall to potential deterioration of the site. This can be especially evident in enclosed interior places, where major humidity and temperature fluctuations related to tourist flows may damage irreversibly materials and finishes. Archaeological sites and historic buildings are particularly vulnerable to souvenir collectors, who remove bits and pieces of historic fabric as first-hand souvenirs of their visit. At Westminster Abbey, for example, where there are as many as 16000 visitors at peak times, pieces of statues have been removed and fragments taken from mosaics.

4.3.3 Local Community

Pressure arising from visitors may negatively affect the quality of life of residents, owing to pollution, noise and litter, or increased costs of living and property prices. Furthermore, tourists may compete with residents for the use of facilities and infrastructure, and increase crowding, inducing irritation of the local population, which may affect the visitor's experience, possibly damaging the destination's image and consequently tourism in the longer term. Social conflicts also arise as a result of the crowding-out phenomenon leading to a tourism monoculture: witness Venice or Bruges. In such situations tourism may come to dominate urban society, leading to higher prices for centrally located land, diminishing the attractiveness of the city for families and firms because of congestion and pollution, and thereby causing the displacement of other activities and functions from the center to the outskirts. Within the context of the scale of the festival, visitor flows may create overcrowding, overwhelm services and the infrastructure, causing conflicts with the local community. However, it is recognized that these events can bring positive economic benefits (e. g. supply of goods, employment opportunities) and make a contribution to revitalizing small, isolated and declining communities. On a larger scale, they can serve to International Cultural Tourism: managements, implications and cases promote cultural events to and for the community whilst also acting as a promotional tool for a city.

4.4 Management Responses

To facilitate discussion and aid clarification the following management responses to actual and potential problems identified are presented in the context of the three broad categories of site used earlier. However, this is not to be taken that the responses presented are mutually exclusive.

4.4.1 Historic Towns and Cities

The management of historic towns and cities is often fragmented among various local and national agencies that control the various aspects of their functions: public services, utilities, etc. The only adequate methodology for managing tourism in such destinations is through a planning process that seeks to ensure cooperation and coordination among all involved agencies. To be effective this process should encompass the following fundamental elements.

(1) Integration in planning process and institutional context.

The process of planning for tourism can provide a general framework to guide the local community, planners and decision makers. This framework consists of principles, goals, objectives and policy measures in regard to tourist development in an area on the basis of the area's distinctive characteristic sand features, respecting local capacities to sustain tourism. Setting limits for sustaining tourism activity in a place involves a vision about local development and decisions about managing tourism, which should be made with the participation of all major actors and the community at large.

(2) Establishing a process of concerted action.

Any tourism management program should work in concert with all stakeholders and interested parties, including government agencies, local communities, non-governmental organizations, developers and tourism businesses. Their participation in the planning and management process is of utmost importance to identify common interests. An agreement on the goals of tourism development will be necessary. Through dialogue International Cultural Tourism: managements, implications and cases and collaboration, site managers and planners may better understand various stakeholders' positions regarding tourism issues and activities that could have an impact on a site. Stakeholders can inform managers about easily misunderstood local cultural differences, help to identify problem areas that may have been overlooked by experts, or provide useful inputs regarding desired conditions at a site, and may better support the implementation of envisaged measures.

4.4.2 Archaeological Sites, Monuments and Temples

In comparison with historic towns and cities, owing to the complexity of their urban situation, site-specific cultural attractions, in general, are more easily managed as they cover a limited and well-defined area. The site itself may be the responsibility of a single management agency and thus under more direct control. Potentially, the major problem for popular sites is that of too many arrivals at the same time or too many visitors in one period. Visitor management tools that can be applied in response to such potential problems primarily aim at reducing congestion and peak time demand. A booking system limiting the number of visitors accessing the site, or a policy aiming at spreading the visitors over space and time, may help to reduce crowding level at a site. Reducing potential queuing at entry points may also be aided by introducing an advanced reservation system to enable groups, in particular, to pre-book, e. g. as practiced for the exhibitions at Palazzo Grassi in Venice. Subject to a well-defined entrance to the site, it is potentially possible to limit the number of visitors admitted in any given period. However, this can create problems elsewhere if not carefully managed and promoted. A more appropriate method, where practical, is to scale entrance fees on the basis of temporal demand (by time of day, by day and by week/month), thereby aiming to smooth peaks and troughs while seeking to maximize revenues and at the same time visitor satisfaction. As regards crowd behavior, suitably designed educational programs, presented within the context of interpretation and presentation of the site, can mitigate visitor impacts by informing visitors on how best to conduct themselves both at the site and with respect to other visitors present.

4.4.3 Festivals

Apart from the specific tasks relating to concept, design and delivery of a festival, the management needs to address all the operational management of cultural and heritage sites' potential problems that may arise in terms of visitors as noted above. Thus, the specific hours of access and departure, projected visitor numbers, crowd control procedures, security and sanitation provisions, insurance requirements, restrictions on the types and locations of temporary structures (e. g. stands and tents), and allowance for placement of sponsor and advertising signs associated with the event all need to be planned. The site itself may require additional attention to safety standards, pathways and so forth depending on anticipated demand and weather conditions. Subject to projected demand, the necessary amenities (rubbish bins, toilets, seating, etc.) will need to be in place.

Possibly the most useful tool available to the event management is that of information management. Ensuring public awareness and forewarning the local community of actual and potential problems, such as along routes to the site, travel times and availability of public transport, any special arrangements and the possibility of noise, e. g. music or fireworks, will all contribute to pre-empting problems. At large festivals and events, crowding represents a characteristic element; many visitors may well expect this in advance of their visit and thus do not experience the same feeling of being crowded as they might in other situations. Even so, management planning should aim to reduce the associated problems likely to arise, such as long queues and access to facilities.

Ⅳ Case Study

The Cold Reality of Cultural Tourism in the Antarctic

While Antarctica may not be seen by many as a destination for cultural tourism, Spennemann (2007) classifies it as a remote heritage area. Documenting the evolution of "tourism" in the Antarctic, he points out that initial visitations were largely scientific until commercial tourism commenced in December 1956 with a LAN Chile DC-6 conducting an overflight tour. In 1958 the first ship-based tours, out of Chile and Argentina, began. By 1969, purpose-built cruise ships visited the waters. Between 1977 and 1980, commercial airlines out of New Zealand and Australia conducted low-level "flight-seeing" tours, taking some 11000 tourists over the area in 44 flights. By the late 1980s, ship-based tours were mounted to the edge of the pack-ice and landing tourists.

Policy development for Antarctica is developed through the Antarctic Treaty System (ATS) or via methods of self-regulation, such as through the International Association of Antarctic Tour Operators (IAATO), and to date all tourism activities have been assessed as having a minor and transitory impact or lower. However, there are two problems in this assessment: the investigations (Environmental Impact Assessments, EIA) are being undertaken by the tourist operators themselves; and no tourist activity has yet to complete a Comprehensive Environmental Evaluation (CEE), the highest level of EIA under the treaty system.

The extant evaluation criteria for activity in Antarctica are vague and, in addition, based on one-off events rather than considering the cumulative impact of activity. Thus, regular visits to a single site are only evaluated as individual occurrences. This is because the current structure is developed around managing the activities of state science programs and is ill-equipped to deal with the impacts of tourism. The implication is that a single tourist cruise can fall well below the environmental capacity of the environment (in terms of pollutants and stress on wildlife) and thus be legitimately allowed under the system. However, because there is a series of these cruises, each below the crucial limits individually, the cumulative impacts may be greater.

France and the UK have put forward a number of working papers to develop a vision and structure for managing tourism, however many of the proposals are not designed as policy instruments but non-mandatory and aspirational tools towards the management of Antarctic tourism. There are some suggestions (O'Brien, 2009) that tourism in Antarctica could/should be regulated according to a "precautionary approach", similar to that of mining (i.e. limited or banned). However, the precautionary position has not advanced far beyond discussion because of the difficulty in linking specific impacts to tourism, even conceptually.

In a destination where international diplomacy is at its most sensitive, policies and agreements by governments about the management of tourism will be slow to develop. In the meantime, the IAATO states that "In more than 40 years of organized tourism to the continent… no discernible impact has been observed" (2012). Furthermore, they position managed visitations to the continent as a positive tool both for conservation and as a cultural tool for international peace and harmony: Tourism is and should continue to be a driving force in Antarctic conservation. Firsthand travel experiences foster education and understanding, with visitors from all over the world—representing more than 100 different nationalities during the 2011-2012 season alone—returning home from Antarctica as ambassadors of goodwill, guardianship and peace for the destination they have visited.

From this case, we can conclude that examining culture, tourism and cultural tourism reveals a complex and convoluted set of philosophies from a policy perspective. Both culture and tourism are often misunderstood, under-valued and neglected, and this can be magnified even more when the two spheres combine under cultural tourism. However, the new global reality of recessionary times, and the need to think outside the "industrial box", has led various territories and regions to realize the true worth of exploring their culture and heritage, and often this is operationalized via tourism. Many regions (as illustrated throughout this book), are exploring tools such as urban (re)generation, tourism development and community enhancement, with culture as a main focal point.

 V Tips

Build a Story around the Cultural Tourism Asset
—William J. Clinton Presidential Library and Museum

Why is it important to talk about experience creation rather than interpretation of cultural values? Interpretation has not become any less important, but it forms just one aspect of the total experience delivered to the visitor. Hopefully that experience is special enough for messages about cultural values to have been conveyed, creating the opportunity for further self-reflection after the visit. It has been suggested that creating an overall favorable experience and engaging visitors with educational/thought provoking messages is achieved through the provision of a series of positive micro-experiences from the beginning to the end of the visit (Law 1999). Brett (1999)

indicates micro-experiences that add up to a "Golden Memory" should be a key objective in planning and management frameworks. Hence, service encounters, the nature of facilities and their management, ambience, lighting, personal comfort and safety, and so on all play a role in visitor engagement. Tactics that take into account the nature of visitor experience, as well as an understanding of basic human nature, are more likely to be successful with tourists.

Alternatively, if the asset does not have the potential to be mythologized, yet is interesting nonetheless, it is possible to build a story around it that will make a visit enjoyable. The story may be based on historic fact or may be based on a fictional character known from popular culture. It matters little, just as long as it is a good enduring story. One attraction that presents a particular narrative about a married couple in politics that want to leave a certain kind of legacy is the William J. Clinton Presidential Library and Museum, Little Rock, Arkansas(Figure 6.3). The library and museum are part of a tradition of valorizing American presidents with titular cultural facilities as a service to history, the community and mostly domestic tourism. The library has temporary exhibitions on a range of political topics or more personal topics (e.g. presidential pets), as well as the permanent exhibition on the Clintons that includes a reconstruction of the Oval Office in the White House and a display of political memorabilia. The basic story told about the couple is very different from what appeared in popular media during the Clinton presidency, and is popular with pro-democrat visitors, with some aspects that even appeal to children. Hence, the narrative tries to incorporate some informal as well as formal moments from the presidency in the experience.

Figure 6.3　Reproduction Oval Office, William J. Clinton Presidential Library and Museum, Little Rock, Arkansas, USA

Ⅵ Dialogue

➢ Conversation 1

(The Museum guide Ben introduces exhibits to the visitor Sally.)

Ben: Good morning, I am your guide and my name is Ben. Welcome to our museum with a remarkable range of exhibits.

Sally: Good morning, Ben. It's my last day in this city and I decided to visit the museum. No matter where I travel, museum is the place I will definitely visit. I can't wait to see what you have there.

Ben: Well, for one thing, we have a fine collection of twentieth and twenty-first century paintings, many by very well-known artists.

Sally: I could even recognize several of the paintings!

Ben: Because this is the most popular gallery that attracts the largest number of visitors, it's best to go in early in the day, before the crowds arrive. Then there are the nineteenth-century paintings. The museum was opened in the middle of that century, and several of the artists each donated one work—to get the museum started, as it were. So they're of special interest to us—we feel closer to them than to other works.

Sally: Wow, that's why I'm so into visiting museums. I hope to learn about the local history, culture and customs of tourist destinations.

Ben: Yeah, people tend to pay more attention to cultural and historical factors in traveling. Let's see "Around the world"—a temporary exhibition. It's created a great deal of interest, because it presents objects from every continent and many countries, and provides information about their social context—why they were made, who for, and so on.

Sally: Let me take some photos of these fantastic exhibits!

➢ Conversation 2

(Sam and Bob are talking about putting restrictions on the tourists who visit to protect the cultural atmosphere.)

Sam: Many of us have more leisure time, and the cost of travelling has become relatively cheaper.

Rob: But here lies the problem. The places we're visiting are becoming more crowded, sometimes spoiling the atmosphere and the beauty—the things we came to see in the first place!

Sam: This is why we're going to discuss how some cities around the world are putting restrictions on the tourists who visit.

Rob: well I would like to talk about Italy, famous for its Colosseum, Trevi Fountain and many other things. The authorities in the city fear that some tourists are showing disrespect to the city and have introduced laws to clampdown on certain behavior.

Sam: I heard that new rules have been introduced to make sure that tourists do not misbehave when they are visiting tourist attractions in Rome.

Rob: Romans don't like to see tourists walking around bare-chested, they don't like to see them wading in their fountains.

Sam: So really the objective is to improve the life of the city for residents and for tourists themselves.

Rob: And to stop tourists misbehaving—that's doing bad or inappropriate things. I'm sure not all visitors misbehave.

Sam: I'm sure not all visitors misbehave—but those who have been, have been wading—that's walking through water—in the famous fountains and men have not been covering up the top half of their bodies—so, going bare-chested.

Rob: Right. These people could destroy the cultural atmosphere of Rome. Many people travel to experience different cultures and misbehaving could affect their experience.

Sam: Not any more, Rob!

Ⅶ Academic Thinking

Community-Based Cultural Tourism: Issues, Threats and Opportunities

Author: Noel B. Salazar

Journal: *Journal of Sustainable Tourism*

Abstract:

Using examples from long-term anthropological fieldwork in Tanzania, this paper critically analyzes how well generally accepted community-based tourism discourses resonate with the reality on the ground. It focuses on how local guides handle their role as ambassadors of communal cultural heritage and how community members react to their narratives and practices. It pays special attention to the time-limited, project-based development method, the need for an effective exit strategy, for quality control, tour guide training and long-term tour guide retention. The study is based on a program funded by the Netherlands-based development agency, Stichting Nederlandse Vrijwilligers (SNV), from 1995 to 2001, and on post-program experiences. Findings reveal multiple complex issues of power and resistance that illustrate many community-based tourism conflicts. The encounter with the "Other" is shown to be central and that the role of professional intermediaries in facilitating this experience of cultural contact is crucial. Tour guides are often the only "locals" with whom tourists spend considerable time: They have considerable agency in the image-building process of the peoples and places visited, (re)shaping tourist destination images and indirectly influencing the self-image of those visited too. The paper provides ideas for overcoming the issues and problems described.

社区文化旅游:问题、威胁与机遇

本文使用来自坦桑尼亚长期人类学田野调查的实例,批判性地分析了人们普遍接受的以社区为基础的旅游业话语与当地现实的共鸣。它着重于分析当地向导如何处理其作为社区文化遗产的"代言人"的角色,以及社区成员如何对他们的叙述和做法做出反馈。它特别关注基于时间和项目的开发方法,有效的退出策略,质量控制、导游培训和长期导游保留的需求。这项研究基于荷兰发展机构 Stichting Nederlandse Vrijwilligers(SNV)从 1995 年到 2001 年资助的一项计划,以及该计划的后期经验。调查结果揭示了许多复杂的权力和抵抗力问题,这些问题说明了许多基于社区的旅游冲突。与"其他"的接触被证明是至关重要的,而且专业中介人在促进这种文化接触经验方面的作用至关重要。导游通常是唯一与游客在一起的"本地人",他们会花费大量的时间:他们在所访问的人民和地方的形象塑造过程中具有重要的作用,(重新)塑造旅游目的地形象并间接影响所访问者的自我形象认知。

Ⅷ Questions

1. What decide the market appeal of tourism products?
2. How to understand the relationship between cultural heritage attractions and tourism?
3. How to correctly handle the opinions of stakeholders in the process of cultural heritage protection and utilization?
4. What role do social networking sites play in tourism?

Ⅸ Key Words and Terms

AM (Arts Management)	艺术管理
AMO (Antiquities and Monuments Office)	文物古迹管理办公室
BBC (British Broadcasting Corporation)	英国广播公司
CHM (Cultural Heritage Management)	文化遗产管理
CM (Cultural Management)	文化管理
DEA (Department of Environment Australia)	澳大利亚环境部

扫码看答案

DMO (Destination Management Organization) 目的地营销组织
EIA (Environmental Impact Assessment) 环境影响评估
HUL (Historic Urban Landscape) 历史城市景观
IATF (Inter-Agency Task Force) 机构间特别工作小组
ICCROM (International Centre for the Study of the Preservation and Restoration of Cultural Property) 国际文化财产保护与修复研究中心
ICH (Intangible Cultural Heritage) 非物质文化遗产
ICOM (International Council of Museums) 国际博物馆协会
ICOMOS (International Council on Monuments and Sites) 国际古迹遗址理事会
IFACCA (International Federation of Arts Councils and Culture Agencies) 国际艺术委员会和文化机构联合会
IGO (Intergovernmental Organizations) 政府间组织
IUCN (International Union for Conservation of Nature) 世界自然保护联盟
IVE (Immersive Virtual Environment) 沉浸式虚拟环境
MOS (Museum of Sydney) 悉尼博物馆
NEA (National Endowment for the Arts) 国家艺术基金会
NGO (Non-Governmental Organization) 非政府组织
NHA (National Heritage Area) 国家文化遗产保护区
New Orleans Jazz & Heritage Festival 新奥尔良爵士乐和文化遗产节
SAR (Special Administrative Region) 特别行政区
UNESCO (United Nations Educational, Scientific and Cultural Organization) 联合国教育、科学及文化组织
UNWTO (World Tourism Organization) 联合国世界旅游组织
WHC (World Heritage Centre) 世界遗产中心
WHC (World Heritage Committee) 世界遗产委员会
WHS (World Heritage Site) 世界遗产
WTTC (World Travel & Tourism Council) 世界旅行和旅游理事会

X Single Choice Questions

Chapter 7
Sustainable Tourism

I Chapter Introduction

The purpose of this chapter is to introduce the sustainable tourism, sustainability is about providing what is needed for something or someone to exist and continue in the future. The growing importance of tourism as a socioeconomic phenomenon, together with the understanding that even apparently profitable tourism firms and destinations endowed originally with the best natural and cultural assets cannot survive the escalating international competition without good managerial practices (Crouch, 2011), has provided a significant momentum for the development of tourism management as a discipline over the last thirty-five years.

Creating sustainable tourism operations is more than just words; it requires action and commitment. Sustainable tourism has taken the lead from work done in sustainable development. As early as 1987, the World Commission on Environment and Development (WCED) defined sustainable development as "meeting the needs of the present without compromising the ability of future generations to meet their own needs". Borrowing from this philosophy, in 1993 the World Tourism Organization, defined sustainable tourism as "meeting the needs of present tourists and host regions while protecting and enhancing opportunity for the future". Destinations and individual tourism businesses are learning to accept that to be sustainable, success must be measured by finding a balance of making a profit while protecting natural and cultural resources so that decisions today do not adversely affect the success of future generations.

II Chapter Objectives

After you have read this chapter, you should be able to:
1. Explain origins and definitions of sustainable tourism.

2. Explain how ecotourism differs from mass tourism.

3. Explain how tourism service providers can fulfill the principles of ecotourism.

4. Describe the benefits that may be achieved through the use of ecotourism practices.

5. Understanding the sustainability of future tourism.

6. Thinking why it is so difficult for tourism service suppliers to achieve sustainable operations.

Ⅲ Reading

1. Sustainable Tourism: Origins and Definitions

The concept of sustainable tourism emerged in the early 1990s. According to Bramwell and Lane (1993) it is defined as "an economic development model conceived to improve the quality of life for the local community, and to facilitate for the visitor a high-quality experience of the environment, which both the host community and the visitors depend on". It was inspired by the already existing concept of sustainable development that emerged in the mid-1980s as a result of increasing interest in environmental protection, and increasing awareness of existing ecological problems. The concept of sustainable development was introduced in *Our Common Future*, also known as the Brundtl and Report, by WCED (1987) and defined thus: Sustainable development is development that meets the needs of the present without compromising the ability of future generations to meet their own needs. It contains within it two key concepts:

(1) The concept of needs, in particular the essential needs of the world's poor, to which overriding priority should be given.

(2) The idea of limitations imposed by the state of technology and social organization on the environments ability to meet present and future needs.

Since the Brundtl and Report, numerous studies of various industries have considered the importance of environmental and ecological variables. Well-known examples are related to: energy production, water management, waste management and recycling, agriculture, among others. Some authors propose general equilibrium models and environmental variables, such as mega models (Hoeller, 1991), and study issues linked to current environmental problems. These models differ from the traditional general equilibrium models by including previously omitted variables such as natural resources, technical progress and demography (Beauma and Schubert, 1994). They describe the interactions between the environment and the economy generally in relation to energy use/saving. Making an important distinction between standard and "green" products, produced respectively by standard (creating solid final wastes unemployable in any other production), and sustainable sectors (clean production resulting in no waste).

2. When Is Tourism Too Much of a Good Thing?

The costs of tourism, especially it's environmental, social and cultural costs, have led many destination residents and tourists alike to become disillusioned with mass tourism. Concerns about mass tourism; the rise of large numbers of working and middle-class travelers; have all add to critics' lament about the continued growth of tourism as they see problems of this growth resulting in:

(1) the architectural pollution of tourist strips;

(2) the herding of tourists as if they were cattle;

(3) the disruption of traditional cultural events and occupations;

(4) the diminished natural environment and beauty of the area;

(5) the low priority paid to local needs with funds used instead to increase tourism amenities to keep the community competitive in the marketplace.

Mass tourism tends to emphasize profit and sacrifice the planet and people resources. The conveniences demanded by mass tourists can strain the environment through the development of more and more infrastructure and superstructure and the increasing wear and tear from the presence and actions of more and more tourists.

2.1 Planet

This boom in tourism has given rise to millions of new jobs and increased economic prosperity in countries across the world, tourism can usher in problems along with economic benefits. The millions of additional tourists have strained the resources of many destinations, sometimes straining natural resources to the point where the initial appeal of an area is diminished and visitation to it declines. Table 7.1 provides one tourism expert's idea of the stages that a destination may go through from beginning to decline. It is important to note that not all destinations decline. If tourism managers are closely monitoring the area's performance, it is possible to anticipate the need to change and enter a phase of rejuvenation before the decline stage begins. Often, rejuvenation is associated with the reallocation of resources, introducing new technologies, or finding a way to reinvent the destination to better meet the needs of existing target markets or develop products and services for new target markets. As tourism numbers have increased, questions about future sustainability of these activities have grown.

Some issues are easier to anticipate and mitigate than others. Climate change is incredibly complex and possibly the greatest impending threat to global tourism. While the existence of climate change may have been debated in popular media, the scientific community agrees that anthropogenic climate change is occurring. This means that although the Earth has experienced natural fluctuations in temperatures in the past, human activity (including greenhouse gas emissions) is now contributing to unprecedented shifts in weather patterns. What does this mean for tourism? Many tourism activities are based on seasonal climates: skiing in the winter, hiking amongst wildflowers in the spring, surfing in the summer, and watching the leaves change color in the fall. These are examples of the many tourist attractions based on existing climate patterns. Think about how many trips you have taken recently that were dependent on certain weather conditions.

Table 7.1 Stages of tourism development

Exploration stage	... small number of visitors discovers the destination area
Involvement stage	... number of visitors increases; more host community members become involved in serving the needs of tourists
Development stage	... tourist arrivals increase rapidly and outside developers build large facilities to serve the seemingly endless demand; tour operators add the destination to tours
Consolidation stage	... growth in the number of visitors ceases, the destination loses its distinctiveness. Professional managers focus on controlling costs and gaining revenue from tour groups. Some environmental and cultural problem begin to appear
Stagnation/Decline stage	... the area has reached full capacity, and businesses try to maintain tourist numbers and revenues by decreasing prices. Maintenance of facilities declines and there sort area begins to look dated. All of the environmental and social problems of tourism appear

Source: Butler R W. The Tourism Area Life Cycle: Applications and Modifications [J]. Channel View, 2016, 1.

Tourism has a complicated relationship with climate change. Not only is tourism likely to be dramatically influenced by climate change in the future, tourism also is an industry that significantly contributes to the human activity that is causing climate change. Climate change is not only a concern for the environmental impacts of tourism. Because tourism is service-oriented, if destinations were to lose tourism demand it would result in job losses and potentially impact the local residents and their quality of life.

2.2 People

Many of the gains realized from tourism are economic and have often been short term in nature. The costs, however, especially to natural and cultural resources of an area, are more likely to be long-lived or even permanent. Too many times, non-local developers relying on "outside money" are the biggest winners, and when the area has become saturated and starts to decline, these developers move on to the next trendy destination with no concern for the damage that may have been done.

Tourism researcher George Doxey studied the effects that "outsiders" have on destination residents and developed an index of these sentiments called the Irridex. The Irridex describes the levels of irritation that locals may feel with the influx in the number of tourists and the changes brought about by this growth. Stage one is Euphoria. In the first phase of tourism development, locals welcome both tourism investors and travelers, recognizing the economic boom tourism can generate. Stage two is Apathy, as residents begin to take tourism for granted, contacts with tourists become businesslike, and communications focus on marketing. Stage three, termed Annoyance, develops when residents become "saturated" with the number of tourists in their area and begin to see the downsides of sharing their home area.

3. What's in a Name?

So far, we have presented quite a list of problems, both environmental and cultural, that can result from tourism. What can be done to minimize these problems? In areas where tourism activities are still developing, long-range planning will address some of the potential problems in developing tourist destinations. In developing areas and in already popular tourist locations, many efforts can be taken that will help safeguard the environment and the people. These efforts are encompassed in a variety of initiatives that can be found under the umbrella of sustainable tourism. As you know, sustainable tourism maximizes the positive impacts and minimizes the negative impacts on profit, the Planet and people. Figure 7.1 illustrates how sustainable tourism is distinct from mass tourism but has a variety of niche markets within it.

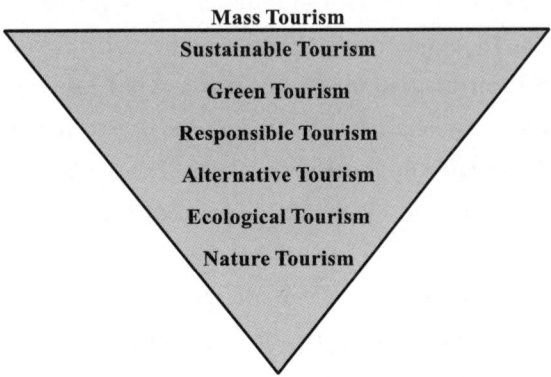

Figure 7.1 Degrees of sustainability

3.1 Ecotourism

Ecotourism? A simple enough word but a complex and often contradictory concept: A fashion, a fad? —Ecological travel is the "next big thing"; the hippest way to travel is to backpack off the beaten track to experience "nature" up close and personal (with all the luxuries of home included).

The foundation of ecotourism is the preservation of the environment. In addition, ecotravelers generally desire to mingle with the local culture and have their travel needs filled by locals in their traditional ways (such as dining on the local gastronomical delights). Compared with other travelers, ecotourists tend to be wealthier, college educated, and willing to spend large amounts of money on extended trips. "Ecotourists are more environmentally concerned and responsible than non-ecotourists. Ecotourism is experiencing double-digit growth that should accelerate as concerns over the environment and global warming rise. The importance of ecotourism, its size, and its influence on economies, environments and peoples were recognized by the United Nations when it declared 2002 as the International Year of Ecotourism.

There are five basic principles to ecotourism development. The core guiding principle is that tourism should be blended with, or assimilated into, the environment and the local culture of an area. The boundary between the tourism industry and the host community should not be startling: Tourism should fit into the community and share in its ways.

The second principle of ecotourism is that the tourist experience should focus on the host community's existing scenic and activity opportunities. In other words, tourism should evolve from the area's natural and historic/cultural attractions rather than developing attractions that do not reflect the authenticity and uniqueness of the region. Third, ecotourism is associated with local ownership and management of all or most services.

To further benefit the host community economically, the fourth principle is that a high proportion of local materials should be used to fulfill tourists' needs, from construction materials to foodstuffs. Finally, the fifth principle highlights the importance of conservation of resources. By using what are called "ecotechniques", local utilities such as water, heat and electricity can be stretched to accommodate the needs of both the tourists and the local population. Ecotechniques include use of solar power, rainwater collection, and bioclimatic design of structures to aid in heating and cooling.

Since its birth, ecotourism has been defined in various ways and used as a marketing term with growing popularity for any number of tourism attractions and tours. It has come to encompass a wide variety of nature-based activities, from hard to soft. This explosion in the use of the term makes some tourism experts now maintain that the word "ecotourism" has been applied so widely that it has in many regards become meaningless.

(1) Attraction of natural environments, so ecotourism is nature based.

(2) Emphasis on learning as an outcome of ecotourism for the tourist that differentiates ecotourism from other more hedonistic forms of "nature-based" tourism, such as the sun, sea and sand; skiing, trekking or rafting.

(3) High desire for sustainability of the natural attraction and the native people of the region.

As mentioned previously, 21st-century ecotourism covers a range of tourism experiences on a continuum of hard to soft activities. For example, a hard ecotourist might travel to coastal sea turtle nesting areas to aid these gentle giants in propagating their species. A soft ecotourist might be a passenger on a cruise ship that stops in Costa Rica and takes a guided day trip to the Cloud Forest.

Ecotourism and ecotechniques can be used by both newly developed and fully developed tourist destinations to try to minimize the negative impacts that large numbers of visitors can have on host communities and the environment. As tourism numbers continue to grow, more and more nations and communities need to apply the principles of ecotourism and conservation to ensure that the tourism industry remains viable.

3.2 Important Guarantee: Establishing the Management System of Ecotourism

The healthy management system of ecotourism is the important guarantee to the sustainable development of ecotourism. Therefore, it firstly should adjust the present management system, tidy up relations among administration management, industry management, ecology management and set up harmony organization and comprehensive management organization of ecotourism sustainable development in term of the principles of reasonable setting and scientific management. Secondly, it should constitute supervising management mechanism, definitely delimit the responsibility and purview of resources managing department, environmental protection department and tour administration department, in particular, it should strengthen the relations and cooperation among different departments.

3.3 Niche Markets

Thanks to the efforts of Jonathan Tourtellot, the senior editor of *National Geographic Traveler* magazine, a new form of tourism, geotourism, which combines all of the prominent features of a destination, from natural resources and culture to lodging and shopping, has found its way into the tourism vocabulary. Geotourism proposes that travelers have various attitudes and behavior toward the cultural heritage, aesthetics, environment and well-being of the local people in the destination. This relatively new form of tourism focuses on the unique culture and heritage of a location while attempting to help visitors enrich these qualities. Geotourism is all about making a place better by encouraging tourists to visit and spend money with preservation in mind. Destinations are encouraged to showcase those things that set them apart as unique.

Destinations are encouraged to showcase those things that set them apart as unique. Efforts such as increased emphasis on volunteering while on vacation are increasing awareness, preservation and protection of all of our resources. Voluntourism, a trip that combines travel activities with charitable work, allows tourists to give back through service projects while they take time to experience a destination. By providing volunteer tourist opportunities to engage their head, hands and hearts,

benefits will be realized by not only the tourists but also the hosting organizations. WWOOF (World Wide Opportunities on Organic Farms) is a segment of voluntourism that is growing in popularity. There is a global network of farms that invite WWOOF to come and stay at the farm to receive education, housing and most meals in return for work on the farm. WWOOF is an excellent example of how voluntourism can immerse themselves in a community; make a contribution to the destination while dramatically reducing their travel costs.

Wildlife tourism is yet another niche market where tourists visit destinations with the intention of seeing native species in their natural habitat. This is in contrast to viewing animals in enclosures at heritage attractions like zoos and aquariums that you read about it. Wildlife tourism is growing in popularity as traditional attractions have been increasingly criticized for lacking sustainable principles.

4. The World Travel Industry: Going "Green"?

Tourism, like other global industries, has been affected by both free trade and globalization, and by the anti-globalization or "fair trade" movement. While not as clearly articulated as in other sectors, there are contradictions and divisions within the tourism industry. Chain hotels, airlines and other multinational tourism companies, even when they support environmental protection and sustainable development, generally favor open borders and free trade. In contrast, one of the tenets of ecotourism is the support of locally owned businesses, local hiring and local purchasing, all practices that are circumscribed under the growing number of international trade agreements and organizations.

Possibly the greatest benefit of ecotourism has been the transfer of the ecotourism philosophy to the preservation of many practices that support mass tourism markets. One simple starting point that is often adopted for identifying sustainable practices is the promotion of the four Rs: Reuse, Recycle, Reduce, and buy Recycled products. Imagine all of the waste that can be generated in a traditional lodging facility.

To sustain the viability of destinations, ecotechniques, developed under the philosophy of ecotourism, are now being used by tourism suppliers to sustain the positive benefits of tourism and reduce and minimize the negative effects it can have on destinations and host communities. In addition, more destination decision makers are using formal planning processes to guide future development and operations to sustain both the marketability of the destination and the quality of life of its residents. From the five ecotourism goals for "establishing standards" discussed earlier, you can see how host communities can gain many potential benefits from incorporating the concepts into sustainable practices rather than simply chasing mass tourism by:

(1) generating more income for more local community members;

(2) promoting understanding between locals and members of different cultures;

(3) educating local populations on matters of health, education, energy use,

business and environmental conservation;

(4) providing a financial incentive to protect and conserve a globally significant natural/cultural resource.

Many of the techniques just described can also be used in already developed tourism areas to improve or sustain the existing tourism industry. Although applying one or two techniques will not change an area from a mass tourism to an ecotourism destination, simply to adopt efforts such as water conservation and sign codes (limiting their size, height and lighting) can help alleviate problems that may have arisen. Research has shown that there are some identifiable barriers that discourage customers from participating in green practices (e. g. , only having sheets changed on stays of three or more nights, using key cards to turn power to the room off and on) including inconvenience, perceptions of cost cutting and concerns about decreased luxury. Interestingly, although customers expressed interest in being green, they are more likely to behave with a higher level of environmental responsibility at home than in a hotel.

There are four levels of certification; starting at certified and then moving up through silver and gold, finally reaching the ultimate level, platinum. Each of these levels is reached by accumulating points in eight categories.

(1) Materials and Resources—consideration for sourcing, transportation and waste.

(2) Indoor Environmental Quality—consideration for air and light quality and sound control.

(3) Location and Linkages—consideration for design choices that include interrelationships with local surrounding.

(4) Innovation and Design—consideration for use of innovative technologies and design.

(5) Regional Priority—consideration for specific regional concerns.

(6) Sustainable Sites—consideration for the entire ecosystem including land and water .

(7) Water Efficiency—consideration for water consumption.

(8) Energy and Atmosphere—consideration for energy sources and use.

Achieving LEED (Leadership in Energy and Environmental Design) certification is definitely within reach of any hotel operation. For example, ITC Hotels which is headquartered in New Delhi was able to obtain LEED Platinum certification for its entire portfolio of hotels. This feat was achieved by doing such things as use biodegradable materials and supplies, using locally grown and processed foods and beverages, promoting fair trade practices, and it even owns a wind farm to supply power to one of its hotels. Other certification programs such as The Green Seal for hotels and Energy Star which have both been certified by the U. S. Environmental Protection Agency and the Green Food Service Alliance which has been certified by the National Restaurant Association are beginning to bring credibility to claims of

sustainability.

5. A Future of Sustainability

Tourists are likely to take vacations that are characterized by elements found in mass tourism, with little awareness or concern for natural and cultural resources in the destination. Tourists are more concerned with convenience and familiarity and can be disconnected from the places and people they visit. Travelers, want to immerse themselves in the destination so they are actively experiencing a place rather than passively observing a place. Travelers will purposefully avoid "touristy" areas and seek authenticity by exploring remote places and meeting local people to appreciate the true meaning of the landscape and the culture. There is a stronger connection and sense of belongingness for a traveler and they are more likely to make a contribution to the destination based on their deeper understanding of its character.

It may seem like an easy solution that everyone should be a traveler, get off the beaten path and follow the ecotourism principles. However, that is not entirely the case and some argue that mass tourism has its own place if it is managed well. What if everyone got off the beaten path? That path could become a road, and that road could become a highway. 47 Ecotourism essentially promotes visitation to remote and fragile areas that are highly sensitive to the impact of tourists.

Now, think back to our discussion of the many different definitions and approaches that have been taken to describe the tourism industry. Do you remember how difficult it has been for industry participants to agree on a singular focus? It seems to be just as difficult to describe sustainable tourism. Yet, as difficult as it may be to define, sustainability is critical to the industry as "tourism contains the seeds of its own destruction; tourism can kill tourism, destroying the very environmental attractions which visitors come to a location to experience". At its root, "sustainable tourism" is an oxymoron because tourism inevitably will have negative impacts on the destination and "true" sustainable tourism development is unachievable. However, if we assume that people will continue to want to travel, the philosophy of sustainability will help minimize the negative impacts and maximize the ability of future generations to see the world.

Ⅳ Case Study

Corporate Social Responsibility and the Sustainable Tourism Practices of Marriott International

1. The Company

Marriott International, Inc. began in 1927 in the United States, when J. Willard

Marriott and his wife opened a small root beer stand, later called the Hot Shoppe, in Washington, DC. In 1939, the Marriott's acquired their first food-service management contract with the U. S. Treasury, growing their business and Hot Shoppes, Inc. In 1957, they opened their first hotel in Virginia (Marriott International, Inc., 2012a). The corporate name of Hot Shoppes, Inc. was changed to the Marriott Corporation in 1967 and the business expanded into airline food service, food production and lodging. In 1969, Marriott opened a hotel in Mexico, its first property outside of the U. S. In 1972, J. W. Marriott, Jr. was named Chief Executive Officer (CEO) and in 1975, the company opened its first European hotel in Amsterdam. Marriott opened its 100th hotel in Hawaii in 1981, began the courtyard concept in 1983, and entered the vacation time-share and senior-living segments of the industry in 1984 (Marriott, 1997). Marriott International, Inc. continues to expand and flourish, with over 3700 lodging properties in 74 countries (Marriott News Center, 2013).

As of 2013, the company operates and franchises hotels under 18 brands; these include Marriott Hotels & Resorts, The Ritz-Carlton, JW Marriott, Bulgari, EDITION, Renaissance, Gaylord Hotels, Autograph Collection, AC Hotels by Marriott, Courtyard, Fairfield Inn & Suites, Springhill Suites, Residence Inn, Townplace Suites, Marriott Executive Apartments, Marriott Vacation Club, Grand Residences by Marriott, and The Ritz-Carlton Destination Club (Marriott News Center, 2013). To staff these properties, it employs more than 300000 people around the world, at its headquarters or in managed and franchised properties. The company reported sales from continuing operations of $12 billion for the fiscal year 2011 (Marriott News Center, 2013).

2. Marriott's Sustainability Efforts

The company's sustainability practices are widespread and substantial. In 2007, the company developed the Marriott Environmental Public Policy Statement and in its sustainability reports for the years of 2009 through 2012, Marriott cited accomplishments in the areas of immigration and integration, global diversity and inclusion, ethics and human rights, poverty alleviation, disaster relief efforts, vitality of children, the environment (energy, water, waste, carbon), green buildings, the supply chain, educating and inspiring associates and guests, and the "Spirit to Preserve"—Juma Reserve and Nobility of Nature projects (Marriott International, Inc., 2009; 2010; 2012). In 2009 alone, the company celebrated its 10-year anniversary of the Women's Leadership Development Initiative, commemorated the 20-year anniversary of its formal programs to promote diversity and inclusion, expanded its portfolio of LEED-certified buildings to include more than 85 hotels and its global headquarters (Matthews, 2011), and was awarded the World Travel and Tourism Council (WTTC) "Tourism for Tomorrow Award for Sustainability"

(Marriott International, Inc., 2009).

It has continued to receive recognition for its sustainability efforts, including being chosen as one of the world's best companies for working women in 2012 (Working Mother, 2012), being ranked the top large hotel chain in terms of its sustainable business practices for three consecutive years (Climate Counts, 2012), and earning the 2013 Work-Life Seal of Distinction from the World at Work's Alliance for Work-Life Progress (AWLP) (Marriott News Center, 2013b). In addition, it has been repeatedly recognized as one of the best companies to work for by *Fortune* magazine and as one of the most environmentally friendly large companies in the U.S. by *Newsweek* magazine (Marriott News Center, 2013a).

3. Key Concepts

Several concepts underlie the sustainability efforts practiced by Marriott. These include fundamental components of sustainable development and CSR efforts, which are threaded throughout Marriott's sustainability initiatives and practices. In addition, Marriott's environmental vision and goals provide a context for the case. Background elements of sustainability that may be helpful for understanding this case, include:

(1) definitions of sustainable development and sustainability (World Commission on Environment and Development, 1987);

(2) foundations of the TBL (Triple Bottom Line) of sustainability (Elkington, 1997; Hawken, 2007; Hawken, 1993; Hawken et al., 1999);

(3) a focus on employees and the community as keys to fostering and supporting the sustainability process (Senge, 2008);

(4) reducing environmental impacts through the reduction of the carbon footprint;

(5) using TBL sustainability reporting systems such as those developed by the GRI (Global Reporting Initiative, 2013), which include integrated reporting that combines the analysis of non-financial performance, comprised of CSR and environmental efforts, along with financial performance;

(6) sustainability and the sustainable development process as a "way of traveling" rather than a destination (Harrison, 2000; GRI, 2013);

(7) the significance of CSR to the well-being of a company and its stakeholders.

Viewing sustainability as a journey (GRI, 2013) or as "a way of traveling" (Harrison, 2000), rather than as an endpoint, suggests that an organization or company does not reach sustainability; instead sustainability is dynamic in nature. As Marriott has increased its brand portfolio and complexity, it shifts and adapts its sustainability focus to fit the needs of its various stakeholders in its efforts to address critical social, cultural and economic issues. Stakeholders in Marriott consist of all those with interests in the firm who may receive benefits, although the interests and needs of these groups may not always be evident (Donaldson and Preston, 1995). These include associates, guests, franchisees, shareholders, communities, suppliers, industry organizations, government, and the wide range of organizations involved in sustainability efforts.

The European Commission (2001) defines CSR as "a concept whereby companies integrate social and environmental concerns in their business operations and in their interaction with their stakeholders on a voluntary basis" and Marriott engages in practices related to this concept throughout its operations around the globe. The John F. Kennedy School of Government's view of CSR is that "it goes beyond philanthropy and compliance and addresses how companies manage their economic, social and environmental impacts, as well as their relationships in all key spheres of influence: the workplace, the marketplace, the supply chain, the community and the public policy realm (Harvard University, 2013)". And as Porter and Kramer (2006) noted, "When a well-run business applies its vast resources, expertise and management talent to problems that it understands and in which it has a stake, it can have a greater impact on social good than any other institution or philanthropic organization. "It is not surprising then to find out that Marriott has long been a champion of CSR within the company itself and via its philanthropic efforts in communities worldwide.

One of the company's focal environmental efforts areas has been to develop a program to help every guest reduce his or her carbon footprint, defined as "the amount of carbon emitted by something during a given period (Merriam-Webster Dictionary, 2012)". Starting in 2009, Marriott guests could make a contribution of a minimum of $10 (equivalent to 10 nights) to offset their carbon footprint online or via post. The company came up with the figure by calculating the electrical and gas consumption in guest rooms and public spaces in almost 1000 of its properties as well as at its headquarters and regional office buildings. Marriott followed the World Resources Institute's Greenhouse Gas Protocol to generate its program and had it independently certified by ICF International, a climate change consulting service (JustGive, 2009; Marriott International, Inc. , 2009).

To report the results of such sustainability projects, Marriott uses the reporting procedure of the GRI (2013), a systematic way to chronicle sustainability efforts, on an annual basis in a manner similar to the way that it reports its financial performance. The GRI has offered organizations around the world a framework for reporting sustainability since 1999. It consists of implementing a reporting cycle that involves data collection, communication and responses. Due to its credibility, consistency and comparability, the GRI framework has become widely accepted as a standard sustainability reporting system around the globe (GRI, 2013).

Marriott continues to pursue its current initiatives while striving to do even more as an effective global corporate citizen in environmental, societal and business

spheres. The company embraces a holistic view of CSR that comprises not only what the company does with its profits to benefit others, but also how it makes its money. It is evident that Marriott has a whole-hearted, whole company, every property, every employee and every guest kind of approach to sustainability. The following analysis demonstrates the company's dedicated efforts in all areas of sustainability.

Ⅴ Tips

The Road:Less Traveled

As we move through the first decade of the new millennium, ecotourism is charting a bold new direction in how we explore the world. Ecotourism has become one of the most rapidly growing and most dynamic sector of the tourism market. Yet it still remains, to paraphrase Robert Frost's poem, the less-traveled road. Hundreds of millions of tourists still go on conventional cruises, sun-and-sea beach holidays, or mass tourism vacations during which distortions of nature are viewed at palm-fringed poolside's, theme parks and overcrowded camp grounds. Much of what is marketed as ecotourism amounts to only ecotourism lite, which offers tidbits of nature or minor environmental reforms such a not changing the sheets daily. Even worse, "greenwashing" scams use environmentally friendly images but follow none of the principles and practices of sound ecotourism. Growing numbers of travelers, however, are walking the path of socially responsible and environmentally respectful tourism.

At the local level, ecotourism principles have become part of many rural struggles over control of land, resources and tourism profits. Wherever people in the world are in conflict over parks and tourism—whether the gold miners in Costa Rica's Corcovado National Park; the Galapagos Islands settlers; the Maasai in East Africa; or the displaced communities around Kruger National Park, St. Lucia Nature Reserve, and elsewhere in South Africa—ecotourism is part of the demand and part of the solution. In the most fragile ecosystems, like the Galapagos, well-run ecotourism is the only option, the only foreign exchange-earning activity that, if done with care and controls, does not lead to irreparable damage to the environment. In other instances, ecotourism is clearly more profitable than the alternative economic activities: for example, studies in three Central American countries found that a stay over ecotourist puts eighteen to twenty-eight times more money into the local economy than a cruise passenger, while a study of game farming in Kenya found that wildlife tourism was fifty times more lucrative than cattle grazing. Other research calculated that a lion is worth $575000, and a single free-flying macaw in Peru is estimated to generate as much as $4700 per year in tourism dollars. In the old Bo-phi that swan a homeland in

South Africa, cattle farming could generate only 80 jobs, whereas six new luxury lodges planned for a game reserve were projected to create 1200 jobs, and ecotourism was estimated to be sixty times more profitable than cattle ranching. Even when pitted against the seemingly lucrative industry of mining in St. Lucia, South Africa, ecotourism is calculated to have the potential to provide more jobs for a longer period of time without destroying the sand dunes and the estuary.

Most common is the distribution of revenue in the form of cash payments or tangible benefits (a road, a clinic, a grinding mill, a classroom, electricity, a truck, etc.) to the local community based on rent for use of land, a set fee per visitor-night, a percentage of park entrance fees, or guest and company donations via travelers' philanthropy projects. Although such compensation can significantly improve daily life in poor rural communities, it may do little to equip local communities with the educational and technical skills and political know-how they will need to assume an active role in ecotourism projects and park management and in negotiations with private-sector participants and government authorities.

The ideal is active community participation in the management and distribution of revenues that gives local residents, in the words of David Grossman and Eddie Koch, "The will, power and skills to improve their standard of living. Through the wise use of wildlife and natural resources". But in reality, many community-based tourism and conservation programs are "relational" rather than participatory: They seek to improve relationships between the community and either the state or the private enterprise through trade-offs, rather than to devolve ownership and management of the protected area or tourism project to the local community. "Without proprietorship," write Grossman and Koch, "most forms of participation become cooperative or collaborative arrangements." Frequently, local communities strengthen their skills and political influence through alliances with national and international environment, development, and human rights organizations, scientists, journalists and academics, which help them, build a counter weight to the power of outside private corporations or negotiate terms with the national government. These external alliances can also help community-owned ecotourism projects develop internationally acceptable standards of accommodation and effective overseas marketing. In recent years, for instance, Kenya has emerged as a leader in community-owned eco-lodges, a number of which have been supported by NGOs as well as white-owned ranches, while Costa Rica has built a network of small-scale local and indigenous ecotourism businesses that have been assisted by local NGOs and the United Nations Development Program (UNDP).

Although alliances with NGOs and experts can provide skills, funds and political clout, it is difficult for community-based ecotourism to take hold and expand without strong government support. As John Akarma observes in discussing Kenya, "For

local community participation to succeed local people need sanctioned authority to enable them to implement programmer responsibilities. " As seen in Kenya, Tanzania and Zanzibar, national governments frequently stifle rural initiatives, hand out lucrative contracts to politically or economically powerful elites, and cede to the private sector or local park officials development responsibilities—construction of roads, wells, schools, and the like—traditionally carried by the state.

Over the last decade, it has been encouraging to see the application of the principles and good practices of ecotourism to more mainstream sectors of the tourism industry. Usually termed "sustainable tourism", these initiatives include efforts to create "greener" practices in the construction of golf courses, ski slopes, larger resorts and hotel chains. While both sustainable tourism and ecotourism continue to grow rapidly, they are still far from transforming the way in which modern, mass tourism is conducted. At its core, ecotourism is about power relationships and on-the-ground struggles. It will take much stronger grass-roots movements, combined with alliances among activists, experts and NGOs, and carefully planned and implemented national ecotourism strategies, to curb the power of the conventional tourism industry. Although this appears unlikely to happen soon, it is still worth the struggle. Along the way, some excellent models are being built; some local communities are being empowered and their members' lives improved; national parks and other fragile ecosystems are receiving more support; and awareness is growing that we cannot continue to play in other people's lands as we have in the past. Despite the constraints, today's traveler does, as Robert Frost suggests, has a choice about which road to take.

Ⅵ Dialogue

(The dialogue is about the world heritage section of sustainable tourism.)

Alice: Hello and welcome to "6 Minute English". I'm Alice.

Neil: And I'm Neil.

Alice: So, Neil, what's the best holiday you've ever had?

Neil: That would be scuba diving on the Great Barrier Reef off the coast of Australia. It was awesome! I saw sharks, sea turtles, manta rays…

Alice: I certainly don't like the idea of coming nose to nose with a shark! But then diving isn't really my thing. I'm more into cultural holidays, you know, visiting the ruins of ancient civilizations.

Neil: That's very worthy, Alice. But tourists are actually damaging a number of important sites around the world— tramping around, dropping litter, scribbling graffiti everywhere…

Alice: I would never drop litter or scribble graffiti!

Neil: Well, we're talking about world heritage sites today, which are places UNESCO considers to be at risk from various threats and in need of protection. Heritage means the things a society considers important to its history and culture, for example art, buildings or natural sites such as the Grand Canyon in the United States.

Alice: And the environment poses a number of different threats. So, Neil, can you tell me which sea creature is a potential threat to the Great Barrier Reef's ecosystem? Is it a starfish, jellyfish or cuttlefish?

Neil: I will go for jellyfish. I'm no expert on marine life, but I have eaten jellyfish and I haven't eaten the other ones.

Alice: Oh, I see. Well, we'll find out later. But now let's listen to the BBC reporter Roger Harradine talking about other types of threat to heritage sites. See how many you can spot!

Roger: The most precious wonders of the natural world—Australia's Great Barrier Reef, America's spectacular Grand Canyon, the Barrier Reef of Belize in South America, second biggest on Earth—all facing threats from humans. The Great Barrier Reef is attracting urgent concern. There's a huge battle over mining and port development. A giant coalmine has just been given the go-ahead by the Queensland government even though scientists warn it may damage the Reef.

Neil: That's the BBC's Roger Harradine. Well, I spotted a couple of threats to heritage sites there—mining and port development. Now, any type of industrial activity can harm them by, for example, encroaching on the natural habitat of animals and plants living there, or by polluting the water that flows into the site.

Alice: Mining is the process of extracting coal or other minerals from the ground, and if you encroach on something, it means you move beyond acceptable limits. The interesting thing is that world heritage sites only constitute 0.5% of the Earth's surface—so why can't people do their mining and industrial development on the remaining 99.5%!

Neil: But there is one human industry that can actually be beneficial for precious sites—tourism.

Alice: But you said earlier that tourism was bad for heritage sites.

Neil: I know. And I was right, up to a point. World heritage sites are some of tourism's main attractions, and more and more people are visiting them. So it's all about getting the balance right between generating money to maintain and restore the sites and minimizing the impact of tourist activities.

Alice: Such as littering and graffiti.

Neil: Exactly. And the term for this is sustainable tourism, or tourism designed to have a low impact on the local culture and the environment, while generating

employment for local people.

Alice: So UNESCO is working to direct governments, site managers and visitors towards sustainable tourism practices in order to keep our world's natural and cultural heritage safe for future generations.

Neil: Wow, you can really talk the talk, Alice. You should work for UNESCO! OK, let's move on now, and listen to Paul Crocombe, of the Snorkeling and Diving Company in Townsville, Queensland, Australia, giving his view on how the Great Barrier Reef will cope with threats to its survival.

Paul: The Reef's fairly dynamic, it's been through a couple of ice ages, and is still here, so its resilience will ensure that the Reef is still here in years to come. But the species diversity and the visual aesthetics of the Reef may change quite considerably, especially if we get an increase in sea temperature, an increase in carbon dioxide in the water, and things like that.

Alice: Paul Crocombe describes the Reef as dynamic and resilient.

Neil: Dynamic means active or capable of changing and resilience means the ability to recover or adapt to change—which all sounds good. But Paul also says that the species diversity—the range of plants and animals—may change.

Alice: For example, a rise in sea temperature would cause a rise in carbon dioxide levels—and this could have a big impact on both the species diversity and the Reef's visual aesthetic—or the way it looks.

Neil: OK, I think it's time now for the answer to today's quiz question, Alice.

Alice: Yes, I think so too. OK, so, I asked you which sea creature poses a potential threat to the Great Barrier Reef's ecosystem. Is it starfish, jellyfish or cuttlefish?

Neil: And I said jellyfish.

Alice: And you got stung, I'm afraid, Neil!

Neil: Ouch!

Alice: The answer is starfish. The crown-of-thorns starfish preys on coral and large outbreaks of these starfish can devastate reefs. Now, can you remind us of some of today's vocabulary, Neil?

Neil: Sure. Heritage/encroach on something/sustainable tourism/dynamic/resilience/species diversity/visual aesthetic.

Alice: Well, that's the end of today's "6 Minute English". Don't forget to join us again soon!

Both: Bye!

Ⅶ Academic Thinking

Prospective Tourist Preferences for Sustainable Tourism Development in Small Island Developing States

Author: Gaetano Grilli, Emmanouil Tyllianakis, Tiziana Luisetti, Silvia Ferrini, R. Kerry Turnera.

Journal: *Tourism Management*

Abstract:

Tourism development is crucial for economic growth in Small Island Developing States, but its management involves trade-offs between ecosystem services and social and cultural identities. This paper aims to contribute to the debate around the achievement of the sustainable development goals through an investigation of the sustainable management of tourism and coastal ecosystem services. The paper presents a choice experiment and latent factor analysis to disentangle relevant aspects of sustainable tourism in Small Island Developing States for potential visitors. Willingness to pay is reported for the different factors revealing preferences variability for previous and prospective visitors. Pro-environmental attitudes influence individual tastes and policy makers should consider these traits in order to attract visitors and private funding. Our findings show that prospective tourists are interested in the wider aspects of the tourism experience which in turn require the careful management of social and environmental resources in Small Island Developing States.

小岛屿发展中国家可持续旅游业发展的潜在游客偏好

旅游业的发展对小岛屿发展中国家的经济增长至关重要,但旅游业的管理涉及生态系统服务与社会和文化特性之间的权衡。本文旨在通过对旅游业和沿海生态系统服务的可持续管理的研究,为围绕实现可持续发展目标的辩论作出贡献。本文提出了一个选择试验和潜在因素分析,以便为潜在游客解开小岛屿发展中国家可持续旅游业的相关方面。支付意愿报告了不同的因素,揭示了以前和未来游客的偏好变化。有利于环境的态度影响个人的品味,政策制定者应该考虑这些特点,以吸引游客和私人资金。我们的调查结果表明,潜在游客对旅游经历的更广泛方面感兴趣,而这又要求小岛屿发展中国家认真管理社会和环境资源。

Ⅷ Questions

1. When can tourism be too much of a good thing?
2. What are the major principles of ecotourism?
3. How can hotel and resort operators create sustainable practices?

4. What benefits may be achieved by a host community through the use of ecotourism practices?

Ⅸ Key Words and Terms

sustainable tourism	可持续旅游
mass tourism	大众旅游
niche market	利基市场
ecotourism	生态旅游
ecotraveler	生态旅行者
ecotourist	生态旅游者
principle of ecotourism	生态旅游原则
ecotechnique	生态技术
geotourism	地质旅游
wildlife tourism	野生动物旅游
establish standards	制定标准
hard ecotourist	严格的生态旅游者
soft ecotourist	一般的生态旅游者
voluntourism	公益旅游，义工旅行，志愿（者）旅游
nature-based tourism	自然旅游

Ⅹ Single Choice Questions

Chapter 8
Trends and Future of Tourism

I Chapter Introduction

The knowledge you have gained through studying the information in this textbook has given you a sound foundation for thinking about the future. Based on this knowledge, you can begin to see some of the challenges and opportunities the tourism industry will face. In this chapter, we gaze into the future by considering some of the emerging trends in the tourism industry.

II Chapter Objectives

After you have read this chapter, you should be able to:
1. Describe emerging trends that will affect future tourism marketing decisions.
2. Describe how emerging market segments will affect the future of the tourism industry.
3. Describe how tourism service suppliers will be affected by changing consumers' needs.
4. Describe how and why tourism service suppliers are becoming larger through mergers, consolidations and alliances.
5. Describe how technological changes will affect the future of the tourism industry.
6. Explain why the human touch will remain important to the future success of tourism service suppliers.

III Reading

1. Innovation and the Future of Tourism
About the Future of Tourism, if the concept were to be strictly, narrowly

understood, it would imply an almost impossible task of primarily considering the endogenous main variables of tourism activity in destinations worldwide, and then, their autonomous progress over time, somehow disregarding global scenarios, trends and paradigm shifts. Much more adequate and interesting seems to explore the subject from a high watchtower, observing and analyzing tourism in the future, i. e. , the role of tourism in the future of our civilization, including its resilience to withstand short-term shocks and its capacity for evolutionary adaptation.

This chapter approaches the future of tourism through the lens of innovation. If our society is to overcome the main challenges of the twenty-first century, it will do so through a combination of reform, re-engineering and disruptive innovation. Tourism may survive or not in its present form, and it may well contribute, resist or even oppose necessary changes. Contemporary cases illustrate all these possibilities, but official prognoses of tourism tend to assume ceteris paribus, business as usual, scenarios. From the oil crises of the 1970s to the last Great Recession, through wars, natural disasters and financial crises, we have been told that tourism is to grow 3%-4% annually long term. No limits to growth, apparently. Even when the first effects of looming climate change are already here with us, we learn that tourism will involve some 1.8 billion international journeys by 2030 and that its resilience contributes to "sustainable growth". However, in other instances tourism is approached from the perspective of an instrument for development. This latter perspective underlies many of the following chapters. Over 50 years ago, back in the 1960s, we began to understand that the exercise of knowledge management, beginning with scientific and technological research and culminating in innovation, does not progress smoothly—in the way of ever going empirical falsification à la Popper—but is rather a process oscillating between times of "normal" paradigm stability (with widely shared concepts and theories) and punctuated periods of radical paradigm shifts and disruptive game-changers. This paradigm-shift approach, proposed in the context of scientific evolution/revolution, was later extended to other human behaviors, such as economics, business and governance.

According to Kuhn, in periods of "normal science", a paradigm is a set of broadly recognized concepts and theories that for a time provide model problems and solutions for a community of practitioners. "Close historical investigation of a given specialty at a given time discloses a set of recurrent illustrations of various theories in their conceptual, observational, and instrumental applications."

In "normal times", in the reign of "business as usual", science, enterprise and governance, including practice in tourism activity, are conducted within the framework of a paradigm. But existing paradigms face major disruptions—paradigm shifts—when the set of problems changes too rapidly and profoundly for the prevailing concepts to apply and problem-solving methods to work. A paradigm-shift is a "game-changer". It involves a dramatic advance in methodology and practice, a major innovation in thinking and planning. And it is especially true in such cases of paradigm-shift that "The Future of Tourism"—or simply "The Future"—depends on innovation.

The concept of innovation has been broadly used in the context of economic growth, "progress", technological breakthroughs, development and elsewhere. Innovation is the bridge to the future, but it is not only scientific and technological (sci-tech) innovation that must be considered, and not every level of innovation has the same significance. Firstly, institutional and governance innovation may imply even deeper changes than technological innovation and often act as the catalyst for the scaling and implementation of sci-tech innovation. Secondly, innovation in processes (so called process re-engineering) is often a harbinger of increased efficiency and bottom-line results, but it does not necessarily imply a disruptive/revolutionary solution to new problems. And then, even disruptive innovations may have quite diverse effects when seen from the perspective of paradigm shifts.

The future of tourism in the twenty-first century will depend on how our civilization deals with the key strategic issues of climate change, development and global governance—tourism being but a transversal activity of contemporary society. However, at this stage, it seems more and more obvious that business as usual is not providing us with the required answers (methods) to build those much-needed bridges towards the future. Reforming and reengineering innovations, useful as they are, fall short in terms of depth and speed of the changes required. Adequate kinds of disruptive—paradigm shifting—innovations, in physics, mathematics/computing and bioengineering to begin with, will be leading the way forward. But then, this is not happening at sufficient scale and speed, especially in the governance field, where it is probably most urgently needed.

Our civilization and tourism within it, is well aware of the historical role of innovation in the "recent" history of humankind. Lip service has been customarily paid to the idea of innovation, even in the context of a rather conservative tourism industry. And, however, there remain wide gaps in the understanding of knowledge management and the resulting innovation, and even more so in the theory and practice of tourism. A preliminary issue concerns of course the actors and mechanisms of innovation.

When referring to the actors of innovation, there is a widespread assumption that it is private sector entities and "youthful minds" there in who lead the way into disruptive new methods and products, capable of changing specific industries and even the goals, means and ways of whole societies. But then, this narrative is biased, reinforcing the widespread neoliberal economics paradigm images of agile private entrepreneurs overcoming the bureaucracy of an overgrown public sector.

However, historical experience shows abundant examples of the key role of the State in providing, not only the stimuli, but the overall control of disruptive forms of innovation. "For many technologies, it has not been Adam Smith's invisible hand, but the hand of government that has proven decisive in their development." This is even more the case in tourism. Because of its transversal nature, bringing in many other economic, socio-cultural and environmental activities, tourism needs to widely involve the public sector in the shaping, positioning, marketing and operation of successful tourism clusters. And, of course, this is not only true of contemporary, highly competitive tourism destinations; it has occurred in quite diverse tourism business paradigms, from eighteenth century elite-traveler models to twenty-first century tourism niche destinations, through the many instances of mass-tourism paradigms.

Of course, the issue here is not to rekindle a centuries-old controversy of the State vs market. Recent examples of the role of the State in innovation leading to development abound anyway—e. g. , in the 1980s in Japan, the 1990s in South Korea, and even in the achievements of dedicated public agencies in the United States and elsewhere. The task is rather to explore the actual processes of innovation in shaping the future of tourism, and even in framing the role of tourism in future society. However, in tourism as in many other activities, innovation is fraught with difficulty. Obviously, it is to be expected that some key stakeholders, whilst paying lip service to "progress" and innovation, have in fact vested interests in preserving the status quo of business as usual. For these, development is to simply be understood as "sustainable growth", with allusions to employment creation and pro-poor tourism.

But, even for entrepreneurs committed to competitive or repetitive strategies, innovation is full of uncertainties, concerning not only the tangible outcomes but also strategic traps, communication challenges and, of course, final economic success. To embrace the cause of (especially disruptive) innovation, entrepreneurs—whether in the private or public sector—must make the best of cost-benefit analyses available, because of "…the intangible nature of certain benefits and the uncertainties associated with achieving the results…" In the case of tourism, the many externalities which often exist, increase the difficulty of estimating the uncertainties involved. In this context, perhaps one of the first steps is reconsidering our discourse: the basic concepts, elements and methods involved in innovation. If "those who tell stories run society" (Plato), it is important to get the discourse right: from the present narrative of courageous private entrepreneurs successfully fighting heavy public sector bureaucracy to recognizing the key role of government and specific public agencies as essential co-creators of disruptive innovation and paradigm shifts.

Many chapters in this book openly embrace the cause of a pro-active public sector in tourism, debunking the myth of government crowding-out private sector activities.

There is in fact growing evidence that public policies—and even direct public measures on tourism—have a crowding-in effect on private initiative. The role of government in helping build the future of tourism must then be not only one of de-risking, but of taking risks; not simply of enabling innovation, but of catalyzing profound change; not of merely fixing markets, but of shaping and creating; and not the deja-vu of levelling the playing field, but of tilting it in favor of innovators. And even this is not the whole story, tourism being an intrinsic, transversal activity of contemporary capitalism, the deep issue of the creation of value remains to be tackled. Should rewards be given to the value-creators or to the value-extractors? Since at least the 1980s, contemporary capitalism has shifted distribution in favor of the latter but it is increasingly difficult to envision a sustainable future within that distribution paradigm. What is the role of government to that respect: redistribution policies or a reappraisal of remuneration to the value-creators?

Of course, this has deep implications for the future of tourism and its macro governance, and concerns directly the distribution of benefits to different stakeholders in destinations and beyond. To begin with, it needs a re-definition of who these stakeholders are, and what they contribute to destination value-creation. It affects their property-rights and control-rights. Therefore, it makes little sense to keep talking about pro-poor tourism, community tourism, over tourism, decent employment in tourism, and even, more ambitiously, about tourism as an instrument for development, without first re-examining the issues of value creation in tourism.

2. The Shape of Coming Tourism Markets

You have read about many of the important tourism market segments of today in previous chapters. Will these segments still be as important in the future? There is no question that tourism markets will change, but what will these markets look like? Two possible scenarios are beginning to unfold. One scenario points to mass markets and a "one-size-fits-all" approach to delivering tourism services; the other points to highly focused services that are targeted toward meeting the needs of specific market niches. In countries growing in economic strength, such as Poland, India, Russia, China, Panama, Vietnam and Brazil, many tourism services will be developed to meet the needs of mass markets. We will see this type of development as levels of disposable income, leisure time and infrastructure improvements in these countries encourage tourism growth.

Increased economic activity will lead to increased levels of leisure travel both domestically and internationally. As more citizens of the world discover the enjoyment that comes from tourism activities, increasing participation in travel will drive the development of new facilities and services. The highly populated, newly affluent countries of China and India will dominate the market as the top two countries for outbound tourists, supplying the world with a huge demand for travel services. There

will also be a large flow of VFR tourists to these countries as former emigrants return to visit relatives in the "homeland" and to learn more about their heritage. Unlike their American and European counterparts, who seek arts and architecture, and active travel experiences, Chinese and other Asian-born tourists are most likely to be motivated to travel to shop and experience cultural values of group engagement, learning and promote geopolitical aspirations.

Tourism markets will probably take a very different path in developed countries such as Canada, France, Germany, Japan, the United Kingdom and the United States. In these countries, we will continue to see mass-market tourism, but marketers will continue to refine and even "tailor-make" their service offerings to meet the needs of increasingly demanding and sophisticated travelers.

2.1 Demographic Shifts

One of the biggest changes that will occur in the tourism market in the 21st century will be the increasing size of the mature traveler segment. The baby boom generations, those tens of millions of post-World War II babies born between the years 1946 and 1964, are retiring in record numbers. As you learned in previous chapters, mature travelers are a very important tourism segment because of their affluence and ability to travel at any time of the year. By 2050, 34.9% of the U.S. population will be 55 years old or older, compared with 26.7% in 2010. According to Statistics Canada and the U.S. Census Bureau, Canada will see an even larger increase in its mature traveler group, and the retirement age population in Japan is also exploding. This explosion in the number of senior citizens is happening in virtually all industrialized countries of the world. Baby boomers are already the most likely age cohort to travel. As retirees, they will be even more likely to travel than their parents and grandparents did, and they will be somewhat different in their tourism interests. Senior baby boomers will be healthier, better educated, and wealthier than seniors of previous generations. The increasing number of SKINs (Spend Kids' Inheritance Now), who are not willing to save their financial assets for their children, have contributed to a growing market of longer holidays. Many will have already traveled throughout their country and in foreign lands, often as students or business people. Therefore, they will be seeking new and exciting adventures in their future travels.

Another demographic shift, which will have an impact on international travel especially, has been the shift in the ethnic mix of North America. During the 19th and first half of the 20th centuries, most immigrants to the United States and Canada were Europeans by birth. These ethnic groups enjoyed traveling to their mother countries and fueled transatlantic tourism in the 20th century. But the majority of immigrants during recent decades have come from Latin and Central America, Asia, and former Soviet Union nations. These individuals, as they become more affluent, will also want to visit the lands of their heritage, generating a substantial increase in travel to their homelands.

These demographic shifts are bad news for some tourism suppliers. Snow holiday resorts will experience a double negative effect. Baby boomers and their parents who have been ski resorts' mainstay market segment are giving up skiing as they age, and unfortunately, many did not turn their children on to the sport. In addition, winter sports have been primarily the pastime of Northern and Western European ethnic groups. These ethnic groups are shrinking as a percentage of the population of the world. Unless members of the growing Asian and all Hispanic ethnic groups can be enticed to learn and participate frequently in winter sports, substantial shrinkage in participation rates will occur in the next 25 years.

Although skiing has decreased in popularity (although being replaced in part by snowboarding) in the traditional ski countries in North America, Europe and Japan, investment in ski resorts continues, and there is development of ski domes at retail malls. The future may see partnerships between North American and European ski companies to bring the classic resorts of Europe into the 21st century. Resort developers are hoping the snowboarders of today will convert to skiers as their age. Future challenges for snow holiday resort developers will be primarily environmental. Growing concerns about human pollution and traffic congestion are being raised whenever and wherever resort expansion is proposed. In the future, resort management and developers will need to develop more environmentally conscious operations.

Whistler Resort in British Columbia, Canada, already has an environmental manager as part of its full-time staff.

The focus will be on development of winter sports resorts, not limiting the market to skiing and snowboarders, as well as the development of winter theme parks that offer plenty to do for the expanding no skier market. Traditional winter season resorts will also expand their entertainment and sports offerings during the other three seasons of the year. There is a need to look at the mountain as a year-round tourism resource and add other desirable alternatives, such as guided nature hikes, cycling adventures and paragliding.

Other members of the tourism industry that will need to change to sustain revenues are theme and amusement parks. The likelihood of visiting a theme park goes down after age 44, so as the average age of the industrialized countries' populations increases, either theme parks will see reduced attendance numbers, or they will need to modify their offerings to appeal to older visitors. You can expect to see theme park growth in some expected locations such as China and Dubai as people seek to travel, but maybe not as far away from home, to experience new adventures, especially virtual relativity options, in comfortable and familiar surroundings.

At the same time theme parks are appealing to an older crowd, they will need to strike a delicate balance as they need to cater to millennials who are current and future patrons with their families. "They're looking for a collection of different kinds of complementary experiences rather than just one main event. 'Curating the experience' is the process of customizing an encounter and controlling how it is shared with the world. This is as simple as choosing a filter on Instagram, finding the right emoji to include in a status update or hash tagging a tweet." These 16 to 34-year-old who have grown up in a tech-savvy digital world are our future customers!

2.2 Travelers with Disabilities and Special Needs

Physical ability is an important determinant of travel. Travelers with disabilities and special needs might have minor limitations, from slight hearing impairments to major mobility obstacles such as confinement to wheelchairs. The United States took the lead to increase accessibility substantially for all by passing *the Americans with Disabilities Act* in 1990. Since that time, access to most major tourism resources and services has greatly improved within the United States. However, access is still a major issue in other countries of the world and seriously restricts the ability to travel for tens of millions of people. The proportion of the world's population that has disabilities will surely grow as the average age in industrialized countries continues to rise.

The Society for Accessible Travel & Hospitality estimates that about 70% of adults with disabilities travel at least once a year. With the increasing size of the mature traveler segment, accessible travel will become more and more of an issue. Although seniors the world over are likely to continue their interest in travel and new sights and experiences, they will begin to have special needs owing to changing health.

2.3 Changes in Business, Professional and Conference Travel

What will happen to the ever-important business and professional travel segment of the tourism market? That is where our crystal ball becomes particularly cloudy: Current trends support the possibility of a decrease or an increase in business and professional travel. Trends in communications, such as computer networking and satellite video image transmission, seem to indicate that business travel will become less necessary. Technological advances allow business people to see each other and share information as if they were in the same room, but will virtual contact replace face-to-face meetings?

Our best guess is that travel for business and professional reasons will continue to increase in spite of further advances in communication technology. Doing business in the future will involve more, not less, collaboration with others. Some of this increased need for interaction among businesses will be satisfied with telecommunications. However, there is no substitute for the personal contact that requires physical travel and meeting with others face-to-face. Yet, business travelers will increasingly find opportunities to tack on a little personal rest and relaxation with their business duties.

We predict that the most popular types of conferences in the future will not be business related but instead will focus on personal lifestyles and interests. Growth in number of conferences and attendees will most likely come in the form of meetings on organized religion, self-improvement/education, hobbies, civic topics, alumni reunions and politics. This trend began in the 1990s when 20% of U. S. citizens traveled to nonbusiness conference events.

3. Emerging Tourism Markets

What tourist activities will be the favored pastimes in the future? We have already mentioned several of the broad tourism trends shaping the face of the industry in previous chapters. Now we will turn our attention to some specific segments that hold promise for future growth. As one travel professional noted, "rather than sit on a beach and sip a main tai, there is a move among travelers to engage themselves in the people and places they visit". In a world where many travelers have "been there and done that", there is a growing desire to do something special or participate in life-changing activities. While there is no question that some specialized niche markets such as slum tourism and dark tourism have evolved, several larger and growing markets should be of interest to all tourism service suppliers.

3.1 Slow Tourism

Despite the fact that slow tourism was inexplicitly defined, there was a general agreement on slow tourism's benefits to both tourists and destinations. Tourists can obtain a more meaningful sustainable tourism experience, getting immersed in the destination and acting like a native, thus achieving a high level of satisfaction and well-being by eventually slowing down. Slow tourism can satisfy tourists' needs of contemporary life, well-being, and finding a true self by providing a relaxing place or creating an authentic local experience. Visitors can easily identify the special characteristics of the locality and achieved a sense of attachment to the destination by slowing down. For destinations, it goes one step further by providing an alternative development pattern from a more green and sustainable way. Slow tourism related to slow cities stresses the unique features and the sense of place and identity of destinations, in contrast to mere destination economic growth. In addition, the concept of "slow" and the "green value" attached to slow tourism can be used as a marketing and management strategy based on place characteristics to attract more tourists.

Slow tourism vacations will develop as an important niche segment of the tourism industry to meet the need of travelers looking for a very different experience. To escape the 21st-century "accelerated" life, more and more travelers will opt out of

high-activity vacations, instead preferring trips with a slower pace than they experience in everyday life, allowing time and opportunities for immersion. These vacations will involve all the five senses and be designed with the goal of experiencing people and places. Research shows that those involved in slow tourism are seeking revitalization and self-enrichment.

This trend suggests that health spas, "zones of tranquility", rural destinations, food tourism venues and cultural tourism opportunities in general will see an increase in popularity. In addition, single-destination, as opposed to autodetonation, trips will be preferred by travelers seeking the immersion of the slow tourism experience. A preferred slow tourism vacation might be a two-week cottage stay in a rural Irish town, walking the green hills and ocean bluffs, soaking in the ambiance of local pubs, and meeting and mingling with the townspeople. "Home-stay holidays" are popular in some countries that offer the opportunity for tourists to live with a family for a period to gain a perspective that is usually not available to casual tourists. Spiritual or religious tourism has also grown rapidly as part of the experience-driven holidays. Spiritual retreats have been offered by historic or religious sites to help tourists enrich their vacation experiences.

3.2　Adventure and Extreme Tourism

Adventure travel is defined as a "trip or travel with the specific purpose of activity participation to explore a new experience, often involving perceived risk or controlled danger associated with personal challenges, in a natural environment or exotic outdoor setting". Like ecotourism, adventure travel focuses on experiencing, not sightseeing. Adventure travel is often split into hard and soft forms, and participants are called hard and soft adventure travelers.

Hard adventure tourism encompasses activities that involve above-average elements of physical challenge and risk. Because of the potential danger involved in many of the hard adventure activities, such as mountain climbing, highly experienced guides often "choreograph" much of the trip for the tourist group.

Recently, researchers have tried to describe the breadth of adventure travelers. Many of the hard adventure tourists in the general enthusiast and active soloist categories are probably grampies, a term for men "who are growing, retired and moneyed, in good physical and emotional health". It is estimated that by 2040 over half of the population in the developed world will be over fifty. This means more people in good health with a more informed global perspective—more grampies—thus more adventure tourists. The lines between adventure and mainstream tourism will become less clearly defined. Adventure will become more accessible and achievable for more people. Moreover, adventure holidays will become more attractive as the collection of experiences begins to undermine the more materialistic elements of consumer society.

3.3 Medical Tourism

Medical tourism, travel to other countries to receive treatments, is becoming very popular. Many already travel for cosmetic surgery or dentistry, experimental drug/surgical treatments, or because treatment is either unavailable or untimely in the country of their residency. In addition to people traveling from high-income countries to low-income countries to seek cheaper medical products, patients from low-income countries travel to high-income countries in search of better care. The estimated gross medical tourism revenues of $40 billion worldwide in 2004 will increase to $100 billion by 2012. With a growing number of health travel agencies, it is becoming easier for travelers to schedule everything from complete physicals to complex surgeries more confidently.

In Singapore, some hospitals and hotels are partnering to offer packages that combine a hotel stay with a treatment package. Thailand's Tourism Ministry has aided the development of packages marketed to rich Arab patients. These packages feature shopping, sightseeing and other activities for family members who are traveling with the loved one who is receiving treatment. The government of South Korea is launching campaigns to promote medical tourism services in their countries. In an interesting twist, Indian nations in Canada are developing private hospitals so fellow Canadians can circumvent the Canadian ban on private-pay medical services by traveling to tribal lands where such laws do not apply.

3.4 Vocation and Real Estate Tourism

Very specialized niches are being served and should grow as tourism service suppliers strive to meet ever-changing needs and expectations. Culinary and heritage tourism definitely fit the concept of travel with a purpose, but new niches are appearing that do more than fulfilling physiological and psychological needs. For example, vocation tourism and real estate tourism are being marketed to meet travelers' needs seeking to combine pleasure with accomplishment.

Vocation and real estate vacations are catching on as travelers seek personal and often tangible benefits by combining relaxation and new experiences into practical leisure-time packages. On a vocation vacation, travelers take time to experience possible new careers before actually making career changes. You can think of these trips as being mini-internships. On a real estate vacation, travelers spend their time gaining in-depth knowledge and perspectives about the area from scheduled meetings with local experts while searching out potential investment opportunities or a second home.

3.5 Space Tourism

Someday in the not-too-distant future, we may be able to fly halfway around the globe in just minutes thanks to developments in scram jet engine technology that will allow for hypersonic flights. We have already witnessed the advent of space tourism as

civilians have joined the ranks of astronauts on space voyages, but the numbers of space travelers will surely grow in coming years as hypersonic travel becomes a commercial reality. Just think, hypersonic travel made possible by scramjet engines will allow passengers to travel from New York to London in 11 minutes at an incredible speed of 18000 miles per hour. This is not science fiction, as engineers around the globe are working on perfecting scramjet technology.

Space travel became a reality when the first space tourist, Dennis Tito, paid for a seat on a Russian Soyuz rocket and spent a week at the International Space Station in 2001 and this experience was repeated by Mark Shuttleworth the year after. The future of space tourism became a reality in 2004 when famed aircraft designer Burt Rutan and his team, with funding from Paul Allen, a Microsoft pioneer, was the first to successfully launch a privately developed manned spaceship, SpaceShip One. They subsequently won the $10 million Ansari X-Prize granted to the first team to launch two successful manned space launches within two weeks of each other. The team's invention gave Richard Branson the confidence to make the significant investment required to commercialize the prototype technology, thus creating the world's first space line, Virgin Galactic.

We realize that there will be competitive offerings, opening up a genuine market place which will ensure that service will improve, safety and reliability will increase, and prices will come down, exactly as has happened with aviation.

3.6　Smart Tourism

Smart tourism is a new buzzword applied to describe the increasing reliance of tourism destinations, their industries and their tourists on emerging forms of ICT that allow for massive amounts of data to be transformed into value propositions.

Smart tourism is an important component of smart cities. However, in many cities, insecurity, safety, fraud and the lack of availability of proper information about resources are the biggest hurdles toward independent mobility. These issues can be overcome via proactive participation of local citizens to help tourists as well as by cooperation between citizens, city administration and tourists. As a result, a number of components of smart cities can be strengthened, from sustainable mobility in tourism development to economic development. This is very challenging, as it requires a combination of societal inputs, advanced smart and effective tools.

Smart tourism development is already under way. In many ways it naturally evolves from the extensive uptake of technology in tourism. However, the systematic and widespread coordination and sharing as well as exploitation of touristic data for value creation is still in its infancy. Smart tourism initiatives around the world are seeking to build viable smart tourism ecosystems but the complexity of the sector makes it extremely difficult to go beyond very specific platform, technology or service innovations. Yet, the technology pushes in the direction of smart tourism is immense and it is expected that tourism will provide the backdrop for pioneering many of these smart technologies.

3.7 Scientific Tourism and Science Tourism

As researchers in emerging economies, scientists are often the first foreign visitors to stay in remote rural areas and, on occasion, form joint venture ecotourism and community tourism projects or poverty alleviation schemes between local agencies or NGOs, the local community and their home institution or agency. They therefore can contribute to avenues for the conservation of natural resources and the development of rural communities as well as influencing the future tourism development through its perceived legitimacy and the destination image it promotes.

Scientific tourism and science tourism, which both deal with scientific knowledge and learning can be understood as extensions of educational tourism. Educational tourism has its roots in the Grand Tour of the 17th-19th centuries and is also divided into two types. In university, college and school, tourism formal learning dominates and tourism experiences are secondary, while educational tourism refers to more general travel for education, including, for example, youth study tours.

It needs to be noted that science tourism is as wide as science itself. It can be related to natural science (e.g., biology and ecology), social science (e.g., sociology and psychology), or even formal science (e.g., mathematics and logic). As the current study focuses on nature-based tourism and its role in promoting environmental sustainability, the focus is on natural sciences that study nature, natural phenomenon and the natural basis of sustainable development. However, we acknowledge that meanings related to nature vary across time, space and culture. Moreover, nature is as much a product of history and culture as a product of biophysical and ecological processes.

Aside from what have been mentioned above, Birth Tourism, Whale Shark Tourism have also shown a growing tendency.

4. Meeting Future Tourists' Needs

All of the changes that have been mentioned will lead to two common forms of market segmentation. Microsegmentation and mass customization have been used for several years, but these two concepts will gain further use in the future. Subsegments, also called "microsegments," are market segments that represent a relatively small group of consumers such as Californian young professional Asian Americans or Manitoban back-country fishing enthusiasts. As companies attempted to lure customers from competitors, they are developing product offerings to meet the needs of smaller and smaller market segments.

Mass customization is the extreme of microsegmentation. A company mass customizes when it produces goods or service to fulfill the unique needs of an individual buyer. An example of how these trends is being manifested in the tourism

industry can be found in hotel developments in locations where real estate has become extremely high priced. In these settings, companies are dual or co-branding two or more hotel brands under one roof. It may seem unique to find a Courtyard and a Residence Inn by Marriott under one roof or a Hampton Inn and Homewood Suites by Hilton under one roof, but how about an Aloft, a Marriott and a Hyatt Place under one roof? In addition to real estate cost savings, there are also operating efficiencies to be gained by sharing laundry, housekeeping, maintenance, and even amenities such as pools and fitness facilities. As companies strive to meet individual customer segments and real estate prices continue to increase, expect to see more co-branding. Tourism businesses in the future will definitely use both microsegmentation and mass customization to attract guests and meet their needs.

Mass customization will allow travelers to customize their service packages and travel itineraries. Hotels specializing in the business and professional segments are building rooms that can be configured to suit individual guests' needs for multimedia presentations, conference calling, telecommunication links and so on. Tour companies will use mass customization to allow more flexibility in touring. As the tourism market becomes more competitive, the empathy component of service quality you learned about in previous chapters will become more and more important. Both micro-segmentation and mass customization can add the personal touch of empathy to a tourism service. "As travel costs increase and as costs, restrictions, social pressures associated with greenhouse gas emissions and climate change continue to evolve, it seems that middle and down-market mass tourism will decrease or become more localized."

One segment of the tourism industry, cruise lines, could face two unique and completely unrelated customer service challenges in the future. The first area of customer concern deals with a perception by some cruisers, especially first time cruisers, that they are being "nicked and dimed" while they are on board. With additional charges for mandatory gratuities, both soft and alcoholic beverages, photographs, upcharges for specialty restaurants, specialty coffees and convenience food choices, the marketing promise of an "all-inclusive price" may start to be questioned. This "sticker shock" realization on the day of disembarkation is especially true for many first-time cruisers. The second and unrelated concern, also occurs on the day of disembarkation. As larger and larger ships are being put into service, current procedures and port terminal facilities are not adequate to efficiently move cruisers off the ship and through the terminal. Technological improvements such as the use of RFID for passenger identification could easily speed up the disembarkation process, but then a bottleneck would quickly occur in the terminal facilities. To alleviate this problem, significant investments will need to be made in these facilities similar to those that had to be made as the airlines put larger and larger aircraft into service.

5. Moving into an Era of Competitive Cooperation and Consolidation

The tourism industry has historically been fragmented, with many different suppliers serving an ever-growing market. This fragmentation has resulted in varying levels of service, quality, availability and pricing. At the same time, the traveling public has gained greater access to information and become more knowledgeable and demanding about tourism services, forcing managers to search for new ways to control costs and improve quality.

Another trend that will move through the tourism industry is cooperative alliances, another concept that was pioneered by airlines to gain greater brand recognition and operating synergies. For example, the alliance between British Airways and American Airlines signaled the importance of gaining dominance in high-traffic corridors such as those serving the North Atlantic marketplace. However, the benchmark for airline alliances is the Star Alliance. This alliance, which was created in 1997 by six airlines with the intent of being the airline of the Earth, has since grown into a global giant.

Airline alliances meet customers' needs by delivering "seamless service—simplified ticketing, better connections, thorough baggage checking and frequent flyer reciprocity". They also provide another important economic benefit by allowing airlines to gain access to landing slots and gates at already crowded international airports. More changes are on the horizon as the number of major participants in the airline industry continues to shrink and the remaining organizations increase their levels of cooperation.

There is no doubt that the airline industry will also continue to cooperate as well as consolidate with more mergers between rival carriers both inside domestic boundaries and across country boundaries. The trend that began in the United States has already spread to Europe and Asia and will only pick up steam in the future. The "Open Skies" treaty between Europe and the United States set in motion the consolidation wave among previously competing airlines. With this treaty, consolidation between airlines no longer means losing lucrative international markets. The combined companies can keep their transatlantic routes and they can fly out of any European city to the United States, not just from airports located in their home country. With these artificial barriers to competition being lifted, the urge to merge will definitely grow.

As we discussed in Chapter 8, the move toward industry partnerships is also accelerating in the food service segment of the tourism industry. Every link in the supply chain, from manufacturers and distributors to operators and customers, is being brought closer together to improve service and reduce operating costs. These efforts have been dubbed efficient food service response or EFR. The partnership

agreements that are evolving through EFR are providing lower food costs, fewer inventory errors, and higher levels of customer satisfaction and value. 36 food service operators, especially franchise operators, will take advantage of the social networking capabilities facilitated by Web 2.0 through enterprise-level networking to share information targeted at improving purchasing and operating efficiencies.

There will also be an increase in subcontracting many functions needed to support guest services. Operations such as cleaning, laundry and food service will be performed by outside contractors who can focus their attention on being extremely efficient in providing one type of service. In some situations, the operating company will own the facilities and equipment and rely on the expertise of outside contractors to provide and manage labor. In other situations, space will be leased to subcontractors, who in turn will make the investments in equipment as well as manage the entire operation. This trend is already becoming evident in the number of fast-food franchised outlets that are appearing in hotels, airports, theme parks, casinos, service stations, food courts in malls and even cruise ships.

Destinations, while competing with each other, have also sensed the need to cooperate with nearby destinations to draw tourists to the region. Developing tourism without considering its impact on neighbors will increase substitution, leading to cut-throat competition and endangering the healthy tourism development in the region. The concept of "coopetition"—simultaneous competition and cooperation among rivals—originally coined in the 1980s by Raymond Noorda, founder of Novell, is an important philosophy or strategy that goes beyond the conventional rules of competition and cooperation to achieve the advantages of both. Regional cooperation in tourism development, promotion and planning could be a win-win situation for all parties involved with a long-term focus. The Eurail train pass is a long-standing example of how this type of cooperation can succeed. The Association of Southeast Asian Nations (ASEAN) can serve as another example of successful regional tourism cooperation. The ASEAN National Tourism Organizations (NTOs) have regularly carried out a number of campaigns to promote the region as a single destination. For example, as part of the ongoing Visit ASEAN Campaign, the NTOs have actively promoted the Visit ASEAN Pass and its corresponding web portal (www.visitASEAN.travel). The ASEAN NTOs have also facilitated travel within and into the region via air travel promotion and enhancement of cruise tourism.

6. Service Enhancements

Services and tourism go hand in hand. It is important to know that these activities make a significant economic impact on almost every nation in the world! Services are growing at a faster rate than all agricultural and manufacturing businesses combined. In fact, tourism-related businesses are the leading producers of new jobs worldwide.

Tourism has developed into a truly worldwide activity that knows no political, one thing is for sure, future service enhancements will revolve around technological advances, and the rate of change in these advancements will continue to increase. To get some idea of future technological changes, think back to the computers you used at home, work, or school just five years ago. How fast could they operate? What software did they run? How were they linked to information sources around the world? What you thought was fast and efficient back then is slow and cumbersome by today's standards; and computing technology is just one facet of the technological changes that will shape the future of the tourism industry. Maybe the changes in service delivery won't come quite this fast, but change will definitely come. As we saw in previous chapters, operators pursue increasing efficiency and effectiveness in everything they do from service delivery to customer connectivity. Although every effort will be made to enhance the guest experience, the human touch will remain the hallmark of hospitality.

6.1 Amplifying Guests' Experiences

A glimpse of what may be in store for hotel guests in the future can be seen at the Fairmont Vancouver Airport hotel, where it is no longer necessary for guests to check in at the hotel's front desk. Check-in takes place in the airline baggage claim area, and the hotel arranges for bags to be delivered straightly to the guest's room. Guests are greeted with a comfortable and cheery room as check-in also activates room lighting and temperature controls that stay in an energy conservation mode until a room is occupied. In-room motion detectors make "Do Not Disturb" signs a thing of the past, because the housekeeping staff can now time their cleaning activities for maximum customer convenience and satisfaction when guests are out of their rooms. And, there are even more changes on the horizon, according to Tad Smith, Senior Vice President, E-commerce, for Starwood Hotels & Resorts Worldwide, Inc.

In the future, your credit card will also have your frequent guest information imbedded in a computer chip. When you walk through the door of the hotels, you'll be automatically checked in, and your credit card will become your key. You won't have to stand in any lines at all. You're going to have an entirely personal experience in your hotel. Your computer screen will be configured to your homepage with your email waiting for you.

Hotel guests now can even check in and select their own room using Apps on their smartphone and then use their phone as a room key and payment device. Hotels have also begun to employ robots to run errands for guests, such as delivering laundry and sundries.

Travelers seeking new adventures will have the opportunity to participate in a real Jules Verne experience as they enjoy an underwater odyssey. Jules' Undersea Lodge in Key Largo, Florida, currently provides the only underwater accommodations

for undersea adventures. However, if architects and developers have their way, larger nautical hotels could be built at offshore sites in Hawaii, Mexico and Sicily.

The importance of the personal touch can be seen in other areas of the tourism industry. For example, travelers are rediscovering the benefits to be gained from the professional knowledge of experienced travel agents. However, now, rather than visiting brick-and-mortar locations, they are accessing these agents through the Internet or phone and the agents are working from home. Consumer satisfaction has led to growth in this segment of the industry and as the need for personalized service grows, so will the number of agents.

Research shows that as more technology is introduced into the service encounter, customers can become dissatisfied if they are placed in a position where they need to deal with technology and service staff at the same time. To solve this problem, it was suggested that service technology interfaces might be designed so that they can be either integrated seamlessly into customer-employee exchanges or that customers should be given both space and time to deal with the technology side of the transaction before engaging in social aspects of the transaction with the service provider.

6.2 Safety and Security Strides

Realistically, the threat of terrorism will continue, so travelers will have no choice other than to accept a decrease in their privacy in exchange for greater security. Security will pervade but hopefully in the future will almost go unnoticed as technologies improve in all aspects of the tourism industry from attractions and sporting events to accommodations and transportation. Surveillance will also become common for all future events and many tourism attractions/congregating sites. In some locales, the future has arrived. "The average visitor to London is now captured on video 300 times in a single day."

Biometrics will become the common form of identification. Most countries will move to globally standardized electronic national identification cards in place of passports. These ID cards may also include drivers' license information along with fingerprint and retinal scan data. In addition, by choice, to achieve better connectedness and better service, travelers will carry more and more personal information from loyalty accounts to personal travel preferences on their smart phones. As security has tightened, airlines have restricted size and weight of baggage to conserve fuel and space. Although, front line airline service personnel have looked the other way as more and more luggage is carried on, this practice will have to cease for both security and operational efficiency reasons. In response, specialty freight companies will enjoy substantial increases in revenue as more and more travelers elect to ship their luggage and adventure "toys".

Owing to the dominance and immediacy of global media, crisis events will have even greater impact on tourism revenues. In response to hyped 24-hour coverage of natural disasters and terrorism attacks, organizations, especially NTOs and their lower-level counterparts, will develop restoration and recovery programs with specialists who communicate through the broadcast and print media and use the power of the Internet to inform travelers of the condition of tourism resources and steps being taken to ensure the safety and security of visitors.

To guard against lost or stolen cash or traveler's checks (for the minority of population still using them), we will move to a truly cashless society. In all venues, making purchases will be easier. Everything from your credit/debit card to your smart phone will be used to make purchases. Making purchases easier for customers means more revenues for service providers through lower transaction fees.

6.3 Keeping the Human Touch

There is no doubt that the business of hospitality and travel is adopting technology at an advanced speed, and organizations as well as travelers are embracing the movement. The personal touch still provides the basis for the reassurance and experience travelers seek, but technology is revolutionizing the way service providers are staying attentive and engaged with their guests. While customer relationship management holds great promise for delivering customized services more efficiently and effectively, "the old-fashion style of customer relations may be the appropriate strategy for many travel and tourism ventures".

To help reduce labor costs, many tourism-related businesses are automating services that until recently were provided by people. More and more businesses within the industry are making greater use of computer terminals and interactive screens to allow travelers to "do it yourself". Although this step depersonalizes service, a growing number of travelers prefer speed and efficiency to the more personal interaction with hospitality service employees. Tourism operators, just like other service providers, will find a balance between the power of technology and human interaction. Customers enjoy the freedom of technology but want to know that when needed there is someone available to serve their needs.

With the shrinking number of available workers owing to the aging populations of industrialized nations and competition for workers who have the skills needed to learn and complete more complex tasks, tourism suppliers will offer better pay and benefits to employees. Greater efficiency through the use of technology and employees who can utilize it will partially compensate for these higher human resource costs. Automation and robots will replace human workers in many back-of-the-house operations and some front-line positions. Employees will be seen as the most important asset for delivering high-quality, highly personalized customer service, so service training and employee empowerment will become the norm industry wide.

7. The Green Frontier

Sustainable tourism is essential for tourism sector development. Environmentally

responsible behaviors and behavioral intentions are important prerequisites for sustainable tourism. Environmental knowledge positively affected behavioral intentions and positively influenced environmental sensitivity and environmental responsibility. Furthermore, environmental sensitivity and environmental responsibility exerted a full effect in mediating the relationship between environmental knowledge and behavioral intentions.

The coming decades will see the rise of mandatory recycling, water and energy conservation, and use of environmentally friendly building products and supplies. The industry will rise to this challenge by focusing on energy efficiency coupled with new energy technologies such as solar, wind and geothermal energy. New Zealand serves as a good example of what is to come, as sizable quantities of thermal energy from hot springs are already used throughout the major tourism city of Rotorua. The lodging industry will increasingly build or convert to "smart rooms" that sense and adjust climate conditions and can be cleaned at least in part with robot technology.

8. Conclusion

It seems that the more things change, the more they stay the same. We may not follow the practice of sticking a fresh pineapple on the front fence, as the old New England ship captains did as a symbol of hospitality, but the welcoming touch provided by service employees will remain a key factor to service success in this growing industry in which the number of jobs created by tourism organizations is projected to continue increasing in record numbers for years to come.

You have made a great start in developing a sound foundation for becoming a professional member of the tourism industry or an informed consumer of tourism services. There will always be new things to do and learn in our rapidly changing world. We hope you decide to become a part of this excitement. You can build a bright professional future by dedicating yourself to lifelong learning and a never-ending desire to improve your knowledge, skills and abilities continually. If you would like to become a part of the growing cadre of tourism professionals, start planning your job search now! For more information on how to enter and succeed in your desired career field, see Cook and Cook. We hope that you have enjoyed the journey through our exploration of the tourism industry, and we hope to see you as industry professionals in our future travels.

Ⅳ Case Study

Will Robots Become the New Normal in the Hospitality Sector?

Pokémon Go is a gaming craze that has got even the hospitality sector hooked.

Australia's Mantra Group launched the world's first Pokémon Go—friendly hotels in Sydney and Melbourne. Pokémon Go fans who use their mobile phones to catch virtual monsters are encouraged to visit one of the hotel bars. A stop at the hotel bar will not only increase the chances of catching one of the monsters but Pokémon Go fans can also take advantage of food and beverage promotions. Pokémon Go is just one of the many examples where technology is at the forefront of the hospitality experience. Trends such as Pokémon Go will certainly come and go but it is technology that is shaping the future within the hospitality sector—a new reality.

Let us, for example, consider the following scenario. A business traveler arrives at a hotel. Instead of being greeted by a human being at the reception desk, the guest will be checked in by a human-looking robot receptionist. Amazingly, the robot receptionist can also speak the guest's native language. The luggage is quite heavy to carry to the room on the third floor. No worries because a robot porter is on hand to transport the case. There is no need for any fiddly keys because the facial recognition system will open the door to the hotel room. As the guest settles in, a personal robot concierge is at hand to answer any questions from providing a weather forecast to dimming the lights. In the evening, the guest is winding down in the hotel bar. The piano is being played by a robot, who is playing quite good. An evening snack is also prepared by a robot chef. Nothing too fancy but it tastes surprisingly good.

This may appear to be far from reality but a robot hotel is coming soon close to you. Robot-staffed hotels, such as the Henn, a hotel in Sasebo, Japan, are already using robots for traditionally human-occupied jobs, such as concierges or porters. And this technology is becoming increasingly mainstream. For example, at the Marriott Hotel in Ghent, Belgium, a humanoid robot named "Mario" welcomes guests and helps with the check-in process. Mario can even dance! In fact, Mario has become not only a new employee but also a mascot for the hotel. Similarly, Royal Caribbean has installed a Bionic Bar on four of its cruise ships, Harmony of the Seas, Quantum of the Seas, Anthem of the Seas and Ovation of the Seas. Two cocktail-mixing robot bartenders, who can also dance, can come up with a cocktail concoction from a selection of 30 spirits and 21 mixers! The movement of the arms were even patterned after Marco Pelle from the New York Theater Ballet. The drinks are also served at the bar by the robots. The hotel chain Hilton is experimenting with a concierge robot named "Connie". Guests can ask Connie questions such as providing information about restaurants and tourist attractions.

This raises the question if robots will become the new normal in the hospitality sector. The development of an ecosystem will certainly mean that service robots will gain wider customer acceptance and no longer be seen as a novelty. Moreover, technological advancements such as improvements in robotic facial expressions will improve the overall service experience. But will robots replace humans in the

hospitality sector? The blurring of real and virtual experiences is certainly redefining everyday lives and robots will be able to assist with routine tasks. However, robots will never be able to replace the human touch—emotion. It will be the concierge who will be able to help to get hold of tickets for a sold-out concert. It will be the bartender who will be able to mix cocktails exactly to the required taste and provide entertaining company. It will be the hotel doorman who has all the local knowledge that is unmatched. Technological innovation will undoubtedly play an increasingly important role within the hospitality sector. It will, however, be the human interaction that will make the difference. Ask any guest!

Question:

(1) Will robots become the new normal in the hospitality sector?

(2) What can robots do in the tourism sector?

(3) Can you compare the advantages of human beings and robots in the hospitality sector?

Ⅴ Tips

What Will the Tourism Industry Be Like in the Future?

Year 2019 has seen many global changes: from an increase in environmental activism and extreme weather events to political uncertainties leading to volatility in the global economy (such as Brexit weakening the British Pound). Whether it's through changing tourist figures or fluctuating room prices, geopolitical shifts and economic trends end up affecting the travel and hospitality industry in the long term in one way or another. And as these changes will likely impact hotel management strategies, staying on top of key hospitality trends is crucial.

So without further ado, here are the top global travel trends we expect to see. What will the tourism industry be like in the future?

1. Innovative technology will shape guests' experiences

From virtual reality to artificial intelligence, technology is innovating at a faster speed than ever before. And to stand out in the competitive hotel industry, hoteliers are shifting to focus more and more on providing an outstanding guest experience by incorporating technology. Using in-room technology can make a guest's stay both more convenient and enjoyable.

Take voice technology, for example. The average human can type 40 words per minute, but speak 150 words during the same amount of time. So by 2020, over 50% of all online searches are done by voice-enabled technology. But it's not just how bookers search for hotels that is changing: a total of 79% of hoteliers have plans to invest in voice technology in the hotel itself. Hotel brands are finding new ways to use smart speakers and voice assistants (such as Alexa or Google Home) to engage guests and drive additional revenue. For example, when guests order room service through voice assistants, the technology can be customized to drive higher margin sales by recommending certain dishes. Innovative technology can also help a hotel become more eco-friendly, bringing it in line with sustainability trends and ensuring it is making a positive environmental impact. Through the implementation of IoT (Internet of Things), a hotel can improve measurement of both energy utilisation and efficiency throughout the building. This can, in turn, help them understand where they stand in terms of industry benchmarks, and drive them towards reaching higher standards.

2. Showing up on Google will become more costly than ever before

While Online Travel Agencies (OTAs) are currently receiving around 51% of bookings, direct bookings are predicted to grow to a 50% share by 2022. But let's forget the debate on who will dominate the booking market next year. At the end of the day, and regardless of who has a higher market share, Google is the true winner.

Owning at least three-quarters of the market, Google dominates online search. Considering that 96% of leisure travelers start their hotel planning with an online search, the online travel industry is one of Google's biggest customers when it comes to advertising. Together with Facebook, Google owns 71% of all online advertising revenue, and the amount that OTAs like Booking.com pay for search marketing is in the billions of U.S. dollars.

Recent months have seen Google getting more aggressive with its tactics by pushing down free search engine listings to make room for even more paid ads. What's more, Google now gives customers the ability to book trips directly through them as well. This means that OTAs (and hotel brands that can afford to compete) must now pay even more to show up higher in search results.

The company has been a rising risk for the travel industry for a while now, making it even more difficult for independent hotels to appear in online searches. As a result, hoteliers will continue to look elsewhere for effective distribution.

And while it's not a new concept, we predict that the Global Distribution System (GDS) will continue to see YOY(Year-on-year percentage) growth by as much as 5% to 10% worldwide. Here's why the GDS is still as important as ever for hoteliers.

3. Travelers will be even more digitally savvy

Millennials and digital nomads continue to change the way in which people travel, which has led to the successes of companies like AirBnB and Uber. The digital maturity of travelers is impacting the hospitality sector and will continue to do so over the next few years. To remain competitive, hotels need to adapt.

As it stands, up to 80% of last-minute bookings are made on a mobile device, and people are now five times more likely to leave a website if it isn't mobile friendly. Mobile bookings grew by 1700% in just four years and the year 2020 saw this trend grow even further. What's even more interesting is that mobile Apps convert five times more than a mobile browser, more independent hotels released their own Apps.

Reviews will be ever more important in the new year as well. Currently, 65% of consumers check online reviews before booking a hotel. A recent Trip Advisor study found that 79% of users are more likely to book a hotel with a higher rating when choosing between two otherwise identical properties, and over 52% agree that they would never book a hotel with no reviews. And this doesn't just stand for online booking sites, reviews on social media platforms are important as well. Hotels can embrace this trend by integrating review management into their marketing strategy going forward.

4. The Chinese outbound tourism market will experience a momentous growth spurt

The Chinese outbound tourism market, which makes up almost a quarter of global tourism spend, is expected to grow at an even faster rate. Thanks to the rising incomes of Chinese people and more open visa policies, Chinese tourists took 160 million outbound trips by 2020.

Hoteliers should see this as an extremely positive trend as on average, Chinese tourists tend to spend more when travelling. The top 10% of Chinese travelers spend an average of 2225 U.S. dollars per day, and according to guests surveyed in a McKinsey study, 34% choose fine dining as the most important factor when deciding where to travel to. There's also some good news for independent hotels. We're seeing an increasing trend of Chinese tourists preferring to stay at authentic, independent hotels to experience local customs.

Hoteliers keen on attracting more Chinese tourists should ensure their website is translated into Chinese, and that they are being promoted on Chinese social networks, such as Weibo.

5. Hotels targeting niche markets will see greatest success

The Internet is increasingly becoming more crowded. Entrepreneurial hoteliers implementing a niche marketing strategy will see the greatest success at attracting new guests.

A niche marketing strategy focuses on targeting one particular section of the market that has a specific set of needs, such as on guest preferences and hobbies, to offer the ultimate travel experience. Hotel owners find that marketing to a niche audience is more cost-effective and brings in larger margins. It also means they have less competition to worry about and can enjoy more brand loyalty as these markets are

often under-served.

To provide an example, an excellent niche market to get into in 2020 is the pet-friendly hotel market. Pet owners see their furry friends as irreplaceable members of their families, and pet industry spending reached an all-time high of 72.56 billion U.S. dollars in 2019. More and more hotels are now offering pet-friendly stays, often including water bowls, outdoor play areas and even doggie room-service to please their guests.

Ⅵ Dialogue

(A and B are talking about the future of A's company and the growth of Australia's tourism industry. At that time, A's company just faced a big opportunity. Let us look at the opportunity waiting for A's company.)

A: Look, Matt. So far the impact is being negligible so you quite rightly point out about 30% of our revenue comes from international VIPs over the last four or five years. We've been diversifying our dependence away from Chinese guests towards the broader Asian growth as well as moved aggressively into premium mass just to diversify that risk and so with that portfolio for the first four months of this year we reported the numbers about two weeks ago at the AGM. Our front money is broadly up on last year, which is quite good. Some of our guests are telling us that there's nervousness in the market and if you look at Macau(China) and you'd know that better than me. There's obviously some of the exuberance left the segment but you know structurally the value proposition that we have which is tailored around experiences and really a high-end tourism offering that continues to be attractive for a long term.

B: OK, so what are you doing then to offset any decline? You just mentioned some of your strategy there but is it focusing more on the domestic component of market here in Australia? I know that you've announced a big expansion to go ahead two million dollars' worth at your properties on the Gold Coast. Would it be fair to say that that's the focal point of your strategy then at the moment?

A: The long-term future of our company is very closely tied to our growth in tourism, the growth in inbound tourism in Australia and that inbound tourism is a multi-decade long growth story if you look at the end of underlying factors demographics wealth creation and changing behaviors. So, there's a big opportunity and for us to really capture that we need more hotel space so a lot of investments that we've put in are really built around creating that hotel space. In fact, we have currently seven hotels in planning or in development and we'd like to do more. As you

point out last week we announced that we had gotten full approval from the government, from all levels of government, to put up to four more hotel towers into our property in the Gold Coast when we're totally completed with that development. We would have up to three thousand keys in Broad Beach in a fantastic location just opposite the beach next to a shopping center and a convention center you know with the size of operation that rivals global resorts and we're really excited about that opportunity but that opportunity is really tailored at inbound tourism and you know that will happen over the next few years.

Ⅶ Academic Thinking

Autonomous Vehicles and the Future of Urban Tourism

Author: Scott A. Cohen, Debbie Hopkins

Journal: *Annals of Tourism Research*

Abstract:

Connected and autonomous vehicles (CAVs) have the potential to disrupt all industries tied to transport, including tourism. This conceptual paper breaks new ground by providing an in-depth imaginings approach to the potential future far-reaching implications of CAVs for urban tourism. Set against key debates in urban studies and urban tourism, we discuss the enchantments and apprehensions surrounding CAVs and how they may impact cities in terms of tourism transport mode use, spatial changes, tourism employment and the night-time visitor economy, leading to new socio-economic opportunities and a range of threats and inequities. We provide a concluding agenda that sets the foundation for a new research sub-field on CAVs and tourism, of relevance to urban planners, policy makers and the tourism industry.

自动驾驶汽车与城市旅游的未来

互联自动驾驶汽车(CAV)有可能扰乱与运输相关的所有行业,包括旅游业。文章通过提供深入构想法探讨互联自动驾驶汽车对城市旅游业的未来可能产生的深远影响,从而开拓了新的领域。围绕城市研究和城市旅游业的主要辩论,文章的讨论围绕互联自动驾驶汽车的魅力和忧虑,以及它们将如何通过在旅游交通方式的使用、空间变化、旅游就业和夜间游客经济方面对城市产生影响,从而带来新的社会-经济机会以及一系列威胁和不平等现象。文章提供了一个最终议程,该议程为有关互联自动驾驶汽车和旅游业的新研究子领域奠定了基础,该领域与城市规划者、政策制定者和旅游业相关。

Ⅷ Questions

1. What are the emerging trends that will affect future tourism marketing decisions?
2. How will tourism service suppliers be affected by changing consumers' needs?
3. As speeds and efficiencies in trains and airplanes increase, do you think that travelers will shift their trips to one or the other of these transportation modes?
4. What are the main types of future tourism markets mentioned in this chapter?
5. Will advances in technology replace the need for the human touch in the tourism industry?

Ⅸ Key Words and Terms

tourism market	旅游市场
business travel	商务旅行
professional travel	职务旅行（专业人士的公务出行）
conference travel	会议旅行
slow tourism	慢旅游
adventure and extreme tourism	冒险与极限旅游
medical tourism	医疗旅游
vocation and real estate tourism	职业与房产旅游
space tourism	太空旅游
smart tourism	智慧旅游
scientific tourism	科考旅游

Ⅹ Single Choice Questions

参考文献
References

[1] Kaghat F Z, Azough A, Fakhour M, et al. A new audio augmented reality interaction and adaptation model for museum visits[J]. Computers & Electrical Engineering, 2020, 84.

[2] LU W, PARK S H, HUANG T. An analysis for Chinese airport efficiency using weighted variables and adopting CFPR[J]. The Asian Journal of Shipping and Logistics, 2019, 35(4).

[3] Lu W, Park S H, Huang T, et al. An analysis for Chinese airport efficiency using weighted variables and adopting CFPR[J]. The Asian Journal of Shipping and Logistics, 2019, 35(4).

[4] Cook R A, Hsu C H C, Taylor L L. Tourism: The business of hospitality and travel[M]. New York: Pearson, 2018.

[5] Jin C, Cheng J, Xu J, et al. Self-driving tourism induced carbon emission flows and its determinants in well-developed regions: A case study of Jiangsu Province, China[J]. Journal of Cleaner Production, 2018, 186.

[6] Rodrigue J P. The geography of transport systems[M]. 5th ed. Routledge, 2020.

[7] Li D, Pang Z. Dynamic booking control for car rental revenue management: A decomposition approach[J]. European Journal of Operational Research, 2017, 256(3).

[8] Qian C, Li W, Ding M, et al. Mining carsharing use patterns from rental data: a case study of Chefenxiang in Hangzhou, China[J]. Transportation research procedia, 2017, 25.

[9] Westcott M, Bird G, Briscoe P, et al. Introduction to Tourism and Hospitality in BC[M]. BC campus, 2014.

[10] Page S. Transportation and tourism: A symbiotic relationship? [C]//The SAGE handbook of tourism studies. Sage Publications, 2009.

[11] Rovos Rail Celebrates 30 Years. [EB/OL][2020-06-27]https://rovos.com/wp-content/uploads/2020/08/RVR-30yr-Press-Release.pdf.

[12] Gonzá lez R M, Román C, Marrero Á S. Visitors' attitudes towards bicycle use in the Teide National Park[J]. Sustainability, 2018, 10(9).

[13] Sheng C W, Chen M C. A study of experience expectations of museum visitors [J]. Tourism management, 2012, 33(1).

[14] Lee H, Jung T H, tom Dieck M C, et al. Experiencing immersive virtual reality in museums[J]. Information & Management, 2019, 57(5).

[15] Cook R A, Hsu C H C, Taylor L L. Tourism: The business of hospitality and travel[M]. New York: Pearson, 2018.

[16] Lee S A, Shea L. Investigating the key routes to customers' delightful moments in the hotel context[J]. Journal of Hospitality Marketing & Management, 2015, 24(5).

[17] Wu C H J, Liao H C, Hung K P, et al. Service guarantees in the hotel industry: Their effects on consumer risk and service quality perceptions[J]. International Journal of Hospitality Management, 2012, 31(3).

[18] McQuilken L, Robertson N. The influence of guarantees, active requests to voice and failure severity on customer complaint behavior[J]. International Journal of Hospitality Management, 2011, 30(4).

[19] Luo C. Big data technology and its application in smart tourism[J]. Tourism Overview, 2013, 8.

[20] Li Y, Hu C, Huang C, et al. The concept of smart tourism in the context of tourism information services[J]. Tourism Management, 2017, 58.

[21] Ocass A, Sok P. An exploratory study into managing value creation in tourism service firms: Understanding value creation phases at the intersection of the tourism service firm and their customers[J]. Tourism Management, 2015, 51.

[22] Hanssens D M, Thorpe D, Finkbeiner C. Marketing when customer equity matters[J]. Harvard Business Review, 2008, 86(5).

[23] Kotler P. Marketing for hospitality and tourism[M]. UK: Pearson Education Limited, 2022.

[24] Armstrong G, Adam S, Denize S, et al. Principles of marketing[M]. Pearson Australia, 2014.

[25] Rust R T, Lemon K N, Zeithaml V A. Driving customer equity: Linking customer lifetime value to strategic marketing decisions[M]. Cambridge, MA: Marketing Science Institute, 2001.

[26] Rust R T, Lemon K N, Zeithaml V A. Return on marketing: Using customer equity to focus marketing strategy[J]. Journal of marketing, 2004, 68(1).

[27] Wiesel T, Skiera B, Villanueva J. Customer equity: An integral part of financial reporting[J]. Journal of Marketing, 2008, 72(2).

[28] Yan L, McKercher B. Travel culture in Eastern Jin China (317-420 AD): The emergence of a travel culture of landscape appreciation[J]. Annals of

Tourism Research, 2013, 43.

[29] PEARCE P L, LEE U-I. Developing the travel career approach to tourist motivation[J]. Journal of travel research, Sage Publications Sage CA: Thousand Oaks, CA, 2005, 43(3).

[30] DU CROS H, JINGYA L. Chinese youth tourists views on local culture[J]. Tourism Planning & Development, Taylor & Francis, 2013, 10(2).

[31] THORNE S. Place as product: a place-based approach to cultural tourism[J]. Municipal World, 2008, 119.

[32] DU CROS H. Emerging issues for cultural tourism in Macau[J]. Journal of Current Chinese Affairs, SAGE Publications Sage UK: London, England, 2009, 38(1).

[33] HUGHES H L. Theatre in London and the inter-relationship with tourism[J]. Tourism management, Elsevier, 1998, 19(5).

[34] Ambrose T, Paine C. Museum basics: the international handbook[M]. Routledge, 2006.

[35] TORRE M de la. Values and Heritage Conservation[J]. Heritage & Society, Routledge, 2013, 6(2).

[36] YANG C-H, LIN H-L, HAN C-C. Analysis of international tourist arrivals in China: The role of World Heritage Sites[J]. Tourism Management, 2010, 31(6).

[37] BANDARIN F, VAN OERS R. The historic urban landscape: managing heritage in an urban century[M]. John Wiley & Sons, 2012.

[38] JØRGENSEN H. Postcolonial perspectives on colonial heritage tourism: The domestic tourist consumption of French heritage in Puducherry, India[J]. Annals of Tourism Research, 2019, 77.

[39] Russo A P. The "vicious circle" of tourism development in heritage cities[J]. Annals of tourism research, 2002, 29(1).

[40] VITTERSØ J, VORKINN M, VISTAD O I. Tourist experiences and attractions[J]. Annals of Tourism Research, 2000, 27(2).

[41] Carr A. Cultural tourism: the partnership between tourism and cultural heritage management[J]. Tourism analysis, 2006, 11(2).

[42] BRYON J, RUSSO A P. The Tourist Historic City[J]. Annals of Tourism Research, 2003, 30(2).

[43] Scott D. Why sustainable tourism must address climate change[J]. Journal of Sustainable Tourism, 2011, 19(1).

[44] Scott D, Becken S. Adapting to climate change and climate policy: Progress, problems and potentials[J]. Journal of Sustainable tourism, 2010, 18(3).

[45] Lu A C C, Gursoy D, Del Chiappa G. The influence of materialism on ecotourism attitudes and behaviors[J]. Journal of Travel Research, 2016, 55

(2).

[46] Baker M A, Davis E A, Weaver P A. Eco-friendly attitudes, barriers to participation, and differences in behavior at green hotels[J]. Cornell Hospitality Quarterly, 2014, 55(1).

[47] Sharpley R. Tourism and sustainable development: Exploring the theoretical divide[J]. Journal of Sustainable tourism, 2000, 8(1).

[48] Benckendorff, Pierre, and Dagmar Lund-Durlacher. International cases in sustainable travel & tourism[M]. Goodfellow Publishers Ltd, 2013.

[49] Grilli G, Tyllianakis E, Luisetti T, et al. Prospective tourist preferences for sustainable tourism development in Small Island Developing States[J]. Tourism Management, 2021, 82.

[50] Fayos-solà E, Alvarez M D, Cooper C. Tourism as an instrument for development: A theoretical and practical study. Emerald Group Publishing, 2014.

[51] Christensen, Clayton M. The innovator's dilemma: when new technologies cause great firms to fail[M]. Harvard Business Review Press, 2013.

[52] Markides C. Disruptive innovation: In need of better theory[J]. Journal of product innovation management, 2006, 23(1).

[53] Fayos-Solà E, Cooper C. Conclusion: The future of tourism—Innovation for inclusive sustainable development[M]//The future of tourism. Springer, Cham, 2019.

[54] Pilkington P. Book review: Mariana Mazzucato, The Entrepreneurial State: Debunking Public vs Private Sector Myths (Anthem Press, London, Delhi and New York 2013) 266 pp[J]. Review of Keynesian Economics, 2015, 3(1).

[55] Potts J. The innovation deficit in public services: The curious problem of too much efficiency and not enough waste and failure[J]. Innovation, 2009, 11(1).

[56] R. Hawkins. Marianna Mazzucato The Entrepreneurial State: Debunking Public vs Private Sector Myths[J]. Science and Public Policy, 2015.

[57] Meng B, Choi K. The role of authenticity in forming slow tourists' intentions: Developing an extended model of goal-directed behavior[J]. Tourism management, 2016, 57.

[58] Oh H, Assaf A G, Baloglu S. Motivations and Goals of Slow Tourism[J]. Journal of Travel Research, 2016, 55(2).

[59] Shang W, Yuan Q, Chen N. Examining Structural Relationships among Brand Experience, Existential Authenticity, and Place Attachment in Slow Tourism Destinations[J]. Sustainability, 2020, 12(7).

[60] Tripathy A K, Tripathy P K, Ray N K, et al. iTour: The Future of Smart Tourism: An IoT Framework for the Independent Mobility of Tourists in

Smart Cities[J]. IEEE Consumer Electronics Magazine, 2018, 7(3).

[61] Gretzel U, Sigala M, Xiang Z, et al. Smart tourism: foundations and developments[J]. Electronic Markets, 2015, 25(3).

[62] Hunter W C, Chung N, Gretzel U, et al. Constructivist Research in Smart Tourism[J]. Asia Pacific Journal of Information Systems, 2015, 25(1).

[63] Neuhofer B, Buhalis D, Ladkin A. Smart technologies for personalized experiences: a case study in the hospitality domain[J]. Electronic Markets, 2015, 25(3).

[64] Gretzel U, Werthner H, Koo C, et al. Conceptual foundations for understanding smart tourism ecosystems[J]. Computers in Human Behavior, 2015, 50.

[65] Gretzel U, Sigala M, Xiang Z, et al. Smart tourism: foundations and developments[J]. Electronic Markets, 2015, 25(3).

[66] Hoarau H, Kline C. Science and industry: Sharing knowledge for innovation [J]. Annals of tourism research, 2014, 46.

[67] Juulia Räikkönen, Miia Grénman. The Experience Economy Logic in the Wellness Tourism Industry[M]// Co-Creation and Well-Being in Tourism. Springer International Publishing, 2017.

[68] Gossling S. Tourism, tourist learning and sustainability: an exploratory discussion of complexities, problems and opportunities [J]. Journal of Sustainable Tourism, 2018, 26(1-3).

[69] Jaramillo J, Goyal D, Lung C. Birth tourism among Chinese women[J]. MCN: The American Journal of Maternal/Child Nursing, 2019, 44(2): 94-99.

[70] Wong C W M, Conti-Jerpe I, Raymundo L J, et al. Whale Shark Tourism: Impacts on Coral Reefs in the Philippines[J]. Environmental Management, 2019, 63(2).

[71] Cohen S A, Hopkins D. Autonomous vehicles and the future of urban tourism [J]. Annals of tourism research, 2019, 74.

教学支持说明

为了改善教学效果,提高教材的使用效率,满足高校授课教师的教学需求,本套教材备有与纸质教材配套的教学课件(PPT)和拓展资源(案例库、习题库等)。

为保证本教学课件及相关教学资料仅为教材使用者所得,我们将向使用本套教材的高校授课教师免费赠送教学课件或者相关教学资料,烦请授课教师通过电话、邮件或加入旅游专家俱乐部QQ群等方式与我们联系,获取"电子资源申请表"文档并认真准确填写后发给我们,我们的联系方式如下:

地址:湖北省武汉市东湖新技术开发区华工科技园华工园六路

邮编:430223

电话:027-81321911

E-mail:lyzjjlb@163.com

旅游专家俱乐部QQ群号:758712998

旅游专家俱乐部QQ群二维码:

群名称:旅游专家俱乐部5群
群　号:758712998

电子资源申请表

填表时间：_____年___月___日

1. 以下内容请教师按实际情况写，★为必填项。
2. 相关内容可以酌情调整提交。

★姓名		★性别	□男 □女	出生年月		★职务	
						★职称	□教授 □副教授 □讲师 □助教

★学校		★院/系	
★教研室		★专业	
★办公电话		家庭电话		★移动电话	
★E-mail（请填写清晰）		★QQ号/微信号	
★联系地址		★邮编	

★现在主授课程情况	学生人数	教材所属出版社	教材满意度
课程一			□满意 □一般 □不满意
课程二			□满意 □一般 □不满意
课程三			□满意 □一般 □不满意
其 他			□满意 □一般 □不满意

教 材 出 版 信 息		
方向一		□准备写 □写作中 □已成稿 □已出版待修订 □有讲义
方向二		□准备写 □写作中 □已成稿 □已出版待修订 □有讲义
方向三		□准备写 □写作中 □已成稿 □已出版待修订 □有讲义

请教师认真填写表格下列内容，提供索取课件配套教材的相关信息，我社根据每位教师填表信息的完整性、授课情况与索取课件的相关性，以及教材使用的情况赠送教材的配套课件及相关教学资源。

ISBN（书号）	书名	作者	索取课件简要说明	学生人数（如选作教材）
			□教学 □参考	
			□教学 □参考	

★您对与课件配套的纸质教材的意见和建议，希望提供哪些配套教学资源：